D0700950

The Sons
of the
Pioneers

Bill O'Neal
and Fred Goodwin

EAKIN PRESS   Austin, Texas

OCM 934491559

For Lloyd "Tommy" Doss—

*one of the greatest of the Pioneers
and a special friend to this project.*

For CIP information,
please access:
www.loc.gov

FIRST EDITION
Copyright © 2001
By Bill O'Neal and Fred Goodwin
Published in the United States of America
By Eakin Press
A Division of Sunbelt Media, Inc.
P.O. Drawer 90159 ✉ Austin, Texas 78709-0159
email: eakinpub@sig.net
🖳 website: www.eakinpress.com 🖳
ALL RIGHTS RESERVED.

1   2   3   4   5   6   7   8   9
1-57168-644-4

Contents

"High Sierras"   Bob Nolan

The high sierras call to me
The wonderful days roll by
The scented breeze, the whispering trees
'Way up in the clear blue sky
The high sierras call to me
I gotta go back there soon
I left my heart
        Among the pines
            Along the trails
Up in the high sierras

Where the dawn breaks upon a wonder-world
And wild creatures greet you with a—
"How-do-you-do Old friend,
We're glad to have you back again
And', Where have you been so long'?

The high sierras call to me
And If they should call you too
You'll leave your heart
        Among the pines
            Along the trails
Up in the high sierras

A Bob Nolan composition in his bold handwriting.

iv

Acknowledgments

Each of us discovered the Sons of the Pioneers during boyhood excursions to the movies, and our admiration has grown with the passing years. Fred has enjoyed a long association with the Sons of the Pioneers, and since the beginning of this project he shared his contacts, as well as his vast collection of Pioneer memorabilia, with Bill.

Through the years Fred had the opportunity to interview most of the Pioneers, along with spouses and other family members and associates. These first-person accounts were invaluable in compiling a history of the Sons of the Pioneers (a list of interviews is included in the bibliography). During the past several months, we are grateful to Tommy Doss for responding to a variety of inquiries. Velma Spencer, Tim's widow, graciously provided two recent interviews. Lynn Farr reminisced at length about Hugh Farr and Pioneer happenings, and she generously loaned photographs from her personal collection. (Photographs not otherwise credited are from the collection of Fred Goodwin.)

Country music historian Charles Cunningham, who lives in Powell, Tennessee, learned of this project and immediately provided an extremely useful videotape of Pioneer performances in Charles Starrett movies. Bev Brown, long-time owner-manager of KGAS Radio in Carthage, Texas, related information about radio transcriptions and music services during the 1940s. Renee Ward, a gifted violinist from Longview, Texas, used her instrument to demonstrate Hugh Farr's "triple-bow" technique. Karon O'Neal assisted with research, constantly encouraged Bill, and converted a handwritten manuscript to computer disk.

FRED GOODWIN
BILL O'NEAL

The roster of active Pioneers at the group's 1972 reunion. Top, L to R: Dale Warren, Luther Nallie. Bottom: Roy Lanham, Lloyd Perryman, Billy Armstrong.

1

Reunion

"What a great heritage to have left the world."
—Rex Allen

*Ticket to the 1972 reunion of the
Sons of the Pioneers.*

THERE WAS A SPOTLIGHT beaming on the Sons of the Pioneers in Los Angeles on April 21, 1972. That Friday was declared "Sons of the Pioneers Day" by Mayor Sam Yorty, who lauded "the first Western singing group to perform at Carnegie Hall." Other accomplishments of the famous group included appearing in nearly one hundred movies, recording hundreds of songs and radio transcriptions, and accumulating an enormous original musical repertory, based primarily on the prolific compositions of Pioneers Bob Nolan and Tim Spencer. Nolan and Spencer had helped found the group, along with the future "King of the Cowboys," Roy Rogers. Roy had left the Pioneers to become a movie star nearly a quarter of a century earlier, and Bob and Tim had retired from the group in 1949. But all three men came to Los Angeles for Sons of the Pioneers Day, and so did charter member Hugh Farr and other former Pioneers, along with current members of the group. Dale Evans came with Roy, and many other relatives, friends, and fans joined them.

Sons of the Pioneers Day climaxed that night with a Pioneer reunion at the Ambassador Hotel. At a reception prior to the banquet the center of attention was a cluster of men, middle-aged or older, who interacted easily with each other. Most of them wore suits with a Western cut, and there were a lot of cowboy hats. Roy and Dale, obviously enjoying themselves, circulated happily among their old comrades. Anticipating his part in the upcoming activities, Roy chuckled shyly: "I get embarrassed when the camera starts."

Rex Allen, Marty Robbins, Jimmy Wakely, and other noted entertainers performed at the banquet, and there were several speakers eager to "pay tribute to the greatest act of its kind in the history of the world." Bob Nolan and Tim

1

Spencer were honored for their compositions. Tim was in fragile health, but Bob, who seldom appeared in public, offered their response. The current Pioneers—Lloyd Perryman, Dale Warren, Roy Lanham, Luther Nallie, and Billy Armstrong—sang "Cowboy Jubilee" and "Along the Santa Fe Trail," and fiddler Armstrong played "Orange Blossom Special." Retired Pioneers Tommy Doss and Ken Carson each sang. Charter member Hugh Farr had not brought his fiddle, but he borrowed Billy Armstrong's instrument for a couple of tunes. Roy and Dale took the stage, and as he prepared to relate the founding of the group he asked for a drink of water. "I get nervous every time I get up in front of anybody," laughed Roy, shaking his head, "after forty years in show business."

Dale sang, then Roy called a square dance, as he had done forty years earlier. Finally all of the Pioneers, past and present, climbed onto the stage, and together performed the group's most famous hit, Bob Nolan's "Tumbling Tumbleweeds."

"The songs written and performed by the Sons of the Pioneers will be sung a thousand years from now; perhaps on other planets," proclaimed Rex Allen that evening. "What a great heritage to have left the world."

Scholars have analyzed the heritage of the Sons of the Pioneers. "The grand masters of the romantic cowboy style," remarked Dr. Bill C. Malone in his landmark study, *Country Music U.S.A.* "Perhaps more than any other group, they preserved a western repertory and exploited the romantic cowboy image."

"Western swing had Bob Wills, bluegrass had Bill Monroe, men who forged entire musical styles," pointed out Country and Western authority Doug Green when considering the beginning years of the group, "and now western music had the Sons of the Pioneers." The encyclopedic *All Music Guide to Country* opened its entry on the Pioneers with the statement: "The Sons of the Pioneers were the foremost vocal and instrumental group specializing in cowboy songs, setting the standard for every group since."

The original compositions of Bob Nolan and Tim Spencer have been properly recognized as a key element in the unique status of the Sons of the Pioneers. "It is difficult for even the most ardent admirer of the Pioneers to fully appreciate the incredible creativity of Bob Nolan and Tim Spencer during their association with Columbia and Republic Pictures," wrote Ken Griffis in his book about the Pioneers, *Hear My Song.* "The importance of Nolan's and Spencer's music cannot be overstated." In an article about Bob Nolan for *The Western Historical Quarterly* in October 1986, Dr. Kenneth J. Bindas stated: "Nolan helped to shape the modern conception of the West in his capacity as leading songwriter for the Sons of the Pioneers—the most popular Western singing group in the United States."

The following month, writing for the November 1986 issue of *Country Sounds*, Gene Davenport thoughtfully discussed the contemporary Pioneers: "Having found their audience over 50 years ago, the Sons of the Pioneers now work, in a radically changed society, to perpetuate and enlarge that audience without sacrificing their integrity of the basic qualities that first lifted them to international prominence and made them not merely an organization, but an American institution."

In 1979 the *Los Angeles Examiner* spoke simply for millions of fans of the Sons of the Pioneers: "They are the essence of Western music."

The grand masters of cowboy style . . . the foremost vocal and instrumental group in Western music . . . an American institution. What were the origins of this remarkable group? The Tumbleweed Trail began early in the twentieth century, with a tough Ohio farm boy, a solitary youngster raised in the Canadian wilderness, a musically inclined boy from Oklahoma and New Mexico, and a pair of immensely gifted brothers from West Texas.

The Sons of the Pioneers in December 1934. Front, L to R: Hugh Farr, Len Slye. Back, Tim Spencer, Bob Nolan. "Big Brother Hugh" inscribed this photo to his guitar-playing sibling, Karl.

2
Founding Fathers

"The phone in our boardinghouse
was ringing morning and night."
—Roy Rogers

THE LAST CHARTER MEMBER of the Sons of the Pioneers died on July 6, 1998. At the age of eighty-six he had become famous worldwide as the "King of the Cowboys," Roy Rogers. But six and a half decades earlier, as Len Slye, a young and ambitious country boy from Ohio, he became the founding force behind the Sons of the Pioneers.

Leonard Franklin Slye was born in Cincinnati on November 5, 1911, the third of four children of Andy and Mattie Slye. The other children were girls: Mary, Cleda, and Kathleen. The Slye family led a hardscrabble existence. When Len was still a toddler, Andy and his brother, who was blind, cobbled together a houseboat from scrap materials. The boat was towed up the Ohio River from Cincinnati to Portsmouth, Andy's hometown.

For the next several years the Slyes lived on the houseboat, while Andy worked at a Portsmouth shoe factory. Hoping to improve his family's living conditions, in 1919 Andy bought an eighty-seven-acre farm twelve miles outside Portsmouth, at the rural community of Duck Run.

But Andy knew nothing about farming. He continued to work in Portsmouth, visiting the farm every other weekend. The Slye children had always helped with household chores, especially because their mother had been crippled early in life by polio. Living on the farm, with their father away most of the time, the workload increased—especially on little Len.

The boy learned to plow, build fences, and tend stock. He worked hard, and eventually he hired out to other farmers to supplement the family income. He helped fill the family larder by hunting in the woods. With his Barlow knife Len fashioned a slingshot, and he regularly bagged squirrels and rabbits for the supper pot. His bag increased when his father bought him a single-shot .22 rifle. Len always had a dog and other pets, and he rode a black mare named Babe

5

bareback. Reveling in his outdoor existence ("I was as happy as a dead pig in the sunshine"), he would be an avid outdoorsman throughout his life.

Running the family farm since boyhood, Len developed a strong sense of responsibility and the tireless work habits of a perfectionist. His compulsive work ethic would be an invaluable asset to his career as an entertainer.

The Duck Run farm had no running water or electricity, and there was no radio. Len saw no more than half a dozen movies during his boyhood and adolescence. When a 4-H triumph with a blue-ribbon pig resulted in a trip to Columbus, the state capital, the awestruck youth spent most of his first day riding the hotel elevator.

As indicated by Len's fascination with an elevator, entertainment opportunities for the Slyes were decidedly limited. Like countless other rural families, the Slyes filled the gap by making music. Andy and Mattie both played the guitar and mandolin by ear, and they taught their children to play these instruments. The family played and sang folk music in harmony. Musically gifted, Len learned to yodel, and he taught himself to play the clarinet. At Saturday night dances Len was captivated by square dance callers. By the time he was ten he had begun to call dances himself (in future Roy Rogers movies, the star sometimes exhibited his calling skills in square dance scenes). He developed a clear, melodic singing style with excellent breath control. Len had a shy streak that would stay with him throughout his life. But he found a deep joy in singing and playing, and even as a boy he sensed that people enjoyed watching him perform. The shy country boy sang unselfconsciously with family members at informal gatherings and at country dances. Gradually, his confidence would grow to the point that he dared dream of performing professionally.

In 1926 Len had to drop out of high school. He had finished only his sophomore year, but family finances dictated that he and his father accept work in a Cincinnati shoe factory. Two of Len's sisters, Mary and Cleda, had married by this time. Andy, Mattie, Len, and Kathleen moved into a rented duplex in Cincinnati. Mattie insisted that Len take night classes in pursuit of a high school diploma. But the grind of his factory job would force him to quit night school.

Mary and her husband had moved to California, and her letters created a powerful attraction for other family members. One morning in 1930, Len and his father climbed out of bed at 4:30 to go to work. Len began talking wistfully about California, then announced that he had saved more than $90, which he was willing to use for a trip. Andy had about the same amount of cash, and that same day the family excitedly began packing for the cross-country trek. Andy and Len quit their jobs, and the Slyes headed west in a 1923 Dodge sedan. Camping out at night and struggling to keep the Dodge running, the Slyes took two weeks to drive to Mary's home in Lawndale.

Helped by Mary's husband, Andy and Len found jobs driving sand and gravel trucks. Len loved California, but after four months Andy insisted upon returning to Cincinnati. Within a few months, though, Len learned that Mary's father-in-law was going to visit California. Offering his services as a driver, Len eagerly returned to California in 1931. His parents soon sold the Duck Run farm and also migrated to California. Len and Andy again found work driving gravel trucks.

But 1931 was the second year of the Great Depression, and the sand and gravel company went bankrupt. Andy and Len, along with cousin Stanley Slye, picked fruit anywhere they could find work. When a job ended, the Slye family piled into the Dodge and joined other migrant workers in searching for jobs. Len had to unlimber his slingshot, again hunting rabbits for supper. After supper the Slyes, including cousin Stanley, would break into impromptu musical performances that attracted crowds of other migrants. Sometimes Len would call for square dancers, and his confidence as a performer continued to grow. Meanwhile, the scarcity of work caused Len to seek odd jobs of any sort. Wiry and quick, he even agreed to box—for fifty cents a round. Because of the desperate poverty of these years, when he became a major star as Roy Rogers, he always carried a large wad of cash in his jeans. "I was broke so long and hunger tore and gnawed so deep into my stomach walls I've never forgot the feel," he said.

Fruit-picking opportunities became so scarce that Andy decided to try to get a job with a Los Angeles shoe factory. He asked his son to join him. But Len had determined to try a musical career.

For several years Western music had been a popular feature on California radio stations. Hundreds of "horse operas" were filmed by Hollywood studios every year, perpetuating Western myths, and there was a natural market in California for music evoking the romantic West. In 1926 Hollywood station KFWB began broadcasting Len Nash and his Original Country Boys. Other popular Western groups included Sheriff Loyal Underwood's Arizona Wranglers, Charlie Marshall and His Mavericks, and the Beverly Hill Billies. The latter group adopted a hillbilly image and played country music, which appealed strongly to California's migrant population from rural areas of the nation. The Beverly Hill Billies debuted over Los Angeles station KMPC in 1930, featuring talented instrumentalists and yodelers and lively country tunes.

Encouraged by the popularity of such groups, Len persuaded his cousin Stanley to perform with him as "The Slye Brothers." This duo played a few dances and parties, but there were no fees. The "brothers" placed a hat in front and collected a little tip money from the partygoers. After a few weeks, Stanley decided to try to find a job with a steady income. Len hooked on with another group of hopefuls, Uncle Tom's Hollywood Hill Billies, but again the pay was scant.

At this point Len's older sister, Mary, persuaded him to appear on a radio talent show. "The Midnight Frolic" aired over Inglewood station KMCS from midnight until 6:00 in the morning, welcoming any amateur performer. Mary stitched a new Western shirt and brought her shy brother to the show.

"I was scared to death," he reminisced. But Len sang and played several songs, and when the little audience applauded enthusiastically, the station took his name and the number of the pay phone where he could be reached.

The next day the manager of a group called the Rocky Mountaineers telephoned to say that he had heard Len and had an offer. The Rocky Mountaineers played a regular radio show on KGFJ. There was no pay, but the show provided publicity for dances and other paying jobs. Like many similar groups, the Rocky Mountaineers were all instrumentalists, and they wanted Len to join as a singer. Len agreed, but said that another singer was needed for harmony. On

September 30, 1931, an ad was placed in the *Los Angeles Examiner*: "YODELER, for old-time act, to travel. Tenor preferred."

Applicants were directed to 1727 E. 65th Street, in south central Los Angeles. The Rocky Mountaineers headquartered at the home of their banjo player. When the banjoist and his wife retired to the bedroom each night, Len and the other Mountaineers pulled the couch adjacent to the day bed, "and we would all sleep across it that way."

Several hopefuls responded to the ad. The most remarkable was a tanned, well-built young man who arrived barefoot, carrying his shoes in his hand. He explained that he was a lifeguard whose professional wardrobe required little in the way of footwear. He bought a new pair of shoes for the audition, but the long walk from the streetcar stop rubbed blisters on his heels. The barefoot musician yodeled, played a bass fiddle and guitar, and displayed a fine singing voice. He introduced himself as Bob Nolan.

He was a Canadian, born Robert Clarence Nobles on April 1, 1908, in the province of New Brunswick. Bob and his younger brother, Earle, were raised on the backwoods farm of their paternal grandparents. Their father, Harry Byron Nobles, had a streak of wanderlust—a quality he passed on to Bob—and often was gone. Their mother, Florence, disappeared from their lives when they were young. The Nobles farm was nearly sixty miles via the St. John River from St. John, on the Bay of Fundy. The 120-mile round trip for supplies was a rare occurrence, and Bob and Earle grew up amid wilderness isolation with little schooling. They were rarely exposed to music, except when revivalists came to conduct religious camp meetings a couple of times a year. At the age of twelve, Bob was sent to live with aunts in Boston so that he could be exposed to educational opportunities. Of course, he also was exposed to various types of music, and he always held fond memories of the two years he spent with his aunts in Boston.

During World War I, Bob's father, Harry, enlisted in the United States Army. Trained in aircraft maintenance, Harry was sent to France. At first assigned to the Royal Air Force, Harry transferred to an American unit in time to be gassed at Belleau Woods. After his discharge, he moved to Tucson, Arizona, to nurture his damaged lungs in the arid desert climate. Feeling that "Nobles" sounded somewhat un-American, Harry changed his last name to Nolan and found work as a tailor.

In 1922, fourteen-year-old Bob traveled by train from Boston to Tucson to live with his father. (Three years later Earle also came to Tucson by way of Boston.) Blessed with the acute sensibilities of an artist, Bob became captivated by the desert, which he found to be "awe-inspiring" and "just outstanding." With a reserved and solitary nature, he spent hours alone in the desert. "At first you see and hear nothing, then the desert comes alive with things few people ever see," he described.

Bob began to write poetry. Impressed by the romantic poets, he worked to adapt desert themes to the style of Robert Burns, John Keats, Percy Bysshe Shelley, and Lord Byron. At Tucson High School, Bob also enjoyed athletics, excelling at track and field. But after high school Bob soon was gripped by wanderlust, happily riding freight trains to far corners of America. In 1928 he married Pearl Fields of Tucson, and the next year they had a daughter, Roberta. Bob could not resist the lure of the rails, however, and he continued his nomadic life. Bob and Pearl divorced a few years later, having never lived together.

In 1929, after a trip to Hawaii aboard a freighter, Bob settled in California, joining a Chatauqua tent show troupe based near Santa Monica. Bob sang and played various instruments and first tried his hand at songwriting, using some of his poetry as lyrics. But the Great Depression had begun, and Chatuaquas produced little income. Bob found work on the beach at Venice, lifeguarding during the day and at night helping to run a concession on the pier. Another concessionaire was Bill Nichols, who shared Bob's interest in music. Bill sang tenor and played the fiddle. Because he fiddled with his eyes closed, he was nicknamed "Slumber."

As the depression worsened, Bob and Bill lost their jobs. Bob was no stranger to bumming around, and he and Bill continued to hang out on the beach. But Bob searched the want ads, responding eagerly to the opportunity of putting his musical talent to work with the Rocky Mountaineers.

Len Slye ran the auditions, and he was immediately impressed by Bob Nolan, notwithstanding the bare feet. Bob also took a liking to Len. Bob demonstrated that he could yodel and sing tenor, and play several instruments as well. Chosen to join the Rocky Mountaineers, Bob soon persuaded the group to take on Bill Nichols, a natural tenor who could perform three-part harmony with the other two singers, allowing Bob to drop to baritone while Len sang lead.

Slye and Nolan worked especially well together, and Bob became intrigued with three-part harmony as a songwriter. Bob wrote "Way Out There," a train-riding song. A flood of tunes soon would follow. But the Rocky Mountaineers were earning little money, despite the exposure afforded by radio. After eight months Bob left the group for a job as a golf caddy at the exclusive Bel Air Country Club. Soon he was able to afford an apartment in West Los Angeles. But the performing bug had bitten deeply, and he compulsively seized songwriting possibilities. He got one idea while looking out his window at wind-driven leaves tumbling down the street. He wrote "Tumbling Leaves," and the Western influence of his career caused him later to re-title it "Tumbling Tumbleweeds."

While Bob Nolan was caddying at Bel Air and writing songs in his apartment, in August 1932 the Rocky Mountaineers ran an ad for another singer. The successful applicant was Tim Spencer.

Vernon Tim Spencer was the eighth of twelve children of Edgar and Laura Spencer. Tim was born on July 13, 1908, in Webb City, Missouri, just outside Joplin. A mining engineer by profession, Edgar Spencer enthusiastically played a fiddle at parties and dances, and sometimes with the Webb City Symphony. Tim's older brother, Glenn, also played the fiddle and piano, and like the other brothers Tim sang well. As a little boy Tim joined his brothers in singing at the Methodist Church.

In 1913 the family moved to an isolated homestead near Springer, New Mexico. The Spencers soon returned to Webb City, then moved back to the homestead. Tim's imagination was captured by the wide-open spaces of New Mexico, which had been a state only since 1912. But soon another mining job beckoned near Joplin, and Edgar left behind his oldest sons to work the homestead while the rest of the family headed for Picher, a boomtown in the north-eastern corner of Oklahoma.

From 1915 until 1930 Picher was the center of the largest zinc-mining area in the world. Although virtually a ghost town today, Picher was a bustling city of more than 20,000 when Tim Spencer lived there. At silent movie theaters he idolized cowboy heroes William S. Hart, Tom Mix, and Hoot Gibson. Tim admired the singing of early recording star Gene Austin. He learned to play various instruments, and he got into trouble with his father when he bought a banjo ukulele on credit. When the high school staged an operetta with a cast of more than 100, Tim won the starring role.

After high school, Tim took a job in one of Picher's mines, but soon he was injured in an accident with an ore car. Freed from the mines, Tim took his banjo to a local hotspot, the Bucket of Blood, where patrons enjoyed his playing and singing. Encouraged by his success as an entry-level professional entertainer, Tim dreamed of pursuing a music career in Los Angeles. His older brother, Glenn, had made his home there, and Tim decided to pay a visit.

Tim took a train from Tulsa to Los Angeles in 1931. Finding a day job at a Safeway warehouse, in the evenings he haunted dances and radio shows that featured Western or hillbilly musicians. As Tim became familiar with the various groups, he especially admired the sound of the Rocky Mountaineers. When he saw a newspaper ad that the Rocky Mountaineers needed a singer, he responded immediately.

In August 1932 Tim Spencer joined Len Slye and Bill Nichols in the trio of the Rocky Mountaineers. Tim quickly learned to yodel, and just as quickly he developed what would prove to be a lifelong admiration of Len Slye.

Another admirer of Len Slye was dark-haired Lucile Ascolese. She regularly attended performances of the Rocky Mountaineers, and in 1933 Len and Lucile were married by a justice of the peace. But conditions proved impossible for the young couple. Nineteen-year-old Lucile was a beauty operator with long workdays, while Len worked at night and was on the road much of the time. She had to stay with her parents, and she was jealous of the attention Len received from female fans. Furthermore, when they married, Len was virtually broke. Divorce proceedings began in 1934, although it took a year and a half to complete the legal termination of the marriage.

Meanwhile, the fortunes of the Rocky Mountaineers did not improve. With no money coming in, the group disbanded late in 1932. Most of the former Mountaineers joined Benny Nawahi's International Cowboys. This grandiose name did not translate to any greater financial success than the Rocky Mountaineers had experienced. Performing for service clubs and other civic groups, the International Cowboys played only for tips. But the band appeared on radio stations KGER in Long Beach and KRKD in Los Angeles. A KRKD employee suggested booking a tour of Arizona, New Mexico, and West Texas, locales where Western music could be expected to enjoy considerable appeal. Len felt that the group "might as well starve to death in a part of the country we hadn't seen."

Tim and Slumber Nichols were willing to give it a try, and so was instrumentalist Cactus Mac Peters, who was supposed to act as manager. Most importantly—because he owned a 1923 Pontiac—a fiddler called "Cyclone" agreed to go. One of the musicians had heard of a famous old ranch, the O-Bar-O, and the group decided to call themselves the "O-Bar-O Cowboys," which had the proper ring for a band of Western entertainers. The O-Bar-O Cowboys piled into Cyclone's vehicle and set out for Arizona in June 1933.

But the booking agent who had suggested the trip had not done much booking. When the O-Bar-O Cowboys reached Yuma, just across the Arizona border, no one had heard of them. The unpublicized group tried to stage a show, but not even one person came to be entertained. Buying a megaphone in a pawn shop, the group drove the streets of each new town, announcing that the O-Bar-O Cowboys had arrived to put on a show. Yet at each performance the entertainers collected no more than a few dollars apiece. Much of the money they collected went for auto repairs, and at one motor court Len had to pay the bill with his wristwatch. When they drove into Miami, near Phoenix, they discovered that the old mining community had become a virtual ghost town.

At Willcox, Arizona, an enthusiastic crowd turned out because Cactus Mac was a hometown boy. The warm reception, however, persuaded Cactus Mac to stay at home, and the O-Bar-O Cowboys departed for New Mexico without him.

At Roswell the group agreed to make unsponsored appearances each night for two weeks over the local radio station. Len persuaded the station owner to loan him a hunting rifle. Just as he had done at the Duck Run farm, Len bagged meat for supper. The boys would mix up gravy in their motor court room. The first night, Len brought in a jackrabbit, but the next day all he could find was a hawk, and the following day there was only a blackbird.

In desperation the group began to talk over the air about their favorite foods. Between numbers, one member talked about fried chicken, another sang the praises of homemade biscuits, and Len announced that his favorite food was lemon pie. After the show a woman called the station with a promise to bake a lemon pie if Len would perform "The Swiss Yodel." Len practiced, then yodeled enthusiastically the next night. Following the show a Mrs. Wilkins and her daughter, Arlene, drove to the motor court with two fresh lemon pies. After visiting with the ladies, the musicians went to their room and devoured the pies.

The next day Mrs. Wilkins invited the group to her house for fried chicken. Her hospitality apparently was influenced by her

TUMBLING . . . CHANDELIERS?

The International Cowboys were invited to take part in a show at the Warner Theater in downtown Los Angeles on Friday, March 10, 1933. That evening a massive earthquake struck, centering on Long Beach, just south of LA. Property damages totaled $60 million, while 118 people were killed.

Tremors struck the Warner Theater just as the International Cowboys were introduced. The audience fled for the exits—except for one man, who stubbornly stayed in his seat. "To this day," reminisced Roy Rogers, "I don't know if he really wanted to hear us perform, or if he was so scared he couldn't move."

The giant chandelier began to sway as the theater reverberated with aftershocks. But the International Cowboys resolutely struck up a lively version of "Tumbling Tumbleweeds" for their audience of one.

daughter. There was an immediate attraction between Len and Arlene, a tall blonde with a sweet and gentle nature. Len saw her daily until the O-Bar-O Cowboys left town. A regular correspondence ensued, and a few years later Len and Arlene would marry.

Tim Spencer also met his future wife on the O-Bar-O Cowboys tour. When the group appeared on a radio station in Lubbock, Texas, a high school senior named Velma Blanton was in the audience. After Tim became acquainted with Velma, he began thinking about work that would be steady enough to support a wife.

Except for meeting a couple of sweethearts, the O-Bar-O Cowboys had suffered a flop on their tour of the Southwest. Straggling back into Los Angeles, the group disbanded. Undiscouraged, Len hooked up with Jack LeFevre and His Texas Outlaws, a group that played a daily sponsored show on KFWB in Hollywood, along with dance hall appearances each Friday and Saturday night. Nichols found a job at a Fort Worth radio station, while Tim Spencer went back to work for Safeway.

The ambitious Len Slye would not give up on his dreams of a distinctive harmony trio. A superb yodeler, he had worked on harmony yodeling with the singers in his miscellaneous groups. No other group offered three-part yodeling, and Len envisioned elevating song harmony to greater heights of expertise. He had enjoyed harmonizing with Bob Nolan and with Tim Spencer. Nolan was a natural baritone with great range, and he was a capable yodeler. Spencer, a tenor, had quickly learned yodeling from Len. Having experienced a mutual rapport with both Bob and Tim, Len was convinced that the three performers could become a standout trio.

Len approached Tim at his Safeway workplace in October 1933. Although Tim enjoyed regular wages, he readily caught Len's dream. The two of them visited Bob at the Bel Air Country Club, waiting for the caddy as he walked off the last hole of the golf course. Bob was reluctant to give up his income as a caddy to resume an unrewarding musical career. He vividly remembered the dead-end struggles with the Rocky Mountaineers. But Len and Tim were persistent, and after a week Bob finally agreed to give music another try.

Len, Bob, and Tim moved to a Hollywood boardinghouse near KFWB, where Len continued to sing with the Texas Outlaws. For $7.50 a week, each boarder received room and two meals a day. The aspiring musicians ate lunch with KFWD employees, hoping to make a key contact. Bob constantly worked on songs that would suit their blend of talents, writing out arrangements for each one and copying lyrics for each singer. Tim also began writing songs for the group, and Len regularly took up pen and paper—for letters to Arlene.

The group agreed to call themselves the Pioneer Trio. At the insistence of Len Slye, they also agreed upon a rigorous regimen of practice. Since boyhood Len had understood the value of ceaseless practice. Len had practiced with a slingshot until he was a deadly threat to birds and small animals. He practiced with a .22 rifle until he was a crack marksman. He practiced with a guitar until he could play to professional standards. And he intended to practice his singing group until they developed close harmony to an unprecedented degree.

Indeed, the group soon to be known as the Sons of the Pioneers always would be distinguished by unusually tight harmony, achieved through talent and unrelenting rehearsal. Only ceaseless hours of practice could produce precise pronunciation and phrasing. Breaths had to be taken at the same instant. Closings had to be exact, especially on diphthongs ("tra-il" instead of "trayul," for example). The singers had to achieve identical rhythm, matching vowels, and simultaneous increase or decrease of volume. Certain vocal traits, especially vibrato and timbre, could not be acquired, so just the right singers had to be enlisted. Through the years, when a Pioneer had to be replaced, someone with a similar voice would be sought. The group refused to settle for similarity of these qualities, working incessantly to achieve sameness, and the precision that they accomplished would elevate the Sons of the Pioneers to a new level.

Len, Bob, and Tim practiced hour after hour at their boardinghouse. Len and Tim sang lead and tenor, respectively, and played guitars, while Bob sang baritone and played bass fiddle. They labored to perfect harmony yodeling as a sound which would distinguish them from other Western groups. Len had yodeled with Bob and Tim on other groups, and the Pioneer Trio determined to develop harmony yodeling as a distinctive feature. Also distinctive were the new songs from the prolific pen of Bob Nolan, as well as tunes that Tim Spencer began to write. After several weeks of practice, the Pioneer Trio could boast a superb blend of voices, harmony yodeling unique to their group, and a collection of songs unavailable to any other.

Confident of the potential of the music they now could offer, the group made a pitch to Harold Hall, electrical engineer at KFWB, and the group decided to offer him $150 to arrange an audition at the station. Len, Bob, and Tim each obtained a fifty-dollar bill. Tim invited Hall to eat at the boardinghouse, and afterward the group brought him to their room. The Pioneer Trio auditioned for Hall, performing their best numbers. Then Tim Spencer spread out the three fifty-dollar bills in front of Hall. Bob Nolan laughed when recalling Hall's immediate reaction: "I can get you an audition."

At their audition, when the trio launched into harmony yodeling in Nolan's "Way Out There," they were hired before they could finish the number. The Pioneer Trio began daily appearances over KFWB with Jack LeFevre and His Texas Outlaws. Soon Benny Milligan, an entertainment columnist who wrote "Best Bets of the Day" for the *Los Angeles Examiner*, singled out the Pioneer Trio's version of "The Last Round-up" as a "Best Bet." The group also was mentioned in other columns in November and December of 1933.

With these publicity boosts, the popularity of the Pioneer Trio soared, as evidenced by fan mail addressed through KFWB. The station pulled the group out of the Texas Outlaws and gave them their own show from 8:00 to 9:00 A.M. The Pioneer Trio also appeared late at night with the Jack Joy Orchestra. Demand became so great that KFWB also put the group on the air, as "The Gold Star Rangers," from 5:00 to 6:00 P.M. The hour-long program was sponsored by the Farley Clothing Company, which paid $35 per week apiece. "I thought I was going to swallow my tongue," reminisced Roy Rogers. "Thirty-five dollars was like a million to me then." In addition to their busy broadcast schedule, the Pioneer Trio enjoyed an upsurge in paid personal appearances. "The phone in our boardinghouse was ringing morning and night," said Roy.

Despite this enormous amount of exposure, the group was determined to continue presenting original music. Bob Nolan churned out tune after tune, while Tim Spencer also composed songs regularly. Nolan always remembered this busy, creative period as his happiest time with the group.

The Pioneer Trio soon decided that a fiddler would improve their instrumentation, while relieving their vocal strain with frequent solo passages. Sensing the strong upward direction of the group, Len, Bob, and Tim determined to add an outstanding fiddler. Musicians were aware that the best fiddler around California was a talented Texan named Hugh Farr.

Thomas Hubert Farr was born on December 6, 1903, in Llano, a small county seat town in the Texas Hill Country. Thomas Benjamin and Hattie Wheatley Farr had five daughters before Hugh was born. (When he finally produced a son, the proud father, who played the fiddle, pointed at Hugh and announced, "There's my fiddler!") Later two more sons, Glen and Karl, rounded out a family of eight. The baby of the family, Karl Marx Farr, was born on April 25, 1909, in another Hill Country town, Rochelle. Thomas Benjamin Farr worked in construction, relocating his family as he moved from job to job in such towns as Llano, Rochelle, San Saba, Breckenridge, and Big Spring.

Thomas and Hattie, playing the fiddle and guitar respectively, often entertained at dances and parties, and they passed on their musical abilities. One of their daughters, Belle, became a fine guitarist. By the age of seven, Hugh was good enough on the guitar to play with his father at Saturday night dances. Hugh's younger brothers, Glen and Karl, also picked up various instruments at young ages.

When Hugh was nine, the gifted youngster began playing a fiddle his father had ordered with cigar coupons. Immediately demonstrating an affinity for the instrument, Hugh soon won a fiddler's contest. Impressed by the talented youngster, a man in the audience gave Hugh his fiddle. Hugh used this instrument for the rest of his life. Rapidly mastering his father's repertoire, Hugh soon was

BOB WILLS AND WESTERN SWING (AND HUGH FARR)

During the 1930s the Dixieland jazz of the Roaring Twenties evolved into a Big Band sound, the "swing" music of Benny Goodman and other bandleaders. Simultaneously, the country counterpart of this popular music was "Western swing," made famous by Bob Wills and His Texas Playboys. Wills was a talented and innovative fiddler who gravitated from West Texas to Fort Worth, where he began to form a band and develop a lively style of music. When Bob Wills and His Texas Playboys began broadcasting over radio station KVOO in Tulsa in 1934, their popularity soared, and Bob became known as the "King of Western Swing." Bob's jazzed-up fiddle breakdowns provided a hallmark for the band.

In California the gifted Hugh Farr, who had no peer as a fiddler, also was creating jazzy breakdowns during these same years. Like Wills, Farr was a native Texan who concentrated upon Western music while being influenced by the wild and fast-paced sounds of jazz. Although the Sons of the Pioneers featured vocal harmony over instrumentation, the movies and recordings of the 1930s and 1940s demonstrate Hugh Farr creating fiddle music as vigorous and inventive as that of Bob Wills.

fiddling at Saturday night dances, while his father backed up the boy on guitar. It was not long before Glen joined in at parties, and little Karl began appearing when he was seven.

Karl started out on a mandolin, backing up his older brothers as they sang and played. Then he took up the banjo, moved on to the guitar, and even fooled around with drums. Like Hugh, Karl exhibited exceptional talent. In 1922, at the age of thirteen, he began playing with a band in the Big Spring area.

Thomas Farr moved from West Texas to California in 1925, finding construction work in Encino. Twenty-one-year-old Hugh got a job with the construction crew at North Hollywood High School. Glen and Karl found miscellaneous employment around Bakersfield. Karl also found a bride, a rancher's daughter named May, and in 1928 they became the parents of Karl, Jr. Hugh had married at eighteen in Texas, but the union did not last long. In California, Hugh had three more brief marriages, before eventually finding a lifelong mate with his fifth bride.

The Farr brothers continued to use their musical talents. In the evenings Hugh fiddled with a combo at Mammy's Shack, a bar on Ventura Boulevard in Sherman Oaks, just east of Encino. Glen and Karl also performed after working the Bakersfield area. After Mammy's Shack burned, Hugh, Glen, and Karl worked as a trio around Southern California. Several times the trio was hired to perform at dances for Los Angeles city employees, and they appeared on radio station KELW in Burbank. But Glen soon drifted away from music, becoming a successful building contractor.

In 1929 Hugh and Karl caught on with a popular group, Len Nash and His Country Boys. From 1929 until 1933, KFOX in Long Beach broadcast "Len Nash and His Country Boys Barn Dance," and the group had recording sessions during this period. Hugh and Karl also were employed as staff musicians at KFOX. Periodically, the Farr brothers would be told to fill in one or two minutes of air time. Hugh would name a key, and the brothers would launch into an impromptu tune. Maturing as musicians during the Jazz Age, the Farr brothers exhibited strong jazz elements in their playing styles. Hugh, as the fiddler, and Karl, as a guitarist, became well known as lively and innovative stylists.

In 1933 the "Barn Dance" show ended, but Nash formed the Haywire Trio, with Hugh, Karl, and a female musician. Then Hugh was approached by the Pioneer Trio. Confident of his abilities and aware of his growing reputation, Hugh had to be persuaded to join the popular new group. Len Slye was an old hand at enlisting musicians, and the Pioneer Trio willingly staged an audition for their prospective fiddler. Impressed ("the hair was standing up on the back of my neck"), Hugh agreed to fiddle for the Pioneer Trio.

Although Hugh could not read music, he had the gift of memorizing hundreds upon hundreds of tunes. He provided rich accompaniment to the Pioneer Trio, while never intruding on the singing. In addition, his deep bass voice was used by the trio for quartet numbers.

Not long after Hugh joined the Pioneer Trio, Harold Hall introduced them over KFWB as "The Sons of the Pioneers." When they later asked Hall why he called them Sons of the Pioneers, rather than the Pioneer Trio, he said that the youthful singers looked too young to be pioneers. Hall insisted that Sons of the

Pioneers was a better fit, and the name stuck. In 1933 and 1934 Len Slye, Bob Nolan, and Tim Spencer had performed as the Rocky Mountaineers, International Cowboys, O-Bar-O Cowboys, Gold Star Rangers, and Pioneer Trio. Finally, as the Sons of the Pioneers, they arrived at an identity which a gifted and energetic band of performers would establish as the preeminent group of Western musicians.

Will Rogers, one of America's most famous and beloved public figures, asked the Sons of the Pioneers to perform with him at a Salvation Army benefit in San Bernardino. This notice by a major star proclaimed that the Sons of the Pioneers were on their way to stardom of their own. Sadly, soon after this appearance, Will Rogers left with pilot Wiley Post for Alaska, where they were killed in a plane crash on August 15, 1935. A couple of years later, when Republic Pictures was searching for a more attractive name for Leonard Slye, one of the reasons he agreed to Roy Rogers was his deep admiration for Will Rogers.

The Sons of the Pioneers made time in their busy schedule to record a series of Standard Transcriptions, featuring old standards along with the new

RADIO TRANSCRIPTIONS

During the 1930s and 1940s, the Sons of the Pioneers recorded several hundred tunes for radio transcription services. These transcriptions were broadcast throughout the nation and abroad, and were instrumental in popularizing the California group.

While radio stations in major cities such as New York, Chicago, and Los Angeles had access to a large pool of talent for live entertainment, stations in smaller communities had a hard time filling their programming slots. Indeed, even large stations needed recorded programming for late hours or for occasions when live entertainers did not arrive. But from the advent of broadcast radio in the 1920s until the mid-1940s, major record companies felt that radio airplay would reduce sales and refused to permit broadcast of their records. Therefore, in the early 1930s, transcription companies began to provide alternate programming in the form of prerecorded music by a wide variety of artists. Transcription discs, which were played at 33 RPM and which usually were sixteen inches wide, were leased to stations for fees commensurate with the approximate size of the listening audience.

In 1934 Jerry King, general manager of KFWB, began organizing a new transcription company, Standard Radio. After recording a few sample acts, he engaged the Sons of the Pioneers to provide the first full series of Standard transcriptions. The transcription sessions were conducted late that summer in Hollywood at Recordings, Inc., located at 5505 Melrose Avenue. The Pioneers recorded 151 songs, everything from the original compositions of

(continued on next page)

compositions of Bob Nolan and Tim Spencer. These radio transcriptions introduced the Sons of the Pioneers to audiences throughout the country.

While recording radio transcriptions, the Sons of the Pioneers signed a contract with a new record company, Decca, guaranteeing them one penny for every record sale. The Sons of the Pioneers first went into a Decca recording studio in Los Angeles on August 8, 1934. (This date also was the first Decca recording session for superstar Bing Crosby.) It was customary to record four sides (two records) during a session. The first four Sons of the Pioneer sides were covered by Len Slye, Bob Nolan, Tim Spencer, and Hugh Farr. Fittingly, all four songs were composed for the Sons of the Pioneers. Bob Nolan had written "Way Out There," "Tumbling Tumbleweeds," and "Ridin' Home," while Bob had collaborated with Tim Spencer on "Moonlight On the Prairie." It was the first of scores of recording sessions during which the Sons of the Pioneers would cut hundreds of sides. And this first recording session produced a hit. "Tumbling Tumbleweeds," destined to become a Western classic, climbed to Number Thirteen on the charts by mid-December.

(*continued from previous page*)
Nolan and Spencer to traditional cowboy songs to hymns. Because editing was not possible on the old wax discs, a mistake meant that the artists would have to start over from the first song. Transcription companies therefore overlooked minor miscues, which helped to promote a more relaxed atmosphere closer to live performances than to commercial recording sessions.

These first Standard discs were sold outright to radio stations, many of which continued to use the Pioneer transcriptions for years, sometimes into the 1950s. Transcription work paid the artists only a fee, but even without royalties the Pioneers reaped a fortune of exposure. Bob Nolan, Len Slye, Tim Spencer, and Hugh Farr were the Pioneers on these initial transcriptions.

The next Pioneer transcriptions were recorded in Chicago in 1940, when the group spent several months in the Windy City. Bob Nolan, Tim Spencer, Lloyd Perryman, Pat Brady, and Hugh and Karl Farr recorded 202 songs for NBC's Orthacoustic Recording Division. These transcriptions were titled *Symphonies of the Sage*. During World War II, the Armed Forces Radio Services broadcast numerous Pioneer recordings. And NBC included the Pioneers in their enormous *Thesaurus* transcription library, utilizing selections from *Symphonies of the Sage*, along with a few new recordings.

Many of the hundreds of transcription songs, which captured the Pioneers at the height of their creativity, were never commercially recorded.

Two days after this initial recording session, Tim Spencer took a bride. Tim had met Velma Blanton the previous year, when the O-Bar-O Cowboys had appeared in Lubbock. A steady correspondence followed, during Velma's senior year at Lubbock High School. By the time she graduated, Tim felt sufficiently successful to assume family responsibilities. Velma journeyed to California, where the couple married on August 10, 1934, at Wee Kirk o' the Heather at Forrest Lawn. (The next year their daughter, Loretta, was born, and their son, Harold, was born in 1936—the day after Tim had left on a five-week tour.)

On March 7, 1935, the Sons of the Pioneers had their second recording session with Decca. All four sides were Bob Nolan compositions, including the haunting "There's a Round-up in the Sky" and the lively "The Roving Cowboy" ("I'm a happy roving cowboy..."). A few days later, the Sons of the Pioneers returned to the studio to record four more sides.

The next two sessions would be seven months later, in October 1935, and by that time another gifted musician had become part of the group. As soon as Hugh Farr joined the Sons of the Pioneers, he began lobbying for the addition of his brother Karl to the group. Karl's talent as a guitarist was comparable to Hugh's gifts as a fiddler, and the brothers had played together since boyhood. With the Sons of the Pioneers enjoying escalating popularity and income, it was decided to make Karl the fifth member of the group. Karl and Hugh were able to back the singers with the same brilliant artistry as the matchless harmony of the trio, and the distinctive sound of the Sons of the Pioneers became fuller and richer.

A couple of years earlier, Bob Nolan had gone to Beverly Hills to see the Beverly Hill Billies when they emerged from station KMPC. But there was a crowd estimated at 10,000, and he could get no closer than a block from the station. On another occasion, Nolan saw fans bring boxes to stand on, hoping that they might catch a glimpse of the Hill Billies through the station windows. By 1935, however, the Beverly Hill Billies had begun to slip in popularity, while the Sons of the Pioneers now were known as the most notable Western singing group in California. Influenced by jazz, especially in the instrumentation of the Farr brothers, and by country music, the Sons of the Pioneers nevertheless developed a predominantly Western image. And for a Western musical group, successful at recordings, radio shows, and personal appearances—and based in Hollywood—the next step had to be motion pictures.

Advertising photo for a daily noon radio show sponsored by "Palace Credit." L to R: Hugh Farr, Bob Nolan, Tim Spencer, Len Slye.

The Farley Clothing Company sponsored a daily show over KFWB featuring the popular Pioneers as the "Gold Star Rangers." Farley applauds the Rangers. L to R: Karl Farr, Hugh Farr, Tim Spencer, Len Slye, Bob Nolan.

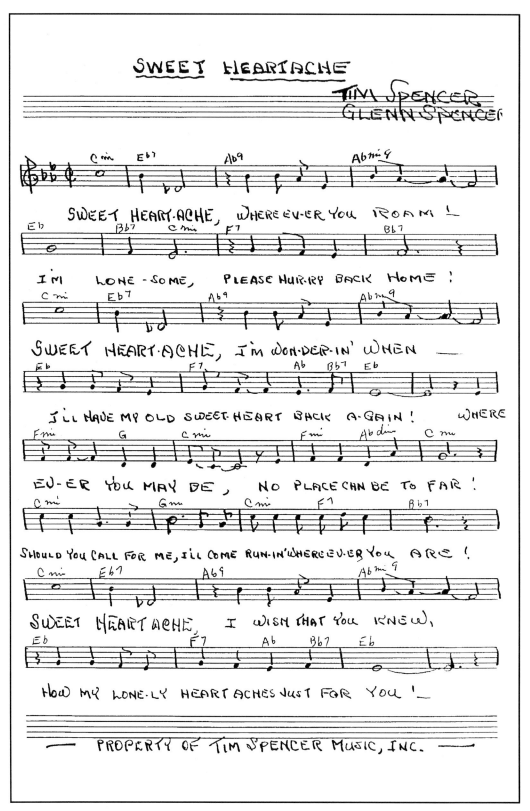

A composition by brothers Tim and Glenn Spencer.

The talented Hugh Farr. When famed conductor Leopold Stokowski was asked whom he considered to be the greatest natural violinist of the century, he replied: "It really has to be two people—the left hand of Fritz Kreisler and the right hand of that fellow who plays with the Sons of the Pioneers—I can't remember his name."

Despite this publicity photo, the Sons of the Pioneers were determined to reject a hillbilly image and emphasize a Western flavor in their music and costumes. L to R: Karl Farr, Len Slye, Tim Spencer, Bob Nolan, Hugh Farr.

*Karl Farr (center) joined the Pioneers in 1935, adding a fuller sound with his "Gallopin' Guitar."
Surrounding Karl, clockwise from top: Tim Spencer, Bob Nolan, Len Slye, Hugh Farr.*

3
On the Silver Screen
(1935-36)

"I'm so happy I've just got to sing!"
—Bob Nolan in *Gallant Defender*

THE SONS OF THE PIONEERS increasingly were in demand for public and radio appearances, and by 1935 the group had launched a promising recording career. And when the silver screen beckoned, the Pioneers began the first of nearly 100 film appearances.

Before the advent of television and, eventually, music videos, musicians were heard over the radio and on recordings, but rarely were they seen in performance by large audiences. A new group, such as the Sons of the Pioneers, could be seen only during personal appearances. Movies, therefore, offered incomparable exposure and the potential for an enormous career boost.

When the Sons of the Pioneers began appearing in motion pictures in 1935, Westerns long had been a staple of the film industry, and it was in these movies that the Pioneers would become nationally known. The Western, with its sweeping scenery and galloping horses, was perfect for the big screen. Motion pictures needed movement, and Westerns *moved*. The historic West of cattle drives and outlaws and gunfighters had only recently passed into history, and young audiences thrilled to the screen adventures of heroic celluloid cowboys sporting six-guns and big hats.

Music was a vital part of Western movies even during the silent film era. When such stars as William S. Hart, Tom Mix, and Ken Maynard flashed across the nation's movie screens, pianos of silent film theaters added to the excitement by banging out musical accompaniment.

Ironically, there was less music in Westerns with the advent of sound films in the late 1920s. Early sound Westerns, in the interest of economy, did not insert background music. Stars such as Ken Maynard and Hoot Gibson had been rodeo and Wild West show performers; they were impressive figures on horseback, but they delivered dialogue awkwardly. Although fans came to Westerns for action, not acting, the action seemed flat without the exciting musical strains provided by silent theater pianists.

Drawing upon the Western musical tradition of hoedowns and cowboy ballads, Ken Maynard tried musical interludes in some of his films, and so did young John Wayne. Wayne's singing voice had to be dubbed, and his experiment as "Singin' Sandy" proved to be brief. Maynard engaged Gene Autry, a radio and recording star, to deliver musical numbers in his movies. After appearing twice with Maynard in 1934, the following year Autry starred in *The Phantom Empire*, a science fiction serial with a Western setting. The role was intended for Maynard, but the cantankerous star was replaced by Autry.

Although Gene was physically unimpressive and uncomfortable as an actor, he was pleasant and sang well, and audiences responded in great numbers. Soon he sang his way through *Tumbling Tumbleweeds*, the first of a series of musical Westerns which established Autry as a major box-office attraction. (Rights to the title of Bob Nolan's song had to be purchased for *Tumbling Tumbleweeds*.) Gene Autry was a screen phenomenon of 1935, and producers—always alert to a new trend—scrambled to find more Western musical talent.

During the mid-1930s about 300 Westerns were filmed every year, and suddenly there was a need for pioneer music in these movies. A great many hillbilly and Western music groups were offered film appearances in the wake of the Autry phenomenom. Being seen by a national audience did little for most of these groups. But the Sons of the Pioneers already had a superior sound, and their lively, fast-paced numbers would prove popular with Western audiences.

In 1935 Warner Brothers brought the group from their radio station, KFWB, to provide music for a comedy short, "Radio Scout," starring a skinny ex-vaudevillian called El (for Elmer) Brendel. It was a modest film debut, but soon the Sons of the Pioneers enjoyed another celluloid assignment—singing for a Universal cartoon entitled *Bronco Buster*.

Then Liberty, a small independent studio, put the Sons of the Pioneers in *The Old Homestead*, a feature based on a Denham Thompson play. Mary Carlisle was the star, and one of the players was Fuzzy Knight, a grizzled Western sidekick. Len Slye, Hugh Farr, and Verne Spence (Tim Spencer) were listed in the cast credits. The Pioneers sang a Bob Nolan tune, "Happy Cowboy," along with "There's a Roundup in the Sky" and "That Old White Mule of Mine."

The group also worked at MGM with the great comedy producer, Hal Roach. *Slightly Static* was a two-reel Hal Roach comedy that featured the Randall Sisters, the Vitaphone Four, and the Sons of the Pioneers: "Bob Nolan, Leonard Slye, Verne Spence, Hugh Farr, Karl Farr." The Pioneers performed "Echoes From the Hills," written by Bob Nolan.

Warner Brothers soon used the Sons of the Pioneers in another short film. *Romance of the West* was advertised as a "Warner Bros.-Vitaphone Musical Technicolor Short, featuring the Sons of the Pioneers." The group sang another Bob Nolan song, "I Follow the Stream."

Mack Sennett, legendary creator of the Keystone Kops, put the Pioneers in another two-reeler, *Way Up Thar*, advertised as "A Young Romance Comedy." Sennett was the producer-director, and the little film starred comedienne Joan

Davis. The cast was rounded out by Myra and Louise Keaton, and by Leonard Slye, Tim Spencer, Hugh Farr, Karl Farr, and Bob Nolan.

On Wednesday, October 9, 1935, the Sons of the Pioneers had a recording session with Decca in Los Angeles. Decca, of course, hoped that the group's movie appearances would increase record sales. It was the first session to include Karl Farr on guitar. Hugh Farr fiddled, and the vocal trio was Len Slye, Bob Nolan, and Tim Spencer. The customary four sides were cut: "Over the Santa Fe Trail," "Song of the Pioneers," "The New Frontier," and "Echoes From the Hills." Five days later the group returned to the studio to cover four more sides, including "Westward Ho."

The next movie assignment would lead to steady work for the Sons of the Pioneers. Columbia Pictures had signed Charles Starrett to star in a series of B Westerns. Starrett had appeared regularly in Hollywood films for several years. He had never worked in a Western, but his performances in such action films as *Return of Casey Jones* and *The Silver Streak* indicated great potential as a cowboy hero. Since Starrett was not a singer, the Sons of the Pioneers were hired to add Western music.

The first Starrett film, *Gallant Defender*, was released in November 1935 (in that same month, two other films featuring the Sons of the Pioneers were released, *Romance of the West* and *Way Up Thar*). *Gallant Defender* had a homesteaders vs. cattlemen plot, and in the movie Starrett was falsely accused of murder. The movie opened with a wagon train on the move, as the Sons of the Pioneers sang a Tim Spencer song, "Westward Ho." In camp the Pioneers sang "The New Frontier," a Bob Nolan tune. At one point in the movie, Nolan announced to Starrett, "I'm so happy I've just got to sing!"

"Well," replied the hero, "go ahead and sing!" Nolan and the other Pioneers led the homesteaders in a rousing version of "Oh, Susanna." At the end of the film, the Pioneers reprised "Westward Ho."

The Pioneers were costumed in scruffy frontier clothes, but their sound was a strong addition to the movie. They appeared in the second Charles Starrett film, *The Mysterious Avenger*. Starrett played a Texas Ranger called to halt rustlers. Joan Perry, who later would marry Columbia studio head Harry Cohn, was the leading lady in both *Gallant Defender* and *The Mysterious Avenger*. The Sons of the Pioneers performed another Bob Nolan song, "Oh, I Miss You So, My Darling."

The Mysterious Avenger was released in January 1936. While Starrett continued to star in his series of Westerns, the Sons of the Pioneers went on to other films and to Decca recording sessions in May, June, and July. But as Charles Starrett films began to find an audience, Columbia executives remembered the work of the Sons of the Pioneers in the first two films.

Warner Brothers had decided to promote Dick Foran as a singing cowboy. The big, handsome Foran had a fine voice, and he was billed as "The Singing Cowboy" in his second film, *Song of the Saddle*, released in February 1936. The Sons of the Pioneers sang "Underneath the Western Sky" and Bob Nolan's lively "Happy Cowboy."

After *Song of the Saddle*, the Sons of the Pioneers appeared in their most important film to date, a Bing Crosby feature for Paramount. The recording superstar began making movies for Paramount in 1931. His films were light romantic comedies with plenty of crooning. Bing's musical talent and easygoing acting style rapidly made him a major box office draw. With the sudden popularity of singing cowboy movies, Paramount decided upon a Western setting for Bing's next musical romance.

Rhythm on the Range was a contemporary Western with opening scenes filmed at the famous Madison Square Garden Rodeo in New York City. Bing played the foreman of the Frying Pan Ranch in Arizona, who was an expert rodeo cowboy. Although Bing was unconvincing as a Westerner, his crooning won the heart of leading lady Frances Farmer and, as a bonus, soothed a dangerous bull. Martha Raye, in her first screen role, was loud and brassy as a man-crazy young lady.

The Sons of the Pioneers were not listed in the cast credits, but they appeared in the film's big production number, "I'm An Old Cowhand." Lasting for several minutes in the last reel of the movie, "I'm An Old Cowhand" was performed during a party scene by Bing, the Pioneers, and just about everybody else in the cast. During the long number Tim, then Len, then Bob each were given small choruses. Bob beat the bass fiddle, Len strummed a guitar, and Tim held a guitar, while the Farr brothers led the instrumentals for the number. Although their appearance was brief, the Sons of the Pioneers now could list a full-length feature from a major studio on their credits.

Next the Pioneers returned to Warner Brothers for another Dick Foran movie, *The California Mail*. While Dick sang and played a Pony Express rider trying to win a mail contract, the Pioneers performed a square dance number and "Underneath a Western Sky." Foran starred in only eight more B Westerns, along with a couple of serials (Warner Brothers dropped the singing cowboy genre), but for years afterward he would remain busy as a supporting actor.

In 1936 the Sons of the Pioneers also appeared in back-to-back Gene Autry movies. *The Big Show* was released by Republic on November 16, just two days after the Warner Brothers release of *The California Mail*.

The Big Show was Gene's twelfth starring

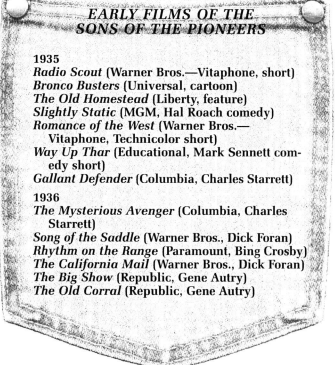

EARLY FILMS OF THE SONS OF THE PIONEERS

1935
Radio Scout (Warner Bros.—Vitaphone, short)
Bronco Busters (Universal, cartoon)
The Old Homestead (Liberty, feature)
Slightly Static (MGM, Hal Roach comedy)
Romance of the West (Warner Bros.—Vitaphone, Technicolor short)
Way Up Thar (Educational, Mark Sennett comedy short)
Gallant Defender (Columbia, Charles Starrett)

1936
The Mysterious Avenger (Columbia, Charles Starrett)
Song of the Saddle (Warner Bros., Dick Foran)
Rhythm on the Range (Paramount, Bing Crosby)
The California Mail (Warner Bros., Dick Foran)
The Big Show (Republic, Gene Autry)
The Old Corral (Republic, Gene Autry)

role. His character was always named Gene Autry, and his films rarely used a historical setting. Like the films of Tom Mix, Gene's movies were set in a contemporary West. On his horse, Champion, Gene regularly galloped after 1930s gangsters driving automobiles down dusty roads. The Western towns in Gene's movies usually boasted a radio station and a night club, along with room to park cars beside horses at the hitching rails. Gene and his talented sidekick, Smiley Burnette, solved most of the problems in his films by singing songs. And young fans loved this curious formula.

In 1936 the *Motion Picture Herald*, which annually listed the Top Ten Box Office Stars, began releasing a separate list of Top Ten Western Stars. In that first poll Gene Autry was in third place, behind top-ranked Buck Jones and George O'Brien. The next year Gene reached Number One, where he stayed for six years, until he left Hollywood for military service in World War II. By 1936, Gene Autry was Hollywood's hottest Western star, and the Sons of the Pioneers were fortunate to appear in *The Big Show*.

The Big Show was one of Gene's best movies. The story opened with scenes of 1930s movie-making, as Gene played a dual role: himself, as usual, and "Tom Ford," a temperamental movie star. Ford skipped out on a personal appearance at the Texas Centennial State Fair in Dallas, but lookalike Gene filled in. The movie was filmed at the 1936 Centennial, resulting in actual footage of this colorful and historic event. Western music was provided by several groups, including the Sons of the Pioneers. The Pioneers performed "Roll, Wagons Roll," "The Wild and Wooly West," and "Nobody's Darling But Mine." During the latter number the group backed Gene Autry in a large radio studio. The Farr brothers sat behind Gene with their instruments. Standing behind the Farrs, Bob worked the bass fiddle, Tim played a fiddle, and Len—wearing a huge black hat—strummed his guitar. Hugh Farr's jazzy fiddle sound was notable during the lively rendition of "The Wild and Wooly West."

In a recording session in Los Angeles on June 18, 1936, the Sons of the Pioneers covered "Ride, Ranger, Ride," by Tim Spencer, and "Blue Bonnet Girl," by Tim's brother Glenn. Back in the Decca studio a couple of weeks later, on July 3, the group recorded four fine songs: "Empty Saddles"; "I'm An Old Cowhand," by popular songwriter Johnny Mercer; the haunting "Blue Prairie," by Bob Nolan and Tim Spencer; and Nolan's "One More Ride."

The Sons of the Pioneers spent several weeks in Dallas in 1936. After filming *The Big Show*, the group appeared regularly at the Texas Centennial. En route from California to Texas, Len Slye stopped over in Roswell to marry Arlene Wilkins in the living room of the Wilkins home. At the same time that the group was performing at the Texas Centennial, a lovely Texas lady was working as a band singer on Dallas radio station WFAA. Her stage name was "Dale Evans."

While appearing in Dallas, the Sons of the Pioneers had a disagreement that caused Tim Spencer to leave the group. Such incidents were common with musical groups. The rift could not have been too deep, because Tim returned within a couple of years. The Sons of the Pioneers did not have to look far to replace Spencer after the Dallas discord, as a standout musician named

Lloyd Perryman had substituted for various members of the group on several occasions.

The youngest of nine children, Lloyd Wilson Perryman was born in rural Arkansas on January 3, 1917. Lloyd attended a two-room school at Zion, where his father farmed and ran a general store. In church Lloyd sang from paperback hymnals with shape notes. Even as a boy he was able to sing harmony, and he began trying to play an old guitar. Lloyd had two uncles who played and sang. He enjoyed Saturday night sings, when the Perrymans and other families would gather around someone's parlor piano or pump organ.

When Lloyd was eleven, the Perrymans moved to Wasco, California, where his father farmed and dabbled in real estate. As a teenager, Lloyd participated in high school musical activities and in amateur radio programs at KERN in nearby Bakersfield. He developed a fine baritone voice with considerable range, and he became a competent guitarist. In 1932, at the age of fifteen, Lloyd decided to try his luck in Los Angeles, where he soon met Len Slye, Tim Spencer, and Bill Nichols—the trio of Benny Nawahi and His International Cowboys. Lloyd worked with a couple of struggling groups, the Sierra Mountaineers and Cyclone and His 4-S Ranch Boys, before catching on with the Beverly Hill Billies. After several months he joined Jack and His Texas Outlaws, then began singing with Jimmy LeFevre and His Saddle Pals. He appeared regularly on the radio with these groups, and he began substituting for members of the Sons of the Pioneers. After Bob Nolan contacted him about Tim Spencer's vacancy, Lloyd officially became a member of the Sons of the Pioneers in September 1936.

The Sons of the Pioneers soon went to work on Gene Autry's next movie, *The Old Corral*. The group was featured as "The O'Keefe boys," and each of the Pioneers was given dialogue. The O'Keefe boys are working up a musical radio act, but early in the movie they feel forced to rob a bus. Sheriff Gene Autry is a passenger on the bus, and soon he and his deputy, Smiley Burnette, ride in pursuit of the gang. Gene and Smiley capture three of the O'Keefe boys, and in their cell they sing "Silent Trails."

Gene asks them to perform at his upcoming show, but they insist that the music is "flat" without the other two boys. So Gene tracks the other two to the Old Corral. Gene subdues both bandits, sending "Buck" (Len Slye) tumbling down a hill.

"You all right, Buck?" asks Gene.

"My right arm's sprained a little," Len replies, rubbing his arm, "my rib's stove in."

"How's your throat?"

"Throat's all right," concedes a puzzled Len.

"Let's hear you," commands Sheriff Autry, and Len obediently yodels.

The next scene has all five O'Keefes in a cell together, dutifully practicing

HORSE OPERETTAS

The Sons of the Pioneers, often called "Aristocrats of the Range," helped to make nearly one hundred Western movies. Western films were nicknamed "horse operas" or "oaters" or "sagebrush sagas." Most of the Pioneer films, of course, were musical Westerns, which were dubbed "horse operettas."

"Silent Trails" (written by Tim Spencer, who also composed "He's Gone Up the Trail"). At the show, held on the town's main street, the O'Keefes perform "Silent Trails" while seated on their horses.

When Chicago gangsters drive through town firing at the leading lady (who witnessed a murder), Sheriff Autry informs the O'Keefes that if they will be his posse, the charges against them will be dropped. The O'Keefes turn over their instruments to a deputy, then follow Gene at a gallop. With their help, Gene rounds up the gangsters.

THE SONS OF THE PIONEERS MEET THE LIGHT CRUST DOUGHBOYS

The Light Crust Doughboys were organized in Texas in 1931. Charter member Bob Wills soon moved on to form his Texas Playboys, while the Light Crust Doughboys, sponsored by a Fort Worth flour company, enjoyed great popularity in the Lone Star State. (Like the Sons of the Pioneers, the Light Crust Doughboys still perform, stressing the nostalgic appeal of their Western swing music.)

In 1936 the Light Crust Doughboys made a brief jaunt to the Los Angeles area. The Sons of the Pioneers were involved in filming two Gene Autry movies, but Hugh and Karl Farr reached out to their fellow Texans by introducing them to the local music scene. The Sons of the Pioneers never backed away from night life, and Bob Nolan and Tim Spencer came along as well. Young banjoist Smokey Montgomery remembered that their favorite destination was the Texas Club in Long Beach. The club closed at 1:00 A.M., whereupon the musicians engaged in a nightly jam session.

The Old Corral was released on December 2, 1936, just two weeks after *The Big Show*. By this time the Sons of the Pioneers had recorded nearly three dozen sides for Decca, and had appeared in thirteen films of various sorts. During 1935 and 1936, the Pioneers worked for eight movie studios, including three independents (Liberty, Educational, and Republic) and five of the eight majors (Warner Brothers, Universal, MGM, Paramount, and Columbia).

The Sons of the Pioneers provided excellent music in their film performances. And, unlike many other groups, they looked right in Western clothes. Most of the so-called "Western" and hillbilly groups seemed out of place in cowboy duds. Many of the performers were chubby, and their hats perched uncomfortably atop their heads. But the well-built Bob Nolan looked every inch the strong frontiersman, while Len Slye and Tim Spencer—as well as Lloyd Perryman and, later, Pat Brady—sported the lean physiques of the typical cowboy. The rugged-looking Farr brothers had been born and raised in Texas ranch country. Each of the Pioneers wore a cowboy hat convincingly (Pat Brady was especially particular about the crease of his Stetson).

The Sons of the Pioneers looked Western and sounded Western, as they proved in film after film in 1935 and 1936. At a time when music was increasingly important in Western movies, the Sons of the Pioneers were establishing themselves as the best singing group in Hollywood. It was only a matter of time until some studio signed them to a contract for regular film work.

The fast-rising Sons of the Pioneers. Top, L to R: Hugh Farr, Karl Farr. Front: Bob Nolan, Tim Spencer, Len Slye.

The Sons of the Pioneers in 1935. L to R: Hugh Farr, Karl Farr, Bob Nolan, Len Slye, Tim Spencer.

The Pioneers surround a pretty lady in 1936.
L to R: Len Slye, Hugh Farr, Tim Spencer, Bob Nolan, Karl Farr.

The Pioneers with Governor James V. Allred at the Texas Centennial. L to R: Texans Karl and Hugh Farr; Tim Spencer, Governor Allred, Len Slye, Bob Nolan.

The Sons of the Pioneers flank Amon G. Carter, in a ten-gallon hat, and another dignitary at the 1936 Texas Centennial. The Pioneers, L to R: Hugh Farr, Bob Nolan, Tim Spencer, Len Slye, Karl Farr.

The Sons of the Pioneers appeared in their first high-profile movie in Rhythm on the Range, starring Bing Crosby, center, with an unidentified man. The Pioneers, standing behind Crosby, L to R: Karl Farr, Hugh Farr, Bob Nolan, Tim Spencer, Len Slye.

Ads for Gene Autry's The Old Corral *gave a prominent credit to the Sons of the Pioneers.*

In 1936 the Pioneers appeared in two Westerns starring Dick Foran, a Warner Brothers singing cowboy. The Pioneers and Foran again worked together in 1950 in John Ford's Rio Grande.

Charles Starrett, with a big smile and bigger hat, is surrounded by the Pioneers in Western Caravans. *From left: Pat Brady, Tim Spencer, Hugh Farr, Karl Farr, Lloyd Perryman, Bob Nolan.*

4
With Charles Starrett
(1937-41)

"I wish I could have kept that group."
—CHARLES STARRETT

BY 1937 THE SONS OF THE PIONEERS were known in Hollywood as recording artists and as a top Western backup group for numerous studios. Their work for Columbia Pictures had been in the studio's first two Charles Starrett Westerns, in 1935. For years Columbia's principal Western stars had been Buck Jones and Tim McCoy. But in 1935 McCoy was signed by another studio, while Columbia chose not to renew the contract of Jones. Columbia determined to build a Western series around Starrett, a big, good-looking actor who had played in diverse films, from *The Sweethearts of Sigma Chi* to *The Mask of Fu Manchu.*

Tyrannical studio head Harry Cohn knew that filmmaking was a tough business. "If you had guts, he'd give you an opportunity," stated award-winning director Frank Capra. "If you didn't, he didn't want you around. . . ." Starrett, whose competitiveness had been honed as a standout football player in college, stayed around for seventeen years and 132 Westerns. And the Sons of the Pioneers would prove instrumental in Starrett's rise as a Western star.

Charles Starrett was born in 1904, the youngest of nine children. His father was a wealthy inventor and manufacturer of precision tools. Charles was a fine athlete who became a three-year starter at fullback for the Dartmouth varsity. In 1924 Richard Dix starred in *The Quarterback*, filmed in part on the Dartmouth campus. Starrett and several other footballers played small roles. Bitten by the acting bug, Starrett ventured to New York in search of stage work.

After playing on and off Broadway for several years, Starrett was signed by a Paramount talent scout in 1929. In Hollywood he appeared in a succession of society dramas and mysteries, and he was a founding member of the Screen Actors Guild. But he made no Westerns until Columbia decided to groom him as a sagebrush star. "I never dreamed I'd be doing Westerns," said Starrett.

37

Columbia had planned to start their 1935-36 Tim McCoy series with *Gallant Defender*. But an independent studio, Puritan, lured McCoy away from Columbia. Handsome Charles Starrett boasted a strong jaw and a strapping physique, and he was inserted into the series intended for McCoy. Starrett was costumed like McCoy, with black clothes, a white hat, and a long white bandana. He was placed astride a magnificent white Arabian, named Raider from a poll of the studio's secretaries (for the best name from such polls, Columbia would pay $15).

The Sons of the Pioneers provided musical interludes in *Gallant Defender* and in the second movie of the Starrett series, *The Mysterious Avenger*. The singing group then went on to other jobs in 1936, appearing in Bing Crosby's *Rhythm on the Range* for Paramount, Dick Foran's *The California Mail* for Warners, and two Gene Autry Westerns for Republic. Periodically the group recorded background music for other Autry films. Meanwhile, Charles Starrett filmed nine more movies, finishing his first series and starting a second series.

By this time Gene Autry had transformed B Westerns with the spectacular success of his singing cowboy films. Tex Ritter was brought to Hollywood from

"CORNED BEEF AND CABBAGE"

Columbia Pictures was founded as a Poverty Row outfit in 1920 by Harry and Jack Cohn and Joe Brandt. Originally called CBC—for Cohn–Brandt–Cohn, but nicknamed "Corned Beef and Cabbage"—the studio was renamed "Columbia" in 1924.

By 1931 hard-nosed Harry Cohn had established himself as studio head. Cohn was a bullying employer who was widely despised and feared in Hollywood, but he deeply loved filmmaking. His goal was to complete a film each week. "I want one good picture a year," said Cohn, who filmed a great many B features and serials to underwrite a few prestige movies. Although the smallest of the majors, Columbia produced more B films, including Westerns, than any other major studio.

Cohn's best director was young Frank Capra, who turned out a classic comedy in 1934. *It Happened One Night* starred Clark Gable and Claudette Colbert. This sparkling film won the Academy Award for Best Picture, and Gable, Colbert, and Capra also were awarded Oscars. *It Happened One Night* was the first motion picture to win Academy Awards in all four major categories and earned Columbia widespread recognition. The studio's reputation was enhanced during the next few years by such Capra gems as *Mr. Deeds Comes To Town* (1936), *You Can't Take It With You* (1938), and *Mr. Smith Goes To Washington* (1939).

Shorter films were the bread-and-butter of Columbia. In 1934 the first of 190 Three Stooges features appeared. The popular Blondie and Dagwood series of comedies began in 1938. Biggest hits among the weekly serials were *The Shadow* (1940), *Terry and the Pirates* (1940), and *Batman* (1943). Through the years the stable of Columbia B Western stars included Buck Jones, Tim McCoy, Wild Bill Elliott, Tex Ritter, and Gene Autry. But none proved as durable as Charles Starrett, who filmed 132 oaters for Columbia from 1935 through 1952.

Broadway to become a singing cowboy, the search was on for other singing cowboys, and music became a prominent element for most Western filmmakers.

Since Charles Starrett did not sing, a tenor named Donald Grayson was added to his films as a second lead. Grayson first appeared in Starrett's sixth movie, *Dodge City Trail*. Grayson would help Starrett battle the bad guys, then break into song. Grayson was a well-trained singer with cultivated diction, but his singing was decidedly un-Western. He also had an unimposing physique. When singing around the campfire or serenading the leading lady, Grayson cut a rather unconvincing figure as a cowboy hero.

After four more films, Columbia signed the Sons of the Pioneers to add Western flavor to the music of the Starrett movies. When Columbia contacted the singing group about a contract, the Pioneers asked Ray Whitley, a friend and experienced musician, to handle negotiations with the formidable Harry Cohn. During the 1930s movie moguls were notoriously tight-fisted with wages (of course, during these depression years most wages were low). Whitley courageously battled Cohn on behalf of the Pioneers. Cohn agreed to allow the Pioneers to record background music at other studios, but his salary offer remained so low—a paltry $33 a week—that Whitely advised his friends not to sign. The Pioneers, however, felt that regular movie appearances would increase their fame and lead to other opportunities—which proved to be true. For a time the Pioneers continued live radio appearances "very early in the morning," recalled Starrett, "and would start working with me at Columbia around seven."

The first Starrett movie with the Sons of the Pioneers under contract was *The Old Wyoming Trail*, released in November 1937. The Pioneers backed up Grayson with "He's Ridin' Home" and "Lovesong of the Waterfall." In the movie, Starrett and Grayson and the Pioneers foiled the plans of the villains, who tried to buy up the farmers' land cheaply because a railroad was planned.

The chief villains were Dick Curtis and George Chesebro. Chesebro played a bad guy in more than 200 Western movies, while the hulking Curtis was equally familiar as a villain. Young fans usually did not know the names of such busy screen scoundrels as Chesebro and Curtis, but there was instant recognition of their surly faces. Chesebro and Curtis both faced off against Starrett on a regular basis. The hulking Curtis had thick lips and squinty eyes, and onscreen he radiated menace. He was as big as Starrett, and most films ended with a slam-bang fistfight between Curtis and the hero.

The athletic Starrett had boxed, and he took pride in his screen brawls. "I did so many fights with . . . Dick Curtis, it got to be called 'The Never Ending Fight.'" During the next four years, as the Sons of the Pioneers helped Charles Starrett contend with evil, that evil usually was personified by Dick Curtis and George Chesebro.

After filming *The Old Wyoming Trail*, Len Slye left the Pioneers to pursue his own movie career. Len already had played a few bit parts, including a bad guy who lost a fight to Gene Autry in *The Old Corral*. "I wanted to be the hero," Roy admitted in his book *Happy Trails*, "and I wanted to be the one whose name was on the movie marquee outside."

When Universal was trying to cast its own singing cowboy in 1936, Len got as far as a screen test. But Bob Baker won the role and began filming his own series in 1937. Ambitious and enterprising, Len continued to seek other opportunities. By the fall of 1937 word was out around Hollywood that Gene Autry was preparing to battle Republic Studios for a pay raise commensurate with the enormous success of his films. Herbert J. Yates, head of Republic, ordered auditions for a new singing cowboy. Yates hoped to intimidate Autry, rather than give him a raise, and if necessary Gene could be replaced by the new singing cowboy.

Len heard about the auditions at Republic when he went to a Glendale hat shop to pick up his Stetson, which had been reblocked. A tall cowboy hopeful named Carter was in the shop talking about buying a hat for the auditions. The next morning Len opportunistically drove to Republic, where he recently had worked on Autry movies. But at the gate he was turned away because he had no appointment pass. Len hung around, hoping to get inside with someone he knew.

After lunch he turned up his collar and pulled his hat brim low, then walked through the gate with a crowd of studio employees returning to work. After only a few steps Len was recognized by the guard. But just as he was about to be tossed out, Len was spotted by producer Sol Siegel, who was conducting the auditions. Familiar with Len's work as one of the Sons of the Pioneers, Siegel assumed that he had come to audition. Siegel told Len to get his guitar and sing a few songs.

The guitar was in Len's car, which was parked several blocks away. While Siegel cleared things with the guard, Len ran to his car and back again. He sang "Tumbling Tumbleweeds" and "Haddie Brown," which showcased his yodeling gifts. A screen test was quickly arranged. Subsequently, Len was released from his Columbia obligations, and he signed a Republic contract on October 13, 1937. It was a standard seven-year contract at $75 a week.

Republic changed his name from Leonard Slye to Dick Weston, and put him in a couple of films. Then, early in 1938, Gene Autry went on strike for higher pay. Gene repeatedly had threatened to strike, and he left the studio just as filming was about to begin on a new feature, *Washington Cowboy*. Republic determined to proceed with filming. Dick Weston would replace Gene, but a hurried

A CONTRACT ON THE LINKS

When Len Slye eagerly signed a contract with Republic in October 1937, he already was under contract to Columbia. The Sons of the Pioneers recently had signed with Columbia to appear in Charles Starrett movies.

In later years, Roy Rogers told his longtime director, William Witney, that he confessed his problem to Irving Briskin, who was in charge of Westerns at Columbia. Briskin charitably agreed to release the ambitious young man, as long as a replacement could quickly take his place on the Sons of the Pioneers. Pat Brady joined the singing group, while Len Slye went off to Republic to become Roy Rogers.

But Witney, who knew Briskin to be "one tough cookie," was somewhat dubious of this generosity. "I have never heard of an incident, before or after, where he made a decision out of his heart."

Perhaps Hugh Farr knew the real story. Since Len Slye was merely an unknown prospect, Farr related that studio heads Harry Cohn and Herb Yates played a round of golf, with the contract going to the winner.

conference produced a new name: Roy Rogers (reminiscent of the beloved Will Rogers). The movie also was retitled, *Under Western Skies*. Although Gene Autry finally returned to Republic, Roy Rogers continued to star in his own series.

While Roy Rogers moved toward stardom, the Sons of the Pioneers had to find a replacement for Len Slye.

The newest Pioneer had been born Robert Ellsworth Patrick Aloysious O'Brady on the last day of 1914 in Toledo, Ohio. Little Bob O'Brady was the only child of vaudeville performers. By the time he was four, Bob was part of the act. When he was twelve, his parents separated. Bob came to California with his father, who shortened their name to Brady.

At the age of twenty Bob Brady was part of a quartet that played clubs in California. He became friends with the Sons of the Pioneers, who played the same clubs. In addition to being a fine singer and yodeler, Brady played bass fiddle and was an irrepressible comedian. When he joined the Sons of the Pioneers in October 1937, he began calling himself Pat Brady, to avoid confusion with Bob Nolan.

Soon, however, the group realized that Brady did not provide quite the right vocal blend with Nolan and Perryman. Brady would continue to be a key member of the Pioneers, proving especially effective onscreen with his comic relief. ("I loved Pat's happy-go-lucky good humor," said Charles Starrett.) Now that the Sons of the Pioneers had a movie contract, Tim Spencer was easily persuaded to rejoin the group, taking over the lead on most numbers. During their years at Columbia, the usual Sons of the Pioneers aggregation would feature the trio of Bob Nolan, Lloyd Perryman and Tim Spencer, along with Hugh and Karl Farr and Pat Brady.

When Len Slye left for Republic, the Sons of the Pioneers had to regroup quickly, because filming was about to start on their second contracted Starrett movie, *Outlaws of the Prairie*. Western film critic Ted Reinhart ranks *Outlaws of the Prairie* as Starrett's best movie. Lovely Iris Meredith was the leading lady; she would be the heroine in nineteen of the Starrett movies with the Sons of the Pioneers. Donald Grayson was the second lead, and Dick Curtis led the bad guys.

There was a grisly piece of villainy in *Outlaws of the Prairie*. Starrett played a Texas Ranger who had his trigger finger cut off by the bad guys. This sadistic act set up a revenge motive, and Starrett put on a glove and began to fan his revolver. (In future Starrett films he usually fanned his sixgun, a flashy movement which added excitement to shootouts. Although it is almost impossible to hit a target when fanning a revolver, Starrett rarely missed—indeed, he repeatedly shot guns out of the hands of the bad guys.)

The public regarded blood violence as unwholesome for young audiences. Accordingly, B Westerns were filled with furious shootouts which rarely produced casualties. Even if someone was wounded, no blood was shown. So when Charles Starrett had his trigger finger cut off, there were complaints from certain quarters.

"After we made that picture," reminisced Starrett to James Horowitz, "the PTA and the church, the Catholic church, put up a big fuss."

Of course, kids in the audiences vividly remembered the scene. There was

B WESTERNS

Charles Starrett was a star of B Westerns. Indeed, of nearly 100 movie appearances by the Sons of the Pioneers, a majority of their films were B Westerns. During the mid-1930s, about 300 B Westerns were filmed every year.

There were eight major studios that filmed A movies, features that were eighty to ninety minutes in length (and sometimes longer). B movies were shorter features, about fifty-five to sixty minutes, and were used for double bills. An A film would provide the feature attraction of a double bill, while the lower half was filled by a B movie (although sometimes a double bill was made up of two B features). Major studios maintained B units to produce Westerns, mysteries, and other short features, and a number of small "independent" studios concentrated their total efforts on B movies.

A cowboy star signed a contract to film a series of six, seven, or eight B Westerns. By using the same actors, director, producer, crew, and even locations, a great deal of money and time could be saved on each movie. It took about one week to film a B Western, with as many as 100 camera "setups" in a single day.

For decades, hundreds of B Westerns were filmed every year. Generations of young Americans grew up cheering cowboy heroes who were brave and strong. Week after week, youthful audiences watched good guys stand up to bad guys, watched justice triumph over evil, watched their heroic Westerners always do the right thing. The men and women who made B Westerns helped countless youngsters to grow up with wholesome values.

much to enjoy in the movie, including fine Western music. Bob Nolan wrote "Open Range Ahead" and "Song of the Bandit." Bob and Tim Spencer wrote the haunting "Blue Prairie." Len Slye wrote "My Saddle Pals and I," sung as the Sons of the Pioneers rode in a wagon. The other tunes were sung in camp or at "Tres Nogales Ranger Station." During the closing bars of "Open Range Ahead," Starrett set up targets, then practiced fanning his revolver at the end of the song.

With as many as four or five tunes per movie, Nolan, along with Spencer, busily composed songs that would be right for the group. Columbia responded to this prolific output by paying an extra $10 or so per song.

Late in 1937 the Sons of the Pioneers worked several recording sessions for the American Record Company (ARC). The group had not recorded for Decca since February 1937. Their first session with ARC was on October 21, 1937. Although Len Slye had signed with Republic only a week earlier, he was permitted to record with the group. At the session, in addition to Len, were Bob Nolan, Lloyd Perryman, Hugh and Karl Farr, and steel guitarist Sam Koki. The group covered seven sides, including "My Saddle Pals and I," written by Len, and Bob Nolan's "Heavenly Airplane."

The Sons of the Pioneers were back in the Los Angeles studio five days later, cutting eleven more sides. Several of these songs, such as "Song of the Bandit" and "Open Range Ahead," were from movie performances with Charles

Starrett. Two days later, on October 28, four more tunes were covered, including the yodeling favorite, "Haddie Brown." When the records were released, the labels listed the artists as "Roy Rogers and the Sons of the Pioneers."

After a couple of months there were two more sessions, on December 14 and 16, 1937. Seven sides were covered each day. The artists were Roy Rogers, Bob Nolan, Lloyd Perryman, Hugh and Karl Farr, and Pat Brady on the bass fiddle.

Curiously, despite their steady output of new movie songs, the Sons of the Pioneers made no more recordings for the next few years. Increasingly popular, the group resumed a busy recording schedule with Decca in 1941.

For the next Starrett movie, *Cattle Raiders*, Nolan wrote "This Ain't the Same Old Range," "Happy Cowboy," "Welcome to the Spring," and "Devil's Great Grandson." The latter number was sung in jail, with Starrett behind bars, falsely accused of murdering the sheriff. For once Starrett chimed in with the music, talking—not singing—his way through a chorus. The Pioneers yodeled, and Pat Brady clowned his way through a loose-limbed dance. As the Pioneers sang "I'm a happy, rovin' cowboy," the Farr brothers were outstanding on guitar and fiddle. Dick Curtis was the villain, Iris Meredith was the heroine, and Donald Grayson was around to horn in on the Pioneer music.

Cattle Raiders was the first release of 1938. The next film was *Call of the Rockies*. Nolan contributed four of the five songs: "A Cowboy Has To Sing," "Following the Sun All Day," "The Hangin' Blues," and "Wind." Along with Iris Meredith, Donald Grayson was in the cast. But this was Grayson's final Starrett movie. He did not project a Western image, and Columbia executives decided that Bob Nolan would be better as Starrett's second lead.

Nolan was assigned the pinto that Grayson had ridden, and he was dressed in tight-fitting Western shirts that displayed his impressive physique. He had handsome features, of course, and he handled dialogue capably. Indeed, by 1939 Harry Cohn had begun to think of Bob Nolan as a potential star. With his good looks and musical ability, he would have been a natural choice to star in a singing cowboy series. Cohn apparently even considered him for larger things. Columbia's big film of 1939 was to be *Golden Boy*, starring Barbara Stanwyck, and he took note of Nolan when the Sons of the Pioneers were walking across the studio lot after a lunch break.

Nolan recalled that Cohn "stopped his whole entourage and pointed a finger at me and said, 'There's my Golden Boy!' My God, it scared the bejeezus out of me! I didn't want that kind of responsibility. So I went out and got drunk and stayed drunk for a week until he gave up on me!"

Nolan laughed when relating this incident, but avoiding stardom was in character for a man who was a loner at heart, who had hoboed around the country and lived on the beach. Besides, Nolan almost compulsively composed music during this period, and he may have realized that stardom would prove a distraction from his greatest gift. Meanwhile, young William Holden was selected as the male lead in *Golden Boy*, a role which made him an immediate star.

Spared the stressful responsibilities of stardom, Bob Nolan played second lead for the first time in *Law of the Plains*, helping Charles Starrett oppose the villainy of Dick Curtis and George Chesebro. *Law of the Plains* was released in May 1938, and the next month *West of Cheyenne* appeared in theaters. For this film Bob Nolan wrote "Biscuit Blues" and, with Lloyd Perryman, "Night Falls on the Prairie."

A month later *South of Arizona* was released. The plot centered around the murder of Iris Meredith's brother. At the graveside the Sons of the Pioneers sang a lovely funeral lament: "There's one more hand on the range, in the rollin' acres of heaven...."

Nolan wrote three more songs for *South of Arizona*. The memorable "Roundup in the Sky" was sung by the Sons of the Pioneers in the bunkhouse, with a sad Iris Meredith listening nearby. In the same bunkhouse, the Pioneers sang "When Pay Day Rolls Around" as they shaved and dressed for a pay day trip into town. During the number, Pat Brady cavorted around the bunkhouse in a comic dance. At the end of the film Starrett and Iris, as newlyweds, rode off in a stagecoach driven and accompanied by the Pioneers, who sang, "Saddle Your Worries to the Wind." Lettering across the canvas cover on the rear of the stagecoach proclaimed: "JUST GOT HITCHED."

The next movie, *The Colorado Trail*, featured "Cottage in the Clouds," by Bob Nolan and Lloyd Perryman, and two more Nolan compositions, "Lone Buckaroo" and "Bound for the Rio Grande."

In October 1938, less than a month after *The Colorado Trail* appeared, *West of Santa Fe* was released. *West of Santa Fe* was the eighth consecutive Starrett film for Iris Meredith. Bob Nolan, as usual, was busy providing music for the movie. The Pioneers sang "Tumbling Tumbleweeds," which had become the theme for the Starrett movies, sung over the title credits and at the end. Other Nolan compositions in *West of Santa Fe* were "When the Prairie Sun Says Good Mornin'," "Hello Way Up There" and "Song of the Prairie," written with Lloyd Perryman.

The prolific Nolan found that writing songs was pleasant and natural for him during the 1930s and 1940s, and by the late 1950s he had published more than 1,500 songs. "Hardly a day went by that I didn't either start or complete a song," he said. He began with an idea, developed the lyrics to express the idea, then worked on the music. His songs were closely suited to the Sons of the Pioneers, who performed them superbly. The repertory of the group increased rapidly, and songs performed on the screen generated widespread requests during personal appearances.

The last film of 1938, *Rio Grande*, provided Nolan with a pivotal role in the plot. Dick Curtis wanted the ranch of the heroine, this time played by Ann Doran instead of Iris Meredith. Curtis ambushed her brother, murdering him with a Winchester shot. Starrett was a friend of the brother, and he sent for the Sons of the Pioneers to help out, since all of the ranch hands had quit in fear of Curtis. Starrett's plan called for Nolan to join Curtis' gang as an undercover man. Starrett and Nolan staged a saloon fight to convince Curtis that Bob was a bad guy. Nolan handled himself impressively in the fight scene. In the end, he was a key figure in conquering Curtis and the other villains.

Nolan provided three musical numbers. The opening scene showcased the Pioneers singing "The West is in My Soul," while washing their clothes at a bunkhouse. Horseplay by the group provided Pat Brady ample clowning opportunities. "Rocky Roads" was performed on a saloon stage, while "Slumber

Time on the Range" was sung around a chuckwagon after supper. Another number, "Old Bronco Pal," was sung while the Pioneers rode down a road, with Pat balancing his bass fiddle on his stirrup.

The musical performances of the Sons of the Pioneers were energetic, pumping life into even a bland plot. With four or five numbers in a film which ran only fifty-five to sixty minutes, the Pioneers frequently dominated the screen. Bob Nolan provided Starrett a strong second lead, while Pat Brady's antics added comedy to each movie. Although Starrett did not sing, the Sons of the Pioneers offered rich Western music unsurpassed in the films of any singing cowboy.

By the end of 1938, the Sons of the Pioneers had become an integral part of Charles Starrett movies. In 1937 Charles Starrett had first appeared on the list of Top Ten Western Stars, in eighth place. The eight films of 1938, featuring Bob Nolan and the Sons of the Pioneers, moved Starrett up to sixth place. And in 1939 Starrett would advance to fifth place.

Nine Charles Starrett films were released in 1939. Iris Meredith was the leading lady in seven of these movies. Bob Nolan continued as Starrett's stalwart pal. He also continued to churn out Western tunes for the Pioneers. The Pioneers usually played cowboys, enlivening each film with three, four, or five numbers. The songs were performed in bunkhouses or around campfires or riding along a trail. Pat Brady clowned around at every opportunity.

Despite the enormous contributions of the Sons of the Pioneers, the greatest asset of the Starrett films was Charles Starrett. The big, good-looking star had a ready smile and a flair for action. Onscreen he radiated confidence and good humor. It was obvious that he enjoyed the role of Western hero, and his films were fun to watch. But the Sons of the Pioneers added greatly to the appeal of Starrett Westerns.

Perhaps the best film of 1939 was *Outpost of the Rockies*, released in September. The Sons of the Pioneers played a squad of Mounties, with Starrett as their sergeant. Bob Nolan wrote "Rocky Road in the Rockies," which the Pioneers sang in camp. A Tim Spencer composition, "Timber Trail," was performed as the Mounties rode along a mountain trail, with a beautiful lake in the background.

The next movie, *Stranger From Texas*, was released in December, and was the first film of the 1939-40 series. By this time the Pioneers were familiar faces around Columbia Studios. The singing group was in and out of the studio, planning songs at story conferences and recording music for the Starrett films. Columbia had started on Poverty Row, among the independent studios on Gower Street. It grew into a major studio, expanding at the same location. The studio lot stretched to Sunset Boulevard, just six blocks west of Warner Brothers. Columbia also acquired a forty-acre ranch in Burbank for location filming. Burbank was only a few miles north of Hollywood, and to the north of Burbank loomed forests and canyons and the San Gabriel Mountains, ideal for Western locations. Although the Sons of the Pioneers continued to travel to personal appearances between films, the Columbia lots provided the setting for their professional life from 1937 through 1940.

The first film released in 1940 was *Two-Fisted Rangers*. Iris Meredith and

Dick Curtis filled their usual roles. But an important newcomer to the Starrett series was director Joseph H. Lewis. The storyline was familiar, with Starrett seeking revenge for the murder of his lawman brother. But Lewis' direction, featuring unusual camera angles, enhanced both Starrett's action and the musical numbers of the Pioneers. Lewis would direct three of the next four Starrett films, all of which were superior entries in the series.

Sam Nelson, Starrett's usual director, returned for the next movie, *Bullets for Rustlers*. Then Joseph Lewis directed *Blazin' Sixshooters*, injecting such freshness that "For once Curtis and Meredith, in their usual roles of villain and heroine respectively, don't look as though they've said their lines countless times before (which, of course, they had)." The number "Don Juan," written by Tim and Glenn Spencer, featured superb guitar work by Hugh Farr and the antics of Pat Brady.

Lewis also directed the next film, *Texas Stagecoach*. Dick Curtis and his henchmen tried to bankrupt Iris Meredith's stagecoach line. The Sons of the Pioneers sang "Hill Country" while repairing the stagecoach road. And at the end of the movie, with the villains vanquished, Bob Nolan drove the stagecoach with Starrett and Iris inside. Pat Brady rode shotgun, and the Pioneers performed a reprise of "Roll On With the Texas Express."

The Durango Kid was next, introducing a masked rider known as the "Robin Hood of the West." The movie ad explained: "Masked in mystery 'til he unmasks his father's killers! The terror of cattle thieves, the idol of thrill lovers!" Starrett played an easygoing character named Steve, who donned a black mask and black clothing to ride against rustlers as the Durango Kid. Astride his white horse, Raider, the Kid fanned his six-shooter and rounded up the bad guys. Lending a hand were Bob Nolan and the Sons of the Pioneers, who sang three songs by Tim Spencer (the latter two written with his brother Glenn): "The Prairie Sings a Lullaby," "There's a Rainbow Over the Ridge," and "Yippi-Yi Your Troubles Away."

In his subsequent films, Starrett continued to play a variety of heroes. But in 1945 he resurrected the Durango Kid character with *The Return of the Durango Kid*. The Durango Kid then became his regular series character, as Starrett played the role in more than sixty films.

After *The Durango Kid*, the Sons of the Pioneers played in four more Starrett movies. The last one, *Outlaws of the Panhandle*, was released on February 27, 1941. Once again the Sons of the Pioneers helped Starrett battle rustlers. Once again Sam Nelson was the director; *Outlaws of the Panhandle* was his seventeenth film with Starrett and the Pioneers. But Iris Meredith and Dick Curtis were not in the movie (Iris had become a semi-regular leading lady for Columbia's other Western star, Wild Bill Elliott). Among the musical numbers was "Ridin' Down the Rio Valley," a Tim Spencer song performed typically, as the Pioneers rode along with a cattle herd.

The Columbia contract for the Sons of the Pioneers came to an end with *Outlaws of the Panhandle*. Counting the first two Starrett Westerns in 1935 and 1936, the Pioneers had appeared in thirty Starrett films. In addition to boosting Starrett's rise in popularity as a Western star, the Pioneers themselves had grown in popularity while at Columbia. Every month or so a new movie appeared featuring several numbers by the Sons of the Pioneers. The constant nationwide exposure of this talented group provided an enviable recognition.

But while considering a contract renewal at Columbia, the Pioneers were approached by Roy Rogers, now being promoted as a star by Republic. No studio made better Westerns than Republic, and Rogers urged his old friends to become part of his movie team. The Pioneers left Columbia and, after several months of radio and recording work in Chicago, signed a standard seven-year contract with Republic.

"I wish I could have kept that group," Charles Starrett later reflected. "Boy, they left a big hole in my pictures when they went over to Republic to join Roy Rogers in his series."

In The Old Wyoming Trail, *as well as the next few Charles Starrett movies, the Sons of the Pioneers were expected to back up tenor Donald Grayson (second from right). Len Slye is in the checked shirt; Bob Nolan is between Len and Grayson; Hugh Farr is on the fiddle; and Lloyd Perryman is behind and above Hugh.*

In The Old Wyoming Trail, as in many of their Western movies, the Sons of the Pioneers provided entertainment at a frontier dance.

With The Old Wyoming Trail *in 1937, the Sons of the Pioneers became regulars in the movies of Charles Starrett (center, white hat, white scarf, white horse). At left in front is Len Slye, wearing nondescript clothing and mounted on a nondescript horse.*

Roy Rogers and Mary Hart in Frontier Pony Express. Her real name was Lynne Roberts, but the studio changed her name so that they could promote "Republic's own Rogers and Hart" as the "Sweethearts of the Range." Rogers and Hart made seven consecutive films together in 1938 and 1939.

The Pioneers and Charles Starrett focus a group stare. L to R: Lloyd Perryman, Karl Farr, Hugh Farr, Bob Nolan, Starrett, Pat Brady.

As he talks to a lawman, Charles Starrett is flanked by Lloyd Perryman and Bob Nolan. While at Columbia, Bob consented to a little plastic surgery, thereby altering "a perfectly good Roman nose."

Bob Nolan readies a noose for a terrified bad guy as Charles Starrett and Pat Brady look on.

Above: *Bob Nolan leads a street shootout in* The Thundering Herd. *Second from left, in the checked shirt, is Lloyd Perryman. Between Lloyd and Bob stands Hugh Farr. Pat Brady, also wearing a checked shirt, stands behind Bob. Karl Farr may be partially seen behind the man in the string tie.* Below: *Last page of a 1939 contract, showing the signatures of the Sons of the Pioneers. Sam Allen (see letterhead in left margin) was the group's agent at this time. Other agents included Art Rush, Ed Gray, and Tim Spencer, although the Pioneers often handled their own booking.*

1
2
3
4
5

EIGHTEENTH: The Artist agrees that the Corporation shall have the exclusive right during the term hereof to make transcriptions or other recordings of the the Artists voice or music of any and all kinds or character and that the Artist will at such times and places as the Corporation may direct, appear and perform such musical numbers, songs, dialogue and any and all sounds required by the Corporation for the purpose of making transcriptions or other recordings thereof.

6
7
8
9

NINETEENTH: The Artist agrees that he will at all times comport and deport himself in such a manner that will reflect favorably on the Corporation; that he will refrain from undue excesses of all kinds and will at all times give his best effort to the furthering of the Corporations' best interests and to the establishment good will for and toward the Corporation and the name "The Sons of the Pioneers".

10

IN WITNESS WHEREOF we have hereunto set our hands this day and year first above written.

THE SONS OF THE PIONEERS, INC.

By ___Karl Farr___
            President

Bob Nolan

Tim Spencer

Pat Brady

Lloyd Perryman

Hugh Farr

Karl Farr

The Sons of the Pioneers preview their dance entertainment in Spoilers of the Range. L to R: Pat Brady (on the bass fiddle), Karl Farr, Hugh Farr, Lloyd Perryman, Tim Spencer, Bob Nolan.

The Sons of the Pioneers serenade Charles Starrett and his frequent leading lady, Iris Meredith. L to R: Pat Brady, Iris, Karl Farr, Starrett, Lloyd Perryman, Hugh Farr, Bob Nolan, Tim Spencer.

Charles Starrett lends a hand with the bass fiddle as the astonished Pioneers watch in Western Caravans. *Hugh Farr is seated in front and Bob Nolan is partially visible at right. Standing, L to R: Karl Farr, Lloyd Perryman, Tim Spencer, Pat Brady.*

The Sons of the Pioneers being fed by other pioneers in Western Caravans. *L to R on the wagon: Karl Farr, Hugh Farr (accepting a cookie), Tim Spencer, Bob Nolan. Starrett, with badge, is in center. Pat Brady, holding a bass fiddle—an unusual item on a wagon train—stands behind Iris Meredith.*

Key players in The Man From Sundown: *Iris Meredith, a grizzled Charles Starrett, Bob Nolan, a scarred bad guy, Hugh Farr.*

Stranger From Texas *was the last of nine Charles Starrett films released in 1939. L to R: Hugh Farr, Tim Spencer, Pat Brady, Bob Nolan, Lloyd Perryman (eyes only), Karl Farr, Starrett.*

The bad guys have the drop on Charles Starrett, Iris Meredith, and the Sons of the Pioneers in Riders of Black River.

The good guys lined up in Stranger From Texas. L to R: Karl Farr, Tim Spencer, Lloyd Perryman, Charles Starrett, Bob Nolan, Pat Brady, Hugh Farr.

The deputy marshal Pioneers at headquarters in Stranger From Texas. *Hugh Farr sits in front cleaning a gun. Tim Spencer leans against a wall, and Lloyd Perryman sits beside him. Pat Brady is on bass fiddle, while Bob Nolan strums a guitar. Karl Farr sits behind Bob.*

Bob Nolan, Iris Meredith, and Charles Starrett in Two-Fisted Rangers, *the first film of 1940. Iris was the leading lady in nineteen Starrett movies.*

Karl Farr (right foreground), Tim Spencer (standing at left), Iris Meredith, Pat Brady, and Bob Nolan help Charles Starrett restore a ramshackle newspaper office in Two-Fisted Rangers.

The Pioneers campaign for Bob Nolan for sheriff in Two-Fisted Rangers. L to R on porch: Karl Farr (with guitar), Hugh Farr, Pat Brady, Tim Spencer, Lloyd Perryman.

The Pioneers share Charles Starrett's concerns in Two-Fisted Rangers. *L to R: Karl Farr, Tim Spencer, Pat Brady, Bob Nolan, Lloyd Perryman.*

The Pioneers with Charles Starrett and Iris Meredith in Blazin' Sixshooters. *Bob Nolan kneels above Iris, and Tim Spencer is in front of her. Hugh Farr sits on the front steps. Karl Farr sits behind his brother. Pat Brady is next to Karl, and Lloyd Perryman leans against the post.*

The Pioneers serenade Charles Starrett and Iris Meredith in a saloon-courtroom in Bullets for Rustlers.

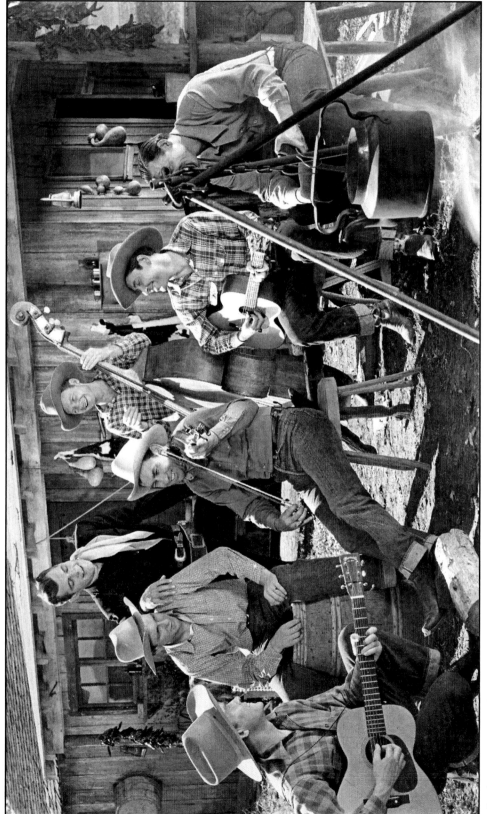

Charles Starrett watches the Pioneers perform in front of their bunkhouse in Blazin' Sixshooters. L to R: Tim Spencer, Lloyd Perryman, Hugh Farr, Pat Brady, Karl Farr, Bob Nolan.

Charles Starrett and Bob Nolan in a tense moment from Texas Stagecoach. *Iris Meredith stands between them.*

The Pioneers have the drop on big Dick Curtis in Texas Stagecoach. *L to R: Pat Brady, Curtis, Tim Spencer, Hugh Farr, Bob Nolan, Karl Farr, Lloyd Perryman.*

The Pioneers take a lunch break from road repairs in Texas Stagecoach. L to R: Hugh Farr, Karl Farr (behind his brother), Tim Spencer, Lloyd Perryman, Bob Nolan, Pat Brady.

Right: *Charles Starrett as the Durango Kid. He first donned the black mask in* The Durango Kid *in 1940. After the Sons of the Pioneers left his series the next year, Starrett would play the "Robin Hood of the West" in more than sixty movies.*

Below: *Charles Starrett with a new leading lady, Marjorie Cooley, in* West of Abilene. *The Pioneers, L to R: Karl Farr, Tim Spencer, Pat Brady, Hugh Farr, Lloyd Perryman, Bob Nolan.*

Charles Starrett, Bob Nolan, and Pat Brady creep up on the bad guys in West of Abilene.

Charles Starrett helps an injured old-timer in The Pinto Kid. *Bob Nolan is kneeling, Pat Brady holds the horses, and Louise Currie is the latest replacement for Iris Meredith.*

Bob Nolan gallops down the familiar main street of Columbia's Western set in a 1938 film. Bob is trailed by Pat Brady and Hugh Farr.

Pat Brady clowning for Charles Starrett's latest leading lady, Frances Robinson, in Outlaws of the Panhandle. *L to R: Karl Farr, Hugh Farr, Lloyd Perryman, Pat Brady, Bob Nolan, and, standing behind Frances, Tim Spencer.*

The Pioneers standing in the background of Outlaws of the Panhandle, *their final movie with Charles Starrett. L to R: Lloyd Perryman, Bob Nolan, Hugh Farr, Karl Farr, Pat Brady, Tim Spencer.*

The first Pioneer movie with Roy Rogers was Red River Valley.

5
Reunited with Roy
(1941-43)

"I've made forty posse rides with Roy and Trigger,
and to this day all I have ever seen was that
long, white tail floating in my face."
—BOB NOLAN

BY 1941, ROY ROGERS had starred in Republic Westerns for three years. Republic filmed the best B Westerns of any studio in Hollywood. With Republic, Gene Autry had made the singing cowboy a movie sensation, and the studio was developing Roy Rogers along similar lines. But Roy Rogers movies would soon take musical Westerns to a higher level. Promoted as the "King of the Cowboys," Roy would become the Number One Western Star, enjoying world-wide popularity and establishing himself as a marketing phenomenon. The foundation stones of this incredible success were the musical Westerns that regularly appeared before adoring audiences. And a vital part of the team that made these Westerns so appealing was the remarkable singing group founded by Roy Rogers, the Sons of the Pioneers.

After leaving the Sons of the Pioneers in October 1937, Len Slye reported to Republic Pictures as "Dick Weston" every day. Aside from small parts in a couple of Westerns, Dick Weston had little to do for several weeks. But he was paid $75 each week, "and I was confident that my big break would come along any day."

The big break occurred when Gene Autry staged a one-man strike. Although the screen's Number One cowboy earned $5,000 per film, Gene learned that the studio was forcing exhibitors to book forty or more Republic features along with the Autry movies. If exhibitors wanted the eight Gene Autry films each year, they had to book the other Republic features. On the strength of the Gene Autry movies, Republic was selling its other films. Gene wanted a larger share of these profits, but Republic head Herbert Yates stubbornly resisted the star's requests. On the first day of the shooting schedule of his next film, *Washington Cowboy*, Gene refused to come to work.

Yates promptly suspended Gene, then summoned Dick Weston to substitute as the lead of *Washington Cowboy*. (Ironically, Gene had received his big break in 1935 in the twelve-chapter serial, *The Phantom Empire*, when he was hired as a late replacement for the scheduled star, Ken Maynard, who was fired for drunken and loutish behavior.) Yates felt that the name "Dick Weston" was too bland for a star. Yates and executives Sol and Moe Siegel met with their new star to select a more fitting name. "Rogers" was reminiscent of the recent icon, Will Rogers, who had died in a 1935 plane crash. "Roy" sounded good with Rogers, and Sol Siegel happily mentioned that in French Roy ("*roi*") means "king." Four years later, Len Slye would legally change his name to Roy Rogers.

The name of the movie also was changed, from *Washington Cowboy* to *Under Western Stars*. The film was directed by Gene Autry's regular director, Joseph Kane, while Gene's comic sidekick, Smiley Burnette, also was on hand. Like other Gene Autry stories, the plot was set in the contemporary West of the 1930s. Roy played a singing Western congressman who brings Dust Bowl issues to Washington.

THE SMARTEST HORSE IN THE MOVIES

William S. Hart and Fritz   Gene Autry and Champion
Tom Mix and Tony   Roy Rogers and Trigger
Ken Maynard and Tarzan

A key to the success of any cowboy hero was a faithful steed. Roy Rogers rode the most memorable horse in the movies, a palomino stallion named Trigger. This handsome and talented animal was foaled in 1932. His sire was a registered palomino who had raced in Mexico, while his dam was half thoroughbred and half quarter horse. This mixture gave him speed, power, size, beautiful coloring, a placid temperament, and the heart of a champion racer.

When he was three, the stout palomino was purchased by Clyde Hudkins. The Hudkins Brothers Stables was one of the rental outfits that provided horses and vehicles for motion pictures. Hudkins recognized the young stallion as a prospective lead horse, and intensive training commenced. He first appeared onscreen as Olivia DeHavilland's mount in the 1938 hit, *The Adventures of Robin Hood*. Not long after this movie was filmed, Republic notified the rental outfits that a new cowboy hero named Roy Rogers needed a lead horse.

The Hudkins Stables brought their palomino, then called "Golden Cloud," to the audition. Roy said as soon as he rode Golden Cloud, "I didn't even consider any of the others." Smiley Burnette helped Roy pick out a more suitable name for a Western horse, "Trigger." Following their first film, *Under Western Stars*, Trigger went back to the Hudkins Stables,

(continued on next page)

To the surprise of everyone at Republic, critics were impressed with the rookie star. Respected *New York Times* critic Bosley Crowther, who usually disdained B Westerns, reviewed *Under Western Stars* with particular enthusiasm for the appealing new lead: "Republic had discovered ... a new Playboy of the Western world in the sombrero'd person of Roy Rogers who has a drawl like Gary Cooper, a smile like Shirley Temple and a voice like Tito Guizar."

Despite the acceptance of Roy Rogers by critics and fans, Herbert Yates quickly agreed to a substantial raise for Gene Autry. But Republic continued producing Roy Rogers movies, even though the budgets were considerably smaller than those for Gene Autry films. After *Under Western Stars*, most of Roy's movies were set in the Old West of the 1800s, and there was greater emphasis on action than music. Roy played historical characters such as Billy the Kid, Wild Bill Hickok, and Jesse James (twice). Joseph Kane continued to direct the Roy Rogers movies, and Roy acquired his own sidekick, the incomparable Gabby Hayes. Roy also rode a spectacular horse, a magnificent palomino named Trigger.

Roy and Trigger and Gabby—and Republic Pictures—quickly proved to be

(continued from previous page)

while Roy left on a three-month promotional tour. During these personal appearances, young fans were repeatedly disappointed at the absence of Trigger. When Roy returned to Hollywood, he asked Clyde Hudkins to buy Trigger, promising to see that Hudkins Stables horses and vehicles would be used for his films. Hudkins offered Trigger to Roy for $2,500, then agreed to keep the horse at his stables until Roy could pay off the price. (Later, when Roy asked Herbert Yates for a raise, the studio head threatened to find another cowboy star to put astride the popular palomino—until Roy happily pointed out that he owned Trigger.)

A trainer named Jimmy Griffin worked with Trigger until World War II, when Griffin took a job in a defense plant. Glen Randall then took over as Trigger's trainer. Trigger could perform sixty tricks, and was billed as "The Smartest Horse in the Movies."

Although Roy was an excellent horseman, his longtime stunt double was Joe Yrigoyen. Trigger had stunt doubles, too, to work the long personal appearance tours as well as dangerous movie scenes. But often Trigger was the only horse good enough to perform the most demanding stunts. "Bring up the old man," went out the call, and Joe Yrigoyen and Trigger would pull off a spectacular scene.

In posse scenes Trigger proudly surged past all other horses. "I've made forty posse rides with Roy and Trigger," said Bob Nolan, "and to this day all I have ever seen was that long, white tail floating in my face."

Trigger co-starred in all of Roy's movies and television shows. He died in 1965 at the age of thirty-three, and Roy had him mounted for his museum.

a popular combination. By 1939 Roy was ranked the Number Three Western Star in Hollywood, behind Gene Autry and William Boyd. Roy remained in third place in 1940. He was convinced that the addition of the Sons of the Pioneers to his team would help elevate Roy Rogers movies to even greater heights, and in 1941 Republic hired the group away from Columbia.

The first Roy Rogers film in which the Sons of the Pioneers appeared was *Red River Valley*. Released on December 12, 1941, *Red River Valley* was the twenty-fifth starring vehicle for Roy Rogers. Roy's regular director, Joseph Kane, worked with the Sons of the Pioneers for the first time. Under Kane they would work fast; he frequently shot a new setup every fifteen or twenty minutes. Kane filmed dialogue scenes as quickly as possible, but he took more care with action sequences. In *Red River Valley* Gabby Hayes again headed up the comic relief, and pretty Gale Storm provided Roy's romantic interest. Trevor Bardette and Hal Taliaferro were familiar Western villains.

The Sons of the Pioneers immediately established themselves in the Roy Rogers formula. Bob Nolan, as in the Charles Starrett films, played second lead to the hero. With the addition of the Sons of the Pioneers, Roy Rogers movies began to place greater emphasis on music. The group sang "Red River Valley" over the titles, then continued to back Roy as he sang this song to Gale Storm in the opening scene.

The film was set in Texas in 1941. Roy played a rancher and radio singer, and the Pioneers were part of his radio act. When Roy asked the group to help him defeat the villains, Tim Spencer remarked, "Well, I'm more of a musician than a G-man."

But the Pioneers helped out, of course. In one scene, Roy and the Pioneers sneaked into the villains' nightclub by waylaying a Mexican band on a break. After subduing

REPUBLIC STUDIOS

Herbert J. Yates, a former tobacco company executive, entered the movie business at the age of thirty-six in 1916. Yates joined Hedwig Laboratories, a film processing business, and within two years he purchased Republic Laboratories. After consolidating other processing plants, in 1927 Yates organized a complete film laboratory service, Consolidated Film Laboratories.

With control of first-rate processing facilities, Yates now aspired to organize a movie studio. He envisioned a studio that would concentrate on B movies, enhancing the steady if spectacular profits of such films by producing streamlined action pictures while exercising strict economy.

Yates approached two independent studios: Monogram, which made fast-paced B Westerns, most notably with a lanky young star, John Wayne; and Mascot, which specialized in serials and headquartered at the old Mack Sennett Studios on Ventura Boulevard in North Hollywood. Yates, who provided additional capital as well as his film laboratory, also pulled in a couple of smaller independent studios. The merger concluded in March 1935 with the formation of Republic Pictures Corporation. The new studio would be located at the former Mack Sennett lot, while Herbert J. Yates would be Republic's president and guiding force.

Mascot had been planning a series of singing Westerns with Gene Autry, and Gene's first feature, *Tumbling*

(continued on next page)

the Mexicans, Roy and the Pioneers donned their costumes and entered the nightclub with sombrero brims pulled low. Walking to the bandstand, they picked up the instruments and played a Mexican tune.

In another scene the Pioneers, incarcerated in a large cell, performed "When Pay Day Rolls Around," the lively number from the 1938 Charles Starrett film, *South of Arizona*. The last scene was a hayride, with Roy and Gale together and the Pioneers singing "Springtime on the Range Today."

Roy carried only one gun on his tooled belt at this stage of his career (soon he would permanently become a two-gun cowboy). He drove the Pioneers around in a three-seat, wood-paneled station wagon (a "Woody") with a rack on top for the instruments. A Woody would be used in most Roy Rogers films.

The Sons of the Pioneers in *Red River Valley* featured the same lineup that had performed together for the past four years: Bob Nolan, Tim Spencer, Lloyd Perryman, Pat Brady, and Hugh and Karl Farr. The Pioneers were comfortable onscreen, and they were in their musical prime. They performed their own numbers with high energy, and when Roy sang lead, they provided rich backup to the performer who had been lead singer of the Pioneers from 1934 to 1937. Pat Brady continued to thump the bass fiddle in *Red River Valley*, while adding comedy with Sally Payne.

Red River Valley was released five days after Pearl Harbor. America's entry into World War II would deeply affect the entire society—including Roy Rogers and the Sons of the Pioneers. Key members of the Pioneers eventually would enter military service, but for a time movie-making at Republic went on as usual.

Red River Valley was the last of eight Roy Rogers films released in 1941. For the third year in a row, Roy finished third among the Top Ten Money-Making Western Stars. But in 1942 Roy

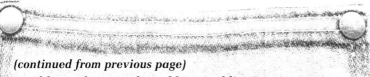

(continued from previous page)

Tumbleweeds, was released by Republic. Gene's success was immediate and spectacular. The popular John Wayne sometimes was loaned out to other studios, and in 1939—while still under contract to Republic—he became a major star with *Stagecoach*.

Republic released about fifty films per year, including Westerns, serials, and mysteries, along with one or two A features. Yates assembled hard-working directors and technicians, sidekicks and stuntmen. Everyone at Republic was expected to be artistic and creative—and to work within budgets. Republic soon was turning out the best B movies in Hollywood. Slick and filled with action, Republic films had an identifiable look and feel (and sound—for gunshot noise the studio used blanks, which gave the films a distinctive, identifiable sound).

Beginning with Gene Autry and John Wayne, Republic enjoyed special success with Westerns. The Three Mesquiteers series, beginning in 1935 and eventually including fifty-one films, was a solid success, and so were Western series starring Bill Elliott (as Red Ryder), Allan "Rocky" Lane, Bob Steele, Johnny Mack Brown, Sunset Carson, Don "Red" Barry, Monte Hale, and Rex Allen. During two decades, 1935 through 1954, Republic released 386 B Westerns. Nearly one-fourth of this output starred the King of the Cowboys, Roy Rogers.

would rise to second-place, and a year later he began a twelve-year reign as the top-ranked Western Star. The addition of the Sons of the Pioneers to Roy Rogers movies was a key factor in boosting him to the top.

The first film of 1942 was *Man From Cheyenne*, released on January 16. Gabby Hayes co-starred, Gale Storm again offered romantic interest, Sally Payne once more was a foil for Pat Brady, and Joseph Kane produced and directed the movie. Taking fuller advantage of the presence of the Sons of the Pioneers, Kane featured the group in eight numbers, including Bob Nolan's "Happy Cowboy" and a specialty by the Farr brothers, "Farr Away Blues."

One month later, *South of Santa Fe* was released. Set in contemporary New Mexico, the plot featured Roy and the Sons of the Pioneers battling gangsters armed with submachine guns, powerful automobiles, and two-way radios. The continuing emphasis on music included six numbers by the Pioneers. "Headin' for the Home Corral," "Yodel Your Troubles Away," and "Open Range Ahead" were especially effective.

The next film, *Sunset on the Desert*, did not offer as much music, but Bob Nolan filled a prominent role. The plot involved mistaken identity, as Roy played himself and a lookalike gunfighter. Bob competed with Roy—unsuccessfully—for the affections of Beryl Wallace. The Sons of the Pioneers provided entertainment at a Red Cross dance, then helped Roy and Gabby Hayes battle the bad guys. The gang of villains was led by Glenn Strange, Douglas Fowley, and Roy Barcroft, but they were vanquished during a rousing gunfight at a livery stable that was prominently labeled "OK Corral." During this shootout, Bob Nolan killed Roy's lookalike.

Glenn Strange and Roy Barcroft again headed up the bad guys in *Romance on the Range*. Armed with imposing size and a gruff voice, Glenn Strange provided opposition for Roy Rogers and a host of other Western heroes. (Later Glenn became a good guy, Sam the bartender in Miss Kitty's Long Branch Saloon on the long-running TV series, *Gunsmoke*.) Roy Barcroft was even more active as a Western villain, and he would battle Roy Rogers more often than any other bad guy.

Romance on the Range opens with Roy, Gabby, and the Sons of the Pioneers singing and yodeling around a campfire. The film closes with the Pioneers serenading Roy and Linda Hayes with "When Romance Rides the Range." But in between the opening and closing scenes, there is little music. For the third time Pat Brady and Sally Payne form a comic couple. Glenn Strange, Roy Barcroft, and the other gang members repeatedly escape pursuit by riding into a cabin, then proceeding through a secret door into a large cave. Otherwise, *Romance on the*

THE COLT .45

During the shootout at the OK Corral at the climax of *Sunset on the Desert*, Roy is shown reloading one of his sixguns. It was an unusual sight, because Roy and other B Western heroes regularly fired their revolvers over and over and over again, while never pausing to reload. After he stopped making movies, Roy enjoyed explaining this phenomenon.

"The reason they call it a Colt .45," he pointed out with a smile, "is because you can shoot it forty-five times without reloading!"

Range is unremarkable and obviously in need of the sheer energy provided by the musical numbers of the Sons of the Pioneers.

Perhaps as a result, the next film was titled *Sons of the Pioneers*. For the first time Bob Nolan received separate billing—"Bob Nolan and The Sons of the Pioneers"—as he had in the Charles Starrett movies. Bob and Tim Spencer provided six songs: "Come and Get It," "Lily of Hillbilly Valley," "The West is in My Soul," "Things Are Never What They Seem," "Trail Herdin' Cowboy," and "He's Gone Up the Trail." Gabby Hayes plays a sheriff plagued by night raiders. Hoping to find a worthy successor, Gabby seeks out Roy Rogers, whose father and grandfather were noted peace officers. Roy is an entomologist in New York City, but he agrees to return to the West and help Gabby. The Sons of the Pioneers help Roy campaign for sheriff, singing "The West is in My Soul." In order to go undercover, Roy pretends to be a murder victim, prompting Gabby and Pat Brady to sing a comic version of "He's Gone Up the Trail." After the bad guys are vanquished, Roy and the Pioneers close the story with "Trail Herdin' Cowboy."

Then Republic assigned the group to work with Gene Autry in *Call of the Canyon*, his fifty-first starring film. Gene not only was the top box-office draw among Western stars, he also was ranked among the Top Ten of all Hollywood stars. His film budgets were considerably larger than Republic allotted for Roy Rogers features, and Gene's films ran longer. (Most B Westerns were about fifty-five minutes long, but Gene Autry films usually ran at least seventy minutes; *Call of the Canyon* was seventy-one minutes long.) *Call of the Canyon* was an entertaining movie, with Gene and Smiley Burnette foiling cattle thieves, and the Sons of the Pioneers joining in the music.

The Sons of the Pioneers were back with Roy Rogers for his next film, *Sunset Serenade*. Roy, Gabby, and "Bob Nolan and the Sons of the Pioneers" foil the efforts of the bad guys, including Roy Barcroft, to cheat Helen Parrish out of her ranch. The half dozen songs from Bob Nolan and Tim Spencer include "Cowboy Rockefeller" and "He's a No Good Son-of-a-Gun." In one scene Roy and the Sons of the Pioneers croon and yodel "Sandman's Lullaby" to a drowsy baby. In another scene the Pioneers help Roy win a saloon brawl, then sing with a player piano while Pat Brady dances a jig.

By the time Republic released *Sunset Serenade*, Gene Autry had left the studio to enter military service. Following *Call of the Canyon*, Gene filmed *Bells of Capistrano*, then enlisted in the Army Air Corps in July 1942. At first the movie star was used for recruiting purposes, entertaining troops, and selling war bonds. But Gene was an avid pilot, and he had not enlisted merely to entertain fellow servicemen. "Everybody ought to think of winning the war ahead of everything else," said the thirty-five-year-old Autry to an interviewer. "I think the He-Men in the movies belong in the Army, Marine, Navy or Air Corps." Gene finally landed a co-pilot's assignment with the Air Transport Command, spending the rest of the war flying C-47 cargo planes to Europe, the South Pacific, and the China-Burma-India theater.

Although Republic had lost Gene Autry, Roy Rogers was a promising replacement. In 1939, 1940, and 1941 Roy ranked as the Number Three Money-Making Western Star, and in 1942, with the Sons of the Pioneers featured in all eight of his films, he moved up to Number Two, just behind Gene Autry. Roy's fan mail was enormous (so was Trigger's—the palomino received hundreds of letters each week).

Republic raised the budgets of Roy's films to $250,000 per movie (most B Westerns carried a budget of only $25,000 to $50,000), and another $200,000 per year for advertising. Gene Autry had been the only B Western star to benefit from such funding. Now Republic bestowed these budgets and promotions on Roy Rogers, as well as the Gene Autry format.

Although Roy often played historical characters of the Old West, Gene always played himself in a contemporary setting. Previous Roy Rogers movies sometimes had been placed in the modern West, but from now on Roy always would play himself in the West of the 1940s (or, later, of the 1950s). Many of the villains wore business suits and fedoras, and drove automobiles along the dusty roads of the Republic back lots. Roy and Trigger, often helped by the Sons of the Pioneers, galloped cross-country after the crooks—and usually caught up with

KING OF THE SIDEKICKS

"Consarn it, you young whippersnapper!"
"Gol durn polecats!"
"You're durn tootin'!"
"Durn persnickety females!"

These lines were made famous by a bewhiskered, cantankerous old coot known to countless young Western fans as Gabby Hayes. He was born George Francis Hayes in 1885 in Wellsville, New York. Hayes began performing in vaudeville as a teenager. He made a silent film in 1923, then left vaudeville for Hollywood in 1929.

By 1931 Hayes was specializing in Westerns. Some of his parts were small, and sometimes he was a bad guy, but increasingly he played sidekicks. He worked with young John Wayne in a dozen B Westerns. He also played opposite Bob Steele, Harry Carey, Tom Tyler, Ken Maynard, Hoot Gibson, Tim McCoy, Buck Jones, Johnny Mack Brown, Gene Autry, and Randolph Scott, among others. Often appearing half-shaven and without his false teeth, Hayes began to create a grizzled but lovable character with a gruff exterior.

In 1935 Paramount began filming one of the most successful of all Western series, Hopalong Cassidy, starring William Boyd as the black-clad hero. Appearing in the first twenty of these movies (when the series ended in 1948 there had been sixty-six Hopalong Cassidy films), Hayes developed a memorable character named Windy Haliday.

When the contract of George Hayes came up for renewal by Paramount in 1939, Republic lured him away for their Roy Rogers team. Since Paramount pressed a legal claim to the character Windy Haliday, Republic named Roy's sidekick Gabby Whitaker.

With a full beard and flowing white hair, the irascible Gabby Whitaker was so unforgettable that George Hayes became permanently identified as Gabby Hayes. But while sitting between takes on a movie set, Gabby habitually read the *Wall Street Journal*. And at night he loved to don evening clothes, insert his teeth, and go nightclubbing with his beloved wife.

their vehicles. Roy himself often drove a "Woody" (a wood-paneled station wagon). Roy sometimes rode into town, dismounted from Trigger, and walked into a radio station for a singing engagement.

It was easy for young fans to imagine that, somewhere out West, it still was possible to experience an adventurous and heroic cowboy's life. In every movie, Roy serenaded lovely leading ladies, usually assisted by the Sons of the Pioneers. The Pioneers commonly were ranch hands who provided a ready-made posse, as well as splendid Western music. Roy Rogers and Republic—and the Sons of the Pioneers—created a Golden West of fine-looking men and women, of adventure and romance, of lively songs and haunting melodies.

Republic expanded the running time of Roy Rogers movies by ten or fifteen minutes, to Gene Autry's length of seventy or more minutes. Although the longer Roy Rogers movies soon would be exciting entertainments, the first few seventy-minute films seemed a bit slow-paced. But the Sons of the Pioneers, as they had with Charles Starrett, noticeably picked up the pace each time they performed one of their animated numbers.

Roy Rogers followed *Sunset Serenade* with *Heart of the Golden West*. Roy played a ranch foreman, and he dressed in work clothes that offered a striking contrast to the gaudy costumes he soon would adopt. The Sons of the Pioneers were part of Roy's crew, but there was not much music. Smiley Burnette brought his Frog Milhouse character to *Heart of the Golden West*, doubling up on the comedy with Gabby Hayes. Screenwriter Earl Felton had fun with the dialogue. At one point, for example, a cattle boat featured in the story departed without Roy and the Pioneers.

"Where does that leave us?" asked Bob.

With a straight face, Roy replied, "Up the creek without the cattle."

The next movie, *Ridin' Down the Canyon*, also did not have as many musical numbers as other entries in the series, although Roy and the Sons of the Pioneers teamed up on the beautiful "Blue Prairie." The plot revolved around a wild horse roundup, and Roy Barcroft was one of the bad guys.

Ridin' Down the Canyon was the last Roy Rogers movie of 1942. *Idaho*, the first film of 1943, was released on March 10. Republic's publicity campaign and Roy's growing popularity made *Idaho* his first movie to open in Loew's chain of first-run theaters.

Idaho ran for seventy minutes, and the increased budget showed onscreen. Smiley Burnette was Roy's sidekick, because Gabby Hayes had been assigned to Republic's newest cowboy star, Wild Bill Elliott (during 1943 and 1944, Gabby played in the first ten Elliott movies, before returning to his natural place beside Roy Rogers). The plot of *Idaho* involved a judge who maintained a "Boy's Town," and who enlisted Roy to help rid the county of an unsavory gambling-drinking emporium operated by villainous Osa Munson. The judge's boys were played by the Robert Mitchell Boys Choir. The choir sang beautifully, while the Sons of the Pioneers performed only three of the movie's seven musical numbers.

Republic next proclaimed Roy "King of the Cowboys" in a film subtly titled *King of the Cowboys*. Smiley Burnette and his horse, Ring-Eyed Nellie, now were becoming familiar to Roy Rogers fans. The Sons of the Pioneers, for the moment, were becoming slightly less familiar. The group performed only "Ride 'em

Cowboy," "Ride, Ranger, Ride," and a few bars of "Red River Valley." But Bob Nolan and the other Pioneers helped Roy break up a saboteur's ring, so that at the end of the film the governor of Texas could make a presentation to "The King of the Cowboys, in grateful recognition of services rendered."

Republic launched a massive promotion of Roy Rogers as King of the Cowboys, spending more than $100,000 for 192 billboard ads, along with a coordinated radio and newspaper advertising campaign. When Roy's next film, *Song of Texas*, was released in June 1943, it opened not only in small-town theaters across the United States, but in more than 125 urban and suburban houses in the Chicago area. And on July 12, 1943, Roy and Trigger were featured on the cover of *Life*, with a "King of the Cowboys" story inside the prominent magazine. *Life* writer H. Allen Smith commented on the recent publicity build-up: "No better example of the hand-tailored human exists today than Roy Rogers, who has been trumpeted into the splendid title 'King of the Cowboys.'" Smith also remarked upon Roy's wholesome image: "He is the protagonist in the American morality play. He is purity rampant— never drinks, never smokes, never shoots pool, never spits. . . . He always wins the girl although he doesn't kiss her. He kisses his horse. His immense public would have it no other way."

In the opening scene of *Song of Texas*, Roy is introduced to a young audience at "Texas Springs Children's Hospital." Leading Trigger into a hospital ward, Roy puts the horse through several tricks. Then, sitting on the bed of "Rosita," a little girl from Mexico City, Roy sings "Mexicali Rose,"

THE MEXICAN CONNECTION

With their extravagant musical numbers, exciting horseback action, and flashy costumes, Roy Rogers movies enjoyed great popularity in Mexico. Republic made a consistent effort to cultivate Mexican audiences. Fiery Estelita Rodriguez was featured in nine Roy Rogers films, often as a romantic-comic foil to Pat Brady. Other Hispanic performers included tenor Tito Guizar, Duncan Renaldo, Conchita Lemus, Nestor Paiva, and Tito and Corinne Valdez. Western actor Duncan Renaldo, who would become famous as television's Cisco Kid, often was consulted by Roy and the Sons of the Pioneers for correct Spanish pronunciation of lyrics and dialogue phrases.

Several of the movies received titles suggestive of Hispanic themes: *Cowboy and the Señorita*, *Song of Santa Fe*, *Lights of Old Santa Fe*, *Bells of Rosarita*, *Hands Across the Border*, *Sunset in El Dorado*, *Bells of San Angelo*, *On the Old Spanish Trail*, and *The Gay Ranchero*. The Sons of the Pioneers usually backed Roy on the title songs, in addition to performing such numbers onscreen as "Mexicali Rose," "Cielito Lindo," and "The Enchilada Man." Bob Nolan wrote "Song of the Vaquero," performed in *South of Santa Fe*. Tim and Glenn Spencer wrote the lively "Don Juan," and Tim also penned "Jumpin' Bean" and "Padre of Old San Antone."

Director William Witney called these songs "commercials" for Mexican release. An obvious commercial was inserted in *Under California Stars*, when Roy, with the Sons of the Pioneers humming in the background, sang a lullaby in Spanish— to a sleepy Anglo boy.

backed by the Sons of the Pioneers. Later in the film a large troupe of dancers, clad in Mexican costumes, perform to "Cielito Lindo," followed by the Sons of the Pioneers singing lyrics in Spanish. Bob Nolan offers a fine baritone solo in Spanish, then Roy sings a solo in English, with a few Spanish phrases.

The Sons of the Pioneers were far more prominent in *Song of Texas* than in the past few movies. Roy and the Sons of the Pioneers were partners in a horse ranch. Bob Nolan competed (unsuccessfully, as usual) with Roy for the beautiful Sheila Ryan, an excellent actress. (The increased budgets placed good talent in Roy Rogers movies, including Sheila Ryan and the principal bad guy, gruff Barton MacLane, a strong presence in A features since the 1930s.) Since neither Smiley Burnette nor Gabby Hayes was in *Song of Texas*, comedy was turned over to Pat Brady, who was listed in the cast credits. The Sons of the Pioneers were involved in brawls and shootouts throughout the movie. During the climax, an action-packed chuckwagon race, Bob Nolan and Roy each drove a wagon, while bad guys drove the other two vehicles. Bob's wagon was wrecked by a dastardly trick, but Roy won the race, thereby saving the ranch and foiling the blustering Barton MacLane. The Sons of the Pioneers performed in seven musical numbers, including the lively instrumental, "Farr Away Blues," featuring Hugh's sweet, jazzy fiddle.

Song of Texas was one of the best of all Roy Rogers movies. A primary factor in the excellence of the film's entertainment was the increased role, in the action as well as the music, of the Sons of the Pioneers. Just as in the Charles Starrett movies, the greater the involvement of the Sons of the Pioneers, the better the Roy Rogers films were. Bob Nolan was stalwart as ever as a second lead. The presence of half a dozen experienced good guys to help Roy offered reassurance in the face of the largest gang of bad guys. Pat Brady's slapstick comedy delighted young fans. And the Sons of the Pioneers, considered by many as the best Western singing group in existence, provided an incomparable asset to any musical Western.

And Republic wisely had decided to make the Roy Rogers Westerns more musical. There were ten numbers in *Song of Texas*, including a lavish dance routine. From this point on, there would be at least one big production number in each movie. Roy always maintained that Herbert J. Yates saw a Broadway performance of the spectacular musical *Oklahoma!*, then returned to Hollywood determined to incorporate the large-scale, colorful, singing-dancing numbers into Roy Rogers films. *Oklahoma!*, the first of nine collaborations between Richard Rodgers and Oscar Hammerstein II, opened on Broadway on March 31, 1943. *Oklahoma!* was a sensation, running for a record 2,212 performances.

It is not known how early in this long run that Herbert J. Yates might have seen *Oklahoma!*, but it is certain that by the summer of 1943 Roy Rogers movies exhibited noticeably more music and lavish production numbers. *Song of Texas* displayed a Roy Rogers version of *Oklahoma!* in the Lone Star State. Other states received Republic's *Oklahoma!* treatment: *Song of Nevada*, *Song of Arizona*, and *Utah*. But just as a greater musical emphasis was introduced into their film work, the Sons of the Pioneers sent one-third of its membership off to war.

Top left: *Roy with Trigger's luxurious trailer on the Republic lot.*

Top right: *Roy and ace trainer Glenn Randall working on another trick with Trigger.*

Bottom: *When new cowboy star Roy Rogers was trying out prospective lead horses, he immediately responded to the magnificent palomino he would name Trigger. "I got on him and it was just like I had put on a pair of pants."*

The Sons of the Pioneers in 1941. Top, L to R: Karl Farr, Hugh Farr, Pat Brady. Bottom: Lloyd Perryman, Tim Spencer, Bob Nolan.

Bob Nolan and Roy Rogers, with Lloyd Perryman in the background. Bob often wore this big black hat, which increased his already impressive screen presence. Roy eventually scaled down the tall crown of his white hat.

The Pioneers on a Western set. Top, L to R: Tim Spencer, Bob Nolan, Hugh Farr. Bottom: Karl Farr, Lloyd Perryman, Pat Brady.

Roy and Gabby on the dance floor in Sunset on the Desert *(1942). Throughout the war, Roy's movies would promote patriotic activities such as Red Cross dances. The Pioneers provide music from the stage.*

Top, L to R: Tim Spencer, Karl Farr, Bob Nolan. Bottom: Hugh Farr, Lloyd Perryman, Pat Brady. After filming was completed, the Pioneers would go to a studio, watch their musical numbers, and, as director William Witney put it, "sing to themselves" while recording the soundtrack.

Cover of a 1942 fan club newsletter, Tumbleweed Topics.

Above: *Roy Rogers at the piano, surrounded by the Pioneers. L to R: Hugh Farr, Pat Brady, Karl Farr, Lloyd Perryman, Bob Nolan, Tim Spencer.*

The Sons of the Pioneers ready for an NBC broadcast. L to R: Pat Brady, Karl Farr, Hugh Farr, Bob Nolan, Tim Spencer, Lloyd Perryman.

In 1942 the Pioneers took time out from Roy Rogers movies to appear in the excellent Gene Autry film, Call of the Canyon. L to R: Smiley Burnette, Tim Spencer, Bob Nolan (background), Karl Farr, Pat Brady (background), Gene Autry, Smiley's sidekick "Tadpole," and Hugh Farr.

The Pioneers provide party music for Gene Autry and friends in Call of the Canyon. The hatless Pioneers are in the background.

Hugh Farr enjoying location filming in 1942.

Top: *When Gabby Hayes (right) and Pat Brady (left) were in the same movie, young fans could expect a double dose of comedy.*

Left: Ridin' Down the Canyon *was the last Roy Rogers movie of 1942.*

George "Gabby" Hayes, the best sidekick in the business.

92

Director William Witney admired Roy's athleticism and horsemanship. "Of all the Western leading men I've worked with, I'd have to give Roy a perfect ten in horsemanship."

After Gene Autry entered military service, Republic promoted Roy Rogers as "King of the Cowboys."

Pat Brady's fellow Pioneers find his efforts on the piano painful to the ears.

In Idaho, *the first film of 1943, Roy examines a wounded man. Pat Brady is in the foreground. Tim Spencer is behind Pat, while Hugh Farr stands behind Roy.*

Atop the wagon, L to R: Tim Spencer, Lloyd Perryman, Hugh Farr. Standing: Karl Farr, Bob Nolan, Roy Rogers, Pat Brady.

Throughout World War II the Pioneers, often alongside Roy Rogers, made countless appearances at military bases. L to R: Bob Nolan, Karl Farr, Pat Brady, Roy Rogers, Hugh Farr, Lloyd Perryman, and Tim Spencer with two servicemen.

6
The Pioneers and World War II

"We tried to get a message in all of [my films],
that right always wins out over wrong."
— Roy Rogers

WHEN THE UNITED STATES entered World War II, in early December 1941, Selective Service—referred to everywhere as "the draft"—had been in effect for just over a year. On October 16, 1940, sixteen million American males above the age of eighteen registered for Selective Service. Men between the ages of twenty-one and thirty-five and classified as I-A began to be selected by lottery for induction into military service (the military greatly preferred inductees at the lower end of the age scale). Husbands and fathers, men with dependents, usually were deferred to Class III, while men working in agriculture or defense plants were placed in Class II. Men with physical shortcomings were classified IV-F, unfit for service. With war raging in Europe it seemed prudent to launch a buildup of America's understrength military.

Following Pearl Harbor, of course, inductions escalated rapidly. The acting profession provided a far higher percentage of inductees than any other occupational group. The 1940 U.S. Census listed 6,931 working actors, and within a few months after Pearl Harbor 3,503 of them—more than half—were in the U.S. Army. Draft boards clearly did not regard acting as an essential occupation, a viewpoint which received strong public support. Indeed, Americans warmly approved the efforts of movie star Jimmy Stewart to join the Army Air Corps. Shortly after the first Selective Service registration, the popular actor tried to enlist. To the relief of MGM executives, the lanky Stewart was rejected because he was underweight. But Stewart ate pasta and drank milkshakes until he passed the physical, and he donned a uniform in March 1941—eight months before Pearl Harbor. (Eventually, Stewart won the Distinguished Flying Cross as a B-24 pilot on combat missions over Europe.) Eight months after Pearl Harbor, thirty-five-year-old Gene Autry entered the service for the duration of the war. In

January 1942, actress Carole Lombard was killed in a plane crash following the first War Bond Campaign. Her bereaved husband, forty-one-year-old superstar Clark Gable, grimly enlisted in the Army Air Corps within a few months, and also was awarded the Distinguished Flying Cross. Many other movie actors enlisted before they could be drafted.

Roy Rogers was thirty and the head of a family when the United States entered the war. Above the optimum age, with a wife and adopted daughter as dependents, Roy was placed in Class III by his draft board. His career was at a pivotal point, with Republic providing him a special buildup when Gene Autry enlisted. In 1942 Roy went on a whirlwind tour of military bases in Texas, making 136 appearances in twenty days. He performed for War Bond sales and at military canteens and base hospitals. Roy's popularity soared as the wartime public sought escapist entertainment. During round after round of public appearances, he continued to perform at military bases and to sell War Bonds. The U.S. Treasury Department eventually awarded Roy Rogers a citation for selling a million dollars worth of war bonds. But by 1945 the Selective Service was desperate for manpower. Even though Roy now was thirty-four and the father of two daughters, he was reclassified I-A. Before he could be inducted, however, Germany surrendered in May 1945. Roy, along with many other men, was returned to Class III for the remaining months of the war.

Like Roy Rogers, the Sons of the Pioneers also performed frequently at military bases. Because of gasoline rationing and other travel restrictions, the Pioneers appeared mostly at bases located in California or nearby states. When the United States declared war, Hugh Farr was thirty-eight and married. Bob Nolan and Tim Spencer both were thirty-three. Tim was happily married and the father of a son and daughter. Bob married in 1942. Clara Nolan, called "Peanuts" by her friends, was Bob's soulmate. They bought a house on a large lot near enough to Republic for Bob to walk home for lunch. Karl Farr was thirty-two and married. Hugh, Bob, Tim, and Karl were not called into the service.

At twenty-four, Lloyd Perryman was the youngest member of the group on December 7, 1941, while Pat Brady was twenty-seven. Both men were called up in 1943. Lloyd went first, in April. His last film appearance was in *Song of Texas*. After training, Lloyd was sent to Burma. Pat entered the army in June, after filming *Hands Across the Border*. Eventually, Sergeant Brady would serve in the European theater, driving a tank with Patton's Third Army. (Years later Dale Warren reminisced about a postwar Pioneer tour of Germany: "We went to all of these little towns, and Pat would say, 'I went through this town.' You could still see the bullet holes in the walls of the old stone buildings. Pat was a hero. He got lots of awards and medals.") Sons of the Pioneers historian Ken Griffis stated that the group continued to pay the salaries of Tim and Pat while they were in uniform.

World War II affected virtually everyone, and the Sons of the Pioneers were no exception. Bob Nolan, Tim Spencer, Lloyd Perryman, Pat Brady, and Hugh and Karl Farr had worked together for more than five years. This group had performed in more than forty films with Charles Starrett and Roy Rogers. They had recorded radio transcriptions and movie scores and records for commercial release. They had traveled incessantly to public appearances, and they had rehearsed tirelessly to develop a unique sound. Now, in 1943, the group and the sound were about to undergo significant change.

After Lloyd Perryman left for the army in April 1943, the Sons of the Pioneers were without a replacement for more than a month. *Silver Spurs* was filmed with only five Pioneers. One of the most action-packed of all Roy Rogers films, *Silver Spurs* featured breathtaking stunt work by the famed Yakima Canutt. Yak's most exciting stunt is seen when the bad guys give chase to a wagon driven by Roy, with sidekick Smiley Burnette riding shotgun. Finally, one of the bad guys leaps off his horse onto the lead pair of the six-horse team, while another gang member jumps onto the wagon to fight Smiley. Roy (Yak) leaves the wagon seat and makes his way out to the lead team. After a brief struggle, both Roy and the bad guy fall beneath the galloping team. The wagon passes over the bad guy, but Roy grabs the rear of the wagon, climbs back in, and throws the other bad guy to the ground. After stopping to let Smiley and leading lady Ruth Terry off, Roy misleads the rest of the gang by driving the wagon off a cliff into a lake. Dressed as Roy, Yak jumps from the falling wagon into the water. It all added up to a better stunt than Yak's more famous drop beneath a galloping team in *Stagecoach*, the 1939 film that made a star of John Wayne.

One of the co-stars of *Stagecoach* was character actor John Carradine, who led the bad guys in *Silver Spurs*. The tall, menacing Carradine was a good example of the first-rate actors who began to appear in Roy Rogers movies.

During this slam-bang film the Sons of the Pioneers helped Roy escape from a false arrest, then participated in a shootout against Carradine's gang in a ghost town. Performing shorthanded, the group played an instrumental featuring the Farr brothers. At the end of the movie, the Pioneers sang a brief version of "Springtime in the Rockies." When they launched into "Tumbling Tumbleweeds," Roy joined in, then also sang lead on "Highways Are Happy Ways." With Roy on lead, Bob and Tim rounded out an excellent trio.

In June 1943 a fine tenor and guitarist, Ken Carson, became the first new member of the group since 1938. Ken had been singing for several years in Chicago, where he headlined his own radio program over WGN. A longtime admirer of the Sons of the Pioneers, he became acquainted with the group during their 1940-41 stay in Chicago. Ken was born in a buckboard on November 14, 1914, when his family was returning to their Oklahoma farm. Within a year his father died. His mother remarried, and his stepfather moved the family to Wichita, Kansas. His mother played guitar and his stepfather was a fiddler, inspiring little Ken to take up a harmonica, and later a guitar and banjo. When he was still a boy, the family migrated to Los Angeles. By the time Ken was seventeen he had developed an excellent tenor voice and was learning to play the guitar. Ambitious and confident, he wrangled an audition with singer-songwriter-actor Stuart Hamblen for his radio program. After a year with Hamblen, Ken and his new friend, future Pioneer Shug Fisher, joined a San Francisco group, the Tarzana Mineral Water Hill Billies.

Presenting himself for film work, Ken landed a small part in a Clark Gable vehicle, *It Happened One Night*, which won the Academy Award for best picture of 1934. With a trio he helped form, the Ranch Boys, Ken moved to Chicago in 1936. Although the Ranch Boys broke up after a few years, Ken became a successful solo act. Certainly, the Sons of the Pioneers were impressed. When Ken was invited to replace Lloyd Perryman, he left Chicago to perform with the best Western group in show business, and to appear in the enormously popular Roy Rogers movies.

Ken's high tenor added a new dimension to Pioneer harmony, and he was an able hand with a guitar. Although his diminutive stature branded him with the nickname "Shorty," he was trim and looked good in Western clothes. His friendly nature came through on the big screen, and he handled his limited acting chores capably.

The amiable Ken Carson was liked by everyone, but he soon learned that the Pioneers preferred not to be with one another during their rare off-duty occasions. "We didn't really socialize off the set," said Ken. "I guess it was because we were up at 5:00 in the morning, going to recording sessions, on tour—fifty-three weeks a year."

Nevertheless, Ken and Tim did "get together a few times." And Hugh Farr quickly warmed to the new Pioneer, even though Ken realized that the gifted fiddler had a strong ego and was temperamental. "Hugh was a little jealous of everybody," observed Ken. "He probably was jealous of Bob most of all. He didn't seem to be jealous of me, because I was a youngster and he played a sort of fatherly role."

Ken learned that Bob was a loner: "He was the Lone Ranger." But Ken had begun to dabble in songwriting, and Bob did not hesitate to solicit his help in working out a new song. Ken remembered, "Sometimes he would call at 1:00 in the morning and say, 'Can you come over? I have an idea for a song. It will only take ten minutes.' It would take two hours. He wrote 'Half-Way 'Round the World' that way."

Bob's nocturnal creativity seemed to rub off on Ken. "I woke up one morning at 5:00 and wrote 'Wondrous Word of the Lord' in about twelve minutes." The Sons of the Pioneers recorded "Wondrous Word" in 1951.

Although Ken was familiar with the work of the Pioneers, understandably he felt the need to rehearse intensively with the group. But Bob and Tim and the Farrs had been together for nearly a decade, and no longer had the inclination to engage in the endless rehearsals of their formative years. The Farr brothers were superb instrumentalists who could improvise any number, while Ken

THE DOUBLE-R-BAR

Roy Rogers and his agent, Art Rush, capitalized fully on the enormous popularity of the King of the Cowboys. Although Roy was never paid more than a few hundred dollars a week by Republic, prosperity was assured by the licensing of more than four hundred products. Carrying the Double-R-Bar brand were cap guns, hats, sheets, boots, holster sets, pocket knives, lunch boxes, and so many other items that the Sears catalogue devoted twelve pages to Roy Rogers products. Sales eventually totaled one billion dollars, and these products from the 1940s and 1950s today are prized collectibles.

"saw a real lethargy with Bob and Tim even then." To his dismay, Ken found that the Pioneers "did most of their rehearsing on the spot." This reluctance to rehearse properly would become more pronounced during the next few years.

Ken joined the group in June 1943, the same month that Pat Brady left for the army. Before being shipped overseas as a soldier in Patton's Third Army, Pat managed to coordinate leave time with a rare wartime recording session. Because wartime rationing included shellac, needed to press records, the amount of shellac allotted to recording companies was limited by the government. Furthermore, in August 1942 the American Federation of Musicians (AFM) went on strike, making financial demands that would offset the growing trend of radio stations to play records rather than employ live musicians. Long-term resistance to this trend proved futile, but the AFM strike lasted for more than a year. Therefore, the Sons of the Pioneers had not recorded commercially since March 1942 when, on December 28, 1943, they entered Decca's Los Angeles studio to cover four tunes: "I Hang My Head and Cry," "Home in San Antone," "There's a New Moon Over My Shoulder," and "Let Me Keep My Memories," which was written by Ken Carson. It was Ken's first opportunity to record with Bob, Tim, Pat, and the Farr brothers. But the rationing of shellac continued to limit wartime recording sessions, and nearly two years would pass before the Pioneers would cut another record.

For Pat Brady, it would be even longer until the next recording sessions. Pat's last film was one of the best of all Roy Rogers movies, *Hands Across the Border*. The genial Big Boy Williams was Roy's sidekick, Ruth Terry was the leading lady, and Roy Barcroft led the bad guys. Duncan Renaldo also was featured.

In the movie, Roy and Big Boy hire on at the Adams Ranch with the Sons of the Pioneers. Early in the film there is a party at the luxurious ranch headquarters. The Pioneers open the festivities by riding up on a wagon singing "Hey Hey": "Hey, hey, yessiree/Don't say it's a gray day/It's a great day/Wait and see..." Next they back Ruth Terry in "The Girl With the High-Buttoned Shoes," then Roy climbs aboard their wagon and sings the title song. There is a lot of exciting horse action as the ranch hands prepare mounts for sale to the cavalry, then test the horses over the cavalry obstacle course. An expert stuntman, doubling for Roy, performs spectacular riding tricks on Trigger, including jumping him over a car.

Hands Across the Border closes with one of the most elaborate production numbers ever staged in a Western. The number lasts for the final ten minutes of the seventy-two-minute running time. A border line is painted down the middle of a large stage, with the Mexican customs house on one side and the U.S. customs house on the other. A twenty-four-girl chorus line includes Anglo dancers and costumed *señoritas*. There are tap dancers, an orchestra, and a violin trio. Trigger performs at one point. The number opens with the Pioneer trio—Bob Nolan, Tim Spencer, and Ken Carson—singing the title song. Later Roy is reinforced by Bob, Tim, Ken, and Pat Brady. (Pat would not make another film for two years.)

Hardly had the Sons of the Pioneers begun adjusting from Lloyd Perryman to Ken Carson than they lost their immensely popular comic and bass fiddle player. Ken strongly recommended another bass fiddler with comedic talent, Shug Fisher, and Tim Spencer gave Shug a call.

George Clinton Fisher was a country boy, born and raised in Oklahoma. His mother, a quarter-blood Choctaw, thought her fourth baby was as sweet as sugar, and he soon was called "Shug." His father was a cotton farmer who once had been a fiddler. Shug inherited a feel and a need for music. When he was ten, Shug traded a saddle blanket for his first instrument, a mandolin. In time he acquired a fiddle and a guitar, and he began to play neighborhood square dances.

When he was seventeen, he attended a traveling medicine show. Shug was drawn to the slapstick comedian, who sported a red wig and blacked teeth. He already had learned to entertain with music, and he was determined to make people laugh.

The next year, in 1925, Shug's father and a friend decided to try their luck in California. They drove west in a Model A Ford, and Shug, now in his eighteenth year, came along for the adventure. He worked variously as a fruit picker and oil rigger. Continuing to entertain at dances, in 1931 he joined the Hollywood Hill Billies and began to play the bass fiddle. Young Ken Carson also was a member, and within a couple of years Ken and Shug moved to the Beverly Hill Billies. Soon Shug was performing with Stuart Hamblen in Los Angeles, before going on the road with "The Lonesome Cowboy," Roy Faulkner. Shug settled down for four years with a radio job in Wheeling, West Virginia. Then he took another radio spot in Cincinnati, where he married Peggy Summer. After the United States entered World War II, Shug moved to Los Angeles to work in defense plants. Art Rush, manager for Roy Rogers, asked Shug to help entertain defense workers.

By 1943 he was a versatile, experienced entertainer who eagerly embraced the opportunity to perform with the Sons of the Pioneers. Like Ken Carson, Shug was a warm, amiable man. The group members responded to him and quickly made him feel that he was a Pioneer. Shug would work with the Pioneers off and on for the next decade and a half.

Shug joined the Pioneers late in 1943, but not in time to take part in the next Roy Rogers movie, *Cowboy and the Señorita*. For this fine film the Pioneers included Bob Nolan, Tim Spencer, Ken Carson, and Hugh and Karl Farr. Big Boy Williams returned as "Teddy Bear," Roy's sidekick. During a chase scene, a posse member actually uses the line, "They went thataway!"

The big production number at the end of the movie begins with a line of *señoritas* performing a Mexican hat dance around a huge sombrero. Slowly the sombrero is lifted, revealing a pair of flamenco dancers. Then Roy and the Pioneers sing "Enchilada Man." The film closes with the title song, "Cowboy and the Señorita."

An entertaining movie in many ways, *Cowboy and the Señorita* is most notable for the introduction of a new leading lady in Roy Rogers films: Dale Evans. Lovely and talented, she was a thirty-one-year-old singer-actress from Texas. The big screen revealed a warm but feisty personality, and when she spoke, a faint Texas twang rang true in the Western setting. A dark-haired beauty in *Cowboy and the Señorita*, in later films she became a blonde. Through the years she switched from blonde to brunette to redhead and back again, but these changes added interesting variation as she played opposite Roy in twenty-eight films. Roy had many pretty leading ladies who could sing well. But Dale was an exceptional singer, and her loveliness had an All-American quality that nicely matched Roy's wholesome good looks. When reviewing *Cowboy and the Señorita*, Phil Hardy commented that Dale "was a versatile workhorse of a singer-cum-dancer whose maternal sexuality complemented Rogers' oddly boy-ish charm."

She was born Frances Octavia Smith in Uvalde, Texas, on October 31, 1912. Her father was a cotton farmer, but when Frances was a child she dreamed of marrying Western movie star Tom Mix. "We would have six children together," she reminisced in *Happy Trails*, "then gallop our horses through the sagebrush." She had the script right, but she would have to cast a different cowboy star as her leading man.

Frances loved to sing and dance and play the piano, and she dreamed of becoming an actress. But the Smith family moved to a farm near Osceola, Arkansas, and when Frances was fourteen she impulsively married another teenager. The next year she had a son, Tom. But her young husband wanted out of the marriage, and the fifteen-year-old mother returned to her parents, who had moved to Memphis. Frances took a secretarial job with an insurance company.

Overhearing Frances singing at work, her boss arranged for her to perform on a Memphis radio show sponsored by the company. Her talent brought her rapid success as a radio singer. She moved with Tom to Chicago, enjoying similar success in a larger market. Later Frances landed a lucrative radio job at WHAS in Louisville, where the station manager changed her name to Dale Evans. She returned to Texas to sing over WFAA in Dallas. She was remarried in 1930, but the marriage did not last. In Dallas in 1937, she married a pianist and musical arranger named Robert Dale Butts.

Returning to Chicago, Dale Evans enjoyed her greatest success to date as a radio and orchestra singer. Beckoned to Hollywood, she took screen tests and signed a one-year contract with Twentieth Century Fox. There was little film work, but Dale recorded for overseas broadcasts and performed more than 500 USO shows at army and navy bases in California and surrounding states. She became the featured singer on the popular Edgar Bergen-Charlie McCarthy radio show, and she appeared on such other important programs as those of Jimmy Durante, Garry Moore, and Jack Carson.

In 1943 Dale signed a one-year contract with Republic Studios. She appeared in several musicals and melodramas, as well as a John Wayne film, *In Old Oklahoma*. Then she was assigned to a Roy Rogers film, *Cowboy and the Señorita*. Dale had never been on a horse since she was a child, and Roy liked to laugh about how much daylight there was between Dale and the saddle. She bounced so badly that the caps popped off her teeth, and the horse Big Boy Williams was riding stepped on them. But she took riding lessons, along with coaching from Roy, and became an excellent horsewoman. *Cowboy and the Señorita* was a fine film, and fan mail began to pour in about Roy's latest leading lady.

Roy and Dale's second movie together, *Yellow Rose of Texas*, was Shug

Fisher's first film appearance. The revamped roster of the Sons of the Pioneers now was set for the next couple of years: Bob Nolan, Tim Spencer, Ken Carson, Shug Fisher, and Hugh and Karl Farr. *Yellow Rose of Texas* was the name of a showboat, and the Sons of the Pioneers were hired as performers when Roy arranged an impromptu audition. In their first performance on the boat they sang "Timber Trail," which they had first aired on-screen with Charles Starrett in 1939 in *Outpost of the Mounties*. Shug performed comic bits, and played a top-hatted "perfesser" during the showboat's minstrel show. The film closed with a musical revue in which the Sons of the Pioneers reprised the beautiful "Timber Trail," and Roy and Dale led the showboat company in the title song.

> ### THE CLASSIC CAST
>
> For a couple of golden years audiences were treated to an incomparable casting combination in Roy Rogers movies: Roy, Trigger, Dale Evans, Gabby Hayes, and the Sons of the Pioneers. This classic cast—the Number One Cowboy Star, the Smartest Horse in the Movies, the ideal leading lady, the most beloved sidekick, and the best Western musical group—worked together in fourteen films:
>
> *Lights of Old Santa Fe* (1944)
> *Utah* (1945)
> *Bells of Rosarita* (1945)
> *Man From Oklahoma* (1945)
> *Sunset in El Dorado* (1945)
> *Don't Fence Me In* (1945)
> *Along the Navajo Trail* (1945)
> *Song of Arizona* (1946)
> *Rainbow Over Texas* (1946)
> *My Pal Trigger* (1946)
> *Under Nevada Skies* (1946)
> *Roll On Texas Moon* (1946)
> *Home in Oklahoma* (1946)
> *Heldorado* (1946)

Dale went on to co-star in twenty consecutive Roy Rogers movies. The popularity of the Roy and Dale pairing grew with every film. Dale found the Republic team to be "like a family." Cast and crew worked from dawn to dark on location or in the studio. Dale was expected to help promote each film with personal appearances, and soon she became a regular with Roy's roadshow cast. When filming, she regularly arose at 4:30 to have her hair and makeup done. Velma Spencer met Dale when Tim brought her home after a day of filming, so that she would not have such a long drive the next morning. Velma was embarrassed that Dale had to be relegated to a folding bed. But Dale was genuinely grateful, and Velma—like almost everyone else who knew her—was won over by her warmth.

The next movie was *Song of Nevada*. An early scene was at a cattle camp, with the Sons of the Pioneers and Roy singing "There's a New Moon Over Nevada." The song featured Ken Carson's increasingly familiar whistling, and Hugh Farr's fiddling and bass harmony. Later the Pioneers, sporting feathers in their hats, added war whoops to "The Wigwam Song." At a frontier costume party they backed Roy in the traditional "Sweet Betsy From Pike." Then they sang backup for Dale as an old-fashioned barbershop quartet. Bob, Tim, Ken, and Hugh were costumed in 1890s suits and handlebar mustaches, which they twirled stylishly throughout Dale's number. But there was not as much action as usual in *Song of Nevada*, and the closing production number, a hokey tribute to Nevada, was flat and disappointing.

Song of Nevada was the last Roy Rogers film for veteran director Joseph Kane. Kane directed each of Roy's first forty-one starring films, and had played a crucial role in making him King of the Cowboys. Republic assigned Kane to direct more ambitious films, including a few John Wayne Westerns. Roy's next movie was directed by John English, but Frank McDonald was assigned to most of the Roy Rogers projects filmed during the rest of the war.

The mediocre *Song of Nevada* was followed by a far more entertaining movie, *San Fernando Valley*. With Yakima Canutt in charge of stunt work, the action was exciting, and the Sons of the Pioneers were important to the plot. The Pioneers played rather lazy cowboys on the horse ranch of Dale and her grandfather. In the film, the Pioneers preferred making music to working at their jobs. After Dale reluctantly fired the boys, she hired a new crew of female rodeo performers. This Rosie the Riveter plot device rang true in a wartime economy in which women in large numbers were replacing men who had entered military service. Roy managed to get a job as ranch cook for the girls, and the

HOLLYWOOD CANTEEN

In 1944 Republic loaned the Sons of the Pioneers to Warner Brothers for a unique wartime movie, *Hollywood Canteen*. The Hollywood Canteen was the most glamorous attraction in Hollywood for the hordes of off-duty servicemen who visited the film capital. Founded by Bette Davis and John Garfield, the Hollywood Canteen opened in October 1942 on Cahuenga Boulevard, just south of Sunset Boulevard. The movie studios provided funding as a patriotic exercise, and most of the food, cigarettes, and refreshments were donated. Almost every important screen or radio entertainer volunteered to perform or serve as hosts or bus boys. Starstruck servicemen enjoyed the presence of Betty Grable, Greer Garson, Dinah Shore, Bette Davis, John Garfield, Fred MacMurray, Red Skelton, Edgar Bergen, and a host of other stars. Anyone wearing uniform was admitted free, and an estimated 100,000 servicemen visited the Hollywood Canteen every month.

When Warner Brothers decided to put the Hollywood Canteen on film, Bette Davis starred as chief hostess. The movie ran for more than two hours, featuring appearances by Joan Crawford, John Garfield, Barbara Stanwyck, Peter Lorre, Ida Lupino, Eddie Cantor, Alexis Smith, Jack Benny, the Andrews Sisters, and others—including the Sons of the Pioneers, Roy Rogers, and Trigger. The Pioneers performed "Tumbling Tumbleweeds," of course, with "Don't Fence Me In" and "Cajun Stomp."

Pioneers returned to serenade them around the swimming pool (no horse ranch being complete without a pool). During a novelty number an orchestra played on the soundtrack, so Karl Farr pretended to blow a trumpet, Bob Nolan a saxophone, and Tim Spencer a clarinet. An even more unusual scene exhibited a rare—if brief—screen kiss between Roy and Dale. The closing production number was fashioned around the popular title song. At the end Roy and Dale, singing "San Fernando Valley," drove off in a Woody hauling Trigger in a horse trailer.

Republic returned Gabby Hayes to Roy Rogers movies with *Lights of Old Santa Fe*. The classic Roy Rogers team now was assembled: Roy, Gabby, Dale, the Sons of the Pioneers—and Trigger. Roy Barcroft, who would appear in more Roy Rogers films than any other bad guy, completed an ideal lineup. Between 1944 and 1947, the combination of Roy, Dale, Gabby, and the Pioneers played together in fourteen films. Although these movies comprise fewer than one-sixth of the total of Roy Rogers films, the repeated appearance together of the Number One Cowboy Star, the ideal Western leading lady, the best sidekick in the movies, and the finest of all Western musical groups made a permanent impression on horse opera fans.

Lights of Old Santa Fe opens with a production number, as Roy, Gabby, and the Sons of the Pioneers hear Dale sing. Roy and the Pioneers, of course, soon break into song, crooning "The Cowboy Polka." Later, jammed into a convertible, Roy and the six Pioneers warble "I'm Happy in My Levi Britches." A few scenes later Roy and the Pioneers launch "Cowboy Jubilee," featuring Hugh's "Flyin' Fiddle," Karl's "Gallopin' Guitar," and Roy's yodeling. Then the Pioneers back Dale and Roy in a duet, before singing the title song around a campfire. The group performs "Ride 'Em Cowboy" over the radio: "Grab your seat and sit 'em tight / The ridin's rough but the pay is right / If you ride 'em cowboy."

In between songs, Roy and the Sons of the Pioneers help Gabby put his faltering rodeo troupe back together again. Roy and Trigger become the rodeo's star attraction, thereby adding several thrilling horse stunts to the film. Late in the movie, the Sons of the Pioneers form a ring as Roy and Roy Barcroft duke it out. When the hero slugs the villain, Barcroft staggers backward into Shug Fisher's arms.

"Shall we dance?" asks Shug.

Barcroft angrily lurches back into the fray, but another blow again propels him back into Shug's arms. "He likes me!" mugs Shug.

"Let me have him, Roy," pleads Bob Nolan. "Shug's tired."

"Here he comes," announces the hero, launching another blow.

"Thanks," Bob says, catching the collapsing villain. "Well, you better sit this one out."

Lights of Old Santa Fe was the last of six Roy Rogers films released in 1944. For the second year in a row, Roy was ranked as the Number One Money-Making Western Star. The successful formula would be continued the next year, beginning with *Utah*.

Utah offered Roy, Dale, Gabby, and the Sons of the Pioneers a plot that had more music than action. Now a blonde, Dale plays a Chicago musical star who decides to sell her Utah ranch to raise the $25,000 needed to back her latest show. Among the showgirls Dale brings to Utah with her is Peggy Stewart, one of Republic's busiest and most beautiful heroines. Roy is the ranch foreman, and the Sons of the Pioneers are his friends and ranch hands. Roy, Gabby, and the Pioneers try various schemes to prevent Dale from selling the ranch. They pick up Dale and her friends at the depot in a Woody, and the Pioneers provide a serenade with "Five Little Miles," featuring their matchless harmony. Bob Nolan, who more than once had lost a leading lady to Roy, has a sweetheart (one of the showgirls) to himself in *Utah*.

Bob again enjoyed his own sweetheart—Adele Mara, who would co-star in a John Wayne movie within a few years—in the next film, *Bells of Rosarita*. The plot involves Dale and Gabby trying to save her circus (her father, manager of the circus, has recently died). The circus is in winter quarters at Gabby's California ranch, where Republic is filming a Roy Rogers movie entitled *Bells of Rosarita*. The Sons of the Pioneers participate in the shooting of the film, and there are some excellent movie-making scenes. Finally, in order to save Dale's circus, Roy calls Republic Studios to enlist fellow cowboy stars as guest performers. In addition to Wild Bill Elliott, Don "Red" Barry, Allan "Rocky" Lane, Sunset Carson, and Bob Livingston (who had played the Lone Ranger in the movies), the Republic casting office sent several circus acts. Roy and his fellow Western stars take time to chase down a gang of bank robbers, then gallop back to town in time for the circus performance.

The Sons of the Pioneers sing "When the Circus Comes to Town" and the beautiful "Trail Herdin' Cowboy." Shug plays a lot of comedy opposite Gabby. Along with romancing Adele Mara, Bob is more active than ever in his role as second lead to Roy. Other Pioneers are featured at different points in the movie.

The Sons of the Pioneers had become far more recognizable than simply another nameless group of musical performers in the background of a film. Like Roy, they were called by their first names. Each of the Pioneers had dialogue, and fans now could place names with faces. Bob was Roy's friend, handsome and strong, and he always was given separate billing: "BOB NOLAN and the Sons of the Pioneers." When Shug appeared onscreen, young fans happily anticipated comedy, just as they had with rubber-faced Pat Brady. Tim and Ken obviously were pleasant cowboys who could sing well, and Hugh was the fiddler with the deep voice. Karl played the guitar and always smiled. As the years passed, movie audiences easily recognized individual Pioneers. This individual recognition, of course, came in the enormously popular films of Roy Rogers. The Sons of the Pioneers were practiced veterans in front of movie cameras, and they enjoyed fame and status unique among Western music groups.

The group was featured on network radio during this period. On November 21, 1944, "The Roy Rogers Show" debuted over the Mutual Radio Network. Sponsored by Goodyear Tires, the half-hour program aired on Tuesdays at 8:30 P.M. The regular cast was Roy Rogers, Bob Nolan and the Sons of the Pioneers, female vocalist Pat Friday, announcer Vern Smith, and Perry Botkin and his band. Budgeted at $3,500 per episode, "The Roy Rogers Show" ran for several months, but went off the air in the spring of 1945 when Goodyear failed to pick up the option. Because of Roy's vast popularity, however, "The Roy Rogers Show" would soon return to network radio.

The Sons of the Pioneers were not as prominent as usual in their next two films, *The Man From Oklahoma* and *Sunset in El Dorado.* In the latter, the Pioneers appear only in an early scene on a tour bus. Dale is on the bus to see the West, and the Sons of the Pioneers are passengers singing a song inspired by Horace Greeley's famous advice: "Go West, go West, young man." Bob, Ken, and Shug each sing a verse. Shug leans over to a meek-looking Easterner in a suit and tie and sings: "I want to go where coyotes feed on city folks that we don't need/Where varmints eat on tenderfeet/That's the land for me!"

The rest of the movie is unusual because Roy, Dale, and Gabby spend almost an hour in the Old West. After Dale leaves the tour bus, she goes to the ghost town of El Dorado, where her grandmother was a saloon singer. In a long dream sequence Dale becomes her grandmother. The adventures which follow are set in the 1800s, and include Roy Rogers being accused of the murder of villain Roy Barcroft. After years of seeing Roy and his team operate in the West of the 1940s, it is refreshing and interesting to watch Roy and his friends ride and shoot and sing in a frontier setting with no automobiles or Eastern gangsters.

PUT US IN THE MOVIES

Before television and music videos made musical artists recognizable stars, singers and groups could achieve visibility only by appearing in movies. Of course, artists were seen at personal appearances, but for Country and Western stars such audiences were small, usually numbering in the hundreds rather than the thousands. Much larger audiences listened to records and radio programs, but to be seen by a large public, Country and Western artists needed movie exposure.

Gene Autry, Tex Ritter, Roy Rogers, and other singing cowboys offered movie appearances for Country and Western groups. Such groups usually had a couple of numbers in each film, presenting their most popular tune and then backing up the star in one or two songs. These groups rarely took part in the action.

In California the locally popular Beverly Hill Billies only managed a few movie appearances. Roy Acuff joined the Grand Ole Opry in 1938, and within a few years Acuff and his Smoky Mountain Boys played to audiences of 15,000. But during the height of their popularity in the 1940s, Roy Acuff and the Smoky Mountain Boys appeared in just eight films. It was 1943 before another Grand Ole Opry star, Ernest Tubb, appeared in *The Fighting Buckaroo* with Charles Starrett. Tubb and his Texas Troubadours made just three other films. It was big news in 1940 when Bob Wills and the Texas Playboys made *Take Me Back To Oklahoma* with Tex Ritter. "The King of Western Swing" and the Playboys were involved in the plot, but they appeared in only half a dozen subsequent movies.

By contrast, the Sons of the Pioneers appeared in nearly one hundred films over a period of two decades. No other Western musical group even approached this regularity and breadth of motion picture exposure, which produced a special degree of popularity for the Sons of the Pioneers.

Sunset in El Dorado was followed by *Don't Fence Me In*, one of the most entertaining of the eighty-eight Roy Rogers movies. Dale's role as newspaperwoman Toni Ames was her favorite. In addition to Cole Porter's popular title song, there were many enjoyable tunes, including "Tumbling Tumbleweeds." The Sons of the Pioneers also sang "I'm Headin' for the Last Roundup" while staging a bogus wake over the "corpse" of Gabby. Tim Spencer leaned over the coffin and whispered, "Gabby, you look better dead than alive."

Gabby played a reformed frontier outlaw, Wildcat Kelly, who supposedly had died decades earlier. Roy owned a dude ranch and the Pioneers were his ranch hands. Roy's father, Reverend John Rogers, had converted Wildcat Kelly in the old days. "Gabby saved Dad's life once," explained Roy, "and Dad saved Gabby's soul."

Dale's feisty character ("I hate namby-pamby heroines") pushed Roy into a swimming pool early in the movie, then later gave chase to the bad guys in a wood-paneled station wagon. Bob (or his stunt double) jumped from his horse to corral two of the bad guys. The film's finale was delightful, with music, dancers, the Sons of the Pioneers, Dale, and Roy presenting a spectacular production number. When Roy and Trigger burst through a paper barn "door," they created perhaps the most memorable scene in any Roy Rogers movie.

The final film released in 1945 was *Along the Navajo Trail*. The action featured exciting stunts by Yakima Canutt and a brawl between the two Roys, Rogers and Barcroft. The music included two dance numbers and "Cool Water" by the Pioneers.

The six films of 1945 again made Roy the Number One Money-Making Western Star, and placed him tenth in the A-list of Top Ten Money-Making Stars. Gabby Hayes ranked just behind Roy as the Number Two Western Star. Roy Rogers movies offered a Western fantasy that was embraced not only by juvenile fans but by war-weary adults. In the same way that audiences of the depression lost themselves in the Fred Astaire-Ginger Rogers dance fantasies, wartime audiences found escape in the happy, romantic, musical West of Roy Rogers. As the war went on, the Roy Rogers formula and team steadily improved. The Sons of the Pioneers, as vital members of the team, enjoyed a steady increase in recognition and popularity.

But would the end of the war bring a change in audience tastes? Certainly it would bring the return of Lloyd Perryman and Pat Brady to the Pioneers. Certainly, too, it would bring an end to the ban on recording, as well as to travel restrictions which cut into personal appearances. An American public suddenly released from the tensions and rationing and restrictions of four years of war would be eager for every form of entertainment. For the Sons of the Pioneers, as for the rest of American society, the postwar years would bring new challenges and new opportunities.

Roy Barcroft was Republic's busiest villain, appearing in 150 Westerns. He was a bad guy in twenty Roy Rogers movies.

The Pioneers entertaining servicemen from atop a makeshift platform.

Bob Nolan and Pat Brady look on as Roy tries to deal with a female admirer in Man From Music Mountain.

Pioneers in the background of Hands Across the Border.

The Pioneer trio led off the longest (ten minutes) and one of the most elaborate production numbers in any Roy Rogers film, Hands Across the Border. Bob Nolan is in the black hat, Ken Carson is at center, and Tim Spencer is at right. Dancing señoritas have just emerged from the Mexican customs house, while American dancers have come from the U. S. customs house.

With Gabby Hayes assigned to Wild Bill Elliott movies, Pat Brady assumed more of the comedy load in such films as Man From Music Mountain.

The Sons of the Pioneers reluctantly lined up behind villain Onslow Stevens in Hands Across the Border. *L to R: Tim Spencer, Bob Nolan, Hugh Farr, Karl Farr, Pat Brady, Ken Carson.*

The Pioneers in front of their photographs at "Grace Purdy's Western Music Corral." A photo of the Pioneers is just above Bob's head, and to the left, a photo of Bob and a shot of Roy Rogers.

Bob Nolan, Dale Evans, Gabby Hayes, and Roy Rogers astride Trigger. The classic cast of Roy, Trigger, Gabby, Dale, and Bob and the other Pioneers appeared in fourteen movies in 1944, 1945, and 1946.

The Pioneers perform "Timber Trail" on the showboat stage in Yellow Rose of Texas. *L to R: Ken Carson, Bob Nolan, Hugh Farr, Tim Spencer, Shug Fisher, Karl Farr.*

Roy and Dale featured in a lavish production number in Song of Nevada.

When Pat Brady left the Sons of
the Pioneers to serve in the
army, Shug Fisher took over
the bass fiddle and the comedy.

*Roy, Dale, and Gabby. Dale was in twenty-eight Roy Rogers movies, while Gabby was Roy's sidekick
in forty films.*

After ranch owner Dale Evans fired the Pioneers as lazy cowboys in San Fernando Valley, the group entertained their female replacements around the swimming pool.

The Pioneers, with Dale Evans and her friends, cluster around a wood-paneled station wagon, a fixture in Roy Rogers movies.

Left: *A scene from* Utah. *L to R: Karl Farr, Hugh Farr, Ken Carson, Roy Rogers, Bob Nolan, Shug Fisher.*

Right: *Gabby Hayes was back with Roy and the Pioneers in* Utah. *L to R: Karl Farr, Tim Spencer, Hugh Farr, Ken Carson, Roy, Bob Nolan, Gabby.*

Roy restrains Gabby while Dale holds back Gabby's tormentor in Man From Oklahoma. *Pioneers in background, L to R: Shug Fisher, Bob Nolan, Karl Farr, Hugh Farr, Tim Spencer.*

Roy and Dale in Bells of Rosarita *(1945). They had an obvious on-screen chemistry.*

Production number from Man From Oklahoma *features Roy Rogers, Dale Evans, Gabby Hayes, and the Sons of the Pioneers—the "classic cast."*

Roy Rogers confers with the Pioneers in Man From Oklahoma. *L to R: Bob Nolan, Karl Farr, Ken Carson, Shug Fisher, Hugh Farr, Tim Spencer.*

Roy and the Pioneers audition in Man From Oklahoma.

Gabby Hayes mesmerizes Shug Fisher in Man From Oklahoma. *Looking on, L to R: Ken Carson, Bob Nolan, Hugh Farr, Roy Rogers, Tim Spencer, Karl Farr (background).*

Bob Nolan takes a back seat as his friends perform in Man From Oklahoma. *L to R: Hugh Farr, Karl Farr, Roy Rogers, Ken Carson, Shug Fisher.*

In Sunset in El Dorado, *Dale Evans flashed back to the Old West, where her grandmother, the notorious "Kansas Kate," fell in love with a cowboy who looked like Roy Rogers. The Pioneers sported long sideburns for Dale's Old West dream sequence. L to R: Ken Carson, Dale Evans, Bob Nolan, Tim Spencer, Karl Farr, Hugh Farr, Shug Fisher.*

When Roy sang with the Pioneers, he usually took the lead. In effect, the group was increased to seven, with a beneficial effect on the music. Top, L to R: Karl Farr, Shug Fisher, Hugh Farr. Front: Roy Rogers, Ken Carson, Bob Nolan, Tim Spencer.

A standoff at the Westward Ho Club in Don't Fence Me In. Dale Evans stated that her role as newspaperwoman Toni Ames was her all-time favorite. L to R: Bob Nolan, Karl Farr, Hugh Farr, Tim Spencer, Shug Fisher, Roy Rogers, Dale Evans, Ken Carson, Gabby Hayes.

Roy and Gabby stand with Trigger in Along the Navajo Trail. *In the saddle, L to R: Shug Fisher, Ken Carson, Tim Spencer, Roy Barcroft, unidentified rider, Bob Nolan, Hugh Farr.*

Left: *Singing lakeside during World War II. L to R: Karl Farr, Shug Fisher, Hugh Farr. Front: Bob Nolan, Tim Spencer, Ken Carson.*

Below: *The Pioneers stage a mock scuffle. L to R: Hugh Farr, Karl Farr, big Bob Nolan being manhandled by Shug Fisher, who uses his tongue for leverage, Ken Carson, and Lloyd Perryman.*

Bottom: *Roy and the Pioneers help Gabby, a reformed outlaw once known as "Wildcat Kelly," play dead in* Don't Fence Me In. *At Gabby's "wake," Tim Spencer (far left), whispered, "Gabby, you look better dead than alive."*

While on the road or location, the Pioneers liked to camp, fish, or sail whenever possible. Bob Nolan (right) and Ken Carson are in the sailboat. In the motorboat are Tim Spencer, Shug Fisher, and the Farr brothers.

RCA publicity photo. Clockwise from the top: Bob Nolan, Karl Farr, Lloyd Perryman, Tim Spencer, Hugh Farr, Pat Brady.

7
The Postwar Years

"...the Studio Executive Committee decided to
discontinue the services of the Sons of the Pioneers...."
—HERBERT J. YATES

ON AUGUST 8, 1945—two days after the first atomic bomb was dropped over Hiroshima—the Sons of the Pioneers covered their first recording session in almost two years. The Pioneers had last recorded with Decca in December 1943. Despite the group's screen exposure, it was difficult to record during the war, and Decca did not renew their contract. Toward the end of the war, RCA Victor signed the increasingly popular Sons of the Pioneers to a recording contract.

RCA intended to produce their recordings with the larger sound of backup instrumentalists. The Sons of the Pioneers always had recorded with their own instruments: the Flyin' Fiddle and Gallopin' Guitar of the Farr brothers, another guitar or two, and a bass fiddle. This classic Pioneer sound was the same as that heard at personal appearances and in the movies. But after Republic increased the musical emphasis of Roy Rogers movies, orchestras often were heard on the soundtracks. Sometimes the orchestra was shown onscreen, usually in an Eastern nightclub where Dale sang, or in an incongruously luxurious club in a dusty Western town. Many times an orchestra swelled the soundtrack as the Pioneers energetically worked their instruments onscreen.

So RCA Victor decided to add four sidemen—backup instrumentalists—to their first session with the Sons of the Pioneers. One of the musicians was Duece Spriggens, who in recent years had substituted with the Pioneers in the absence of Pat Brady or Shug Fisher. Shug was with the group at the first RCA session, along with Bob Nolan, Tim Spencer, Ken Carson, and Hugh and Karl Farr.

The group covered four songs, three composed by individual Pioneers: Bob Nolan's "Cool Water"; Tim Spencer's "Timber Trail"; and "Forgive and Forget" by Shug Fisher. The biggest hit of the session was a Bob Wills number, "Stars and Stripes on Iwo Jima." The famous Battle of Iwo Jima was fought in February and

March of 1945, and within a few months Wills released his song, which quickly rose to Number One on *Billboard*'s "Juke Box Folk Records" chart. RCA's Pioneer version hit the charts in October 1946, topping out at Number Four. The flip side of "Stars and Stripes on Iwo Jima" was "Cool Water," which also made the charts. "Cool Water" rose to Number Four in March 1947, and a year and a half later the Pioneer standard would enjoy another run on the charts.

The Sons of the Pioneers returned to RCA's Hollywood studio on January 7, 1946. This time there were five sidemen. In addition to the Pioneers' instruments, there were two violins, a steel guitar, a piano, and drums. The Pioneers again covered four songs, but none of these tunes reached the charts. The Pioneer roster was the same for this second session as the first. But by the time RCA produced a third session, two months later, Pat Brady and Lloyd Perryman had rejoined the group.

Just as Pat and Lloyd missed the first postwar recording sessions, they also were not discharged in time to help make the first few postwar films. (Discharges were awarded on a point system: one point for every month in the service, five points for each campaign star or combat decoration, and twelve points for each child. A total of eighty-five points was necessary for discharge eligibility.) When Lloyd was preparing to leave Burma to return to the United States, his commanding officer delivered "the nicest backhand compliment" he ever received. "Perryman," said the officer, "you're a good soldier, but you're a better top tenor. Go on back to your first love, the Sons of the Pioneers."

The first movie released in 1946 was *Song of Arizona*. Bob, Tim, Ken, Shug and the Farrs, along with Roy and Dale, help Gabby pay off the note on his "Half-a-Chance Ranch" for wayward boys. One of the bad guys is Dick Curtis, the hulking villain with whom the Pioneers had worked in so many Charles Starrett films. During one light-hearted number, the Pioneers sing to the boys about how "Michael O'Leary-O'Bryan-O'Toole was the toughest of cowboys, the fight'nist fool...."

The next movie, *Rainbow Over Texas*, opens with Roy and the Pioneers riding along singing the title song. Movie stars Roy Rogers and the Sons of the Pioneers leave on a nationwide personal appearance tour. Dale has a crush on Roy, singing duets with his records while sailing on her father's yacht. By happy coincidence, her father owns a luxurious ranch near the Western town where Gabby is sheriff, and where everyone soon comes together. On a saloon stage the Pioneers perform a "Cowboy Camp Meetin'," a humorous church revival with deep-voiced Hugh Farr as the preacher. The action includes an exciting horse race, which utilized footage from *Hands Across the Border*. After the bad guys are shot, a barbeque is held around the ranch swimming pool. Roy, Dale, and the Pioneers reprise the title song to end the movie.

Lloyd Perryman was back in time to work in the next movie, *My Pal Trigger*. Purporting to tell the story of how Roy acquired his superb horse, *My Pal Trigger* was Rogers' favorite film. Gabby and Dale run the "Golden Horse Ranch." When Roy looks at the newborn animal, he remarks, "You're kind of quick on the trigger, son."

"What are you gonna name him, Roy?" he is asked.

"I just did!" exclaims Roy.

In *My Pal Trigger*, Bob Nolan and the other Pioneers work for Gabby. During a party at the ranch, Bob is the caller for a *mounted* square dance, while the other Pioneers provide the music. Later, at the El Dorado Club in town, the Pioneers expertly perform "El Rancho Grande," one of their finest numbers on film.

The action scenes, controlled by Yakima Canutt, are superior throughout the movie. Roy "trains" Trigger, affording the horse an opportunity to display numerous tricks. Roy engages in two hard-hitting brawls, and Trigger wins a stallion fight. Roy and Trigger also win the climactic race, filmed at the popular Santa Anita Race Track in Pasadena.

Both Lloyd Perryman and Pat Brady were back in Hollywood for RCA's third recording session, on March 15, 1946. There were seven sidemen—and seven Pioneers: Bob, Tim, Lloyd, Pat, the Farr brothers, and Ken Carson.

After Lloyd's return, Ken Carson was hired by NBC radio in Los Angeles. Although Ken no longer toured or made movies with the Pioneers, he continued to record with the group for another year and a half. In 1959 he married Gretchen Myers in San Franscisco, then moved to New York, where he was a regular on Garry Moore's TV show. He later was proud of being invited to perform at the weddings of Tricia and Julie Nixon. In 1979 Ken relocated to Florida. Although Shug Fisher also left the Pioneers early in 1946, he soon would return to the group for a longer tenure.

At the March 15 recording session, the Pioneers covered five tunes: Bob Nolan's "Tumbling Tumbleweeds"; Tim Spencer's "Cowboy Camp Meetin'," from the recent movie *Rainbow Over Texas*; "Out California Way"; "Grievin' My Heart Out For You"; and "No One To Cry To," which climbed to Number Six on the charts.

Republic assigned the Pioneers to a quick appearance in *Home on the Range*, the first starring film for their latest cowboy hero, Monte Hale. Having bolstered Hale's initial movie, the Pioneers also appeared in *Ding Dong Williams*, a minor film about jazz and teenagers. "Ding Dong Williams" is a jazz clarinetist hired to work at a movie studio. Ding Dong is a fan of cowboy star "Steve Moore." On the set of Steve's latest movie, Ding Dong watches a scene around a campfire with the star, the leading lady, and the Sons of the Pioneers. The Pioneers sing a superb version of "Cool Water."

Back with Roy, the Pioneers helped film *Under Nevada Skies*. Bob Nolan's role was somewhat larger than usual, and he handles the part with spirit and the practiced skill of a movie veteran. Lloyd Perryman and Pat Brady were in the film, but Tim Spencer was absent. So the Pioneer roster consisted of Bob, Lloyd, Pat, Shug, and the Farr brothers. Between Gabby, Pat and Shug, there was plenty of comedy. During most of the movie the Pioneers sang and played backup to Roy and Dale. But they dressed as pirates for a novelty number, "The Cowboy-Sailor." Sporting a peg-leg and eye patch, Pat chanted, "Rope the mainsail/Brand the deck...." "Foghorn" Farr was featured, rumbling out: "Oh give me a home/On the billowy foam/Where the deer and the mermaids play...."

The Pioneers had two more recording sessions in August 1946, and another in September. RCA also produced a separate session for the Farr brothers on August 29. Hugh and Karl performed "Farr Away Blues," "Texas Skiparoo," "South in My Soul," and "Farr Brothers Stomp." On August 15 Bob, Tim, Lloyd,

Ken, Pat, Hugh, and Karl covered a trio of Pioneer classics: Tim's "Everlasting Hills of Oklahoma"; Bob's heartfelt "Chant of the Wanderer"; and Bob and Tim's hauntingly beautiful "Blue Prairie." Instrumentation included a nine-piece orchestra with strings. Six days later the Pioneers recorded "Trees," and on September 2 the group covered four more songs. "Baby Doll" found the charts, rising to Number Five in February 1947.

Also in September 1946 *Roll On Texas Moon* was released. *Roll On Texas Moon* was the first Roy Rogers movie directed by William Witney, who was a veteran director of serials. Witney had been in military service, and *Roll On Texas Moon* was his first assignment for Republic in four years. Gene Autry also had returned from the war, and Frank McDonald, who had been working with Roy, was assigned to direct Gene's first film, *Sioux City Sue*. So Witney directed *Roll On Texas Moon*, then went on to direct twenty-six more Roy Rogers movies, until the series ended in 1951.

Before the war, Witney had directed two dozen action-packed serials, along with a few Western films. Under his direction, Roy Rogers movies would feature more action and stunts, with less emphasis on music and gaudy costumes. The pace would become faster, with more fights and chases and shootouts. But this development meant that there would be less of what the Sons of the Pioneers did best.

Although there were several songs in *Roll On Texas Moon*, most of the music involved Roy and Dale. The Pioneers helped Roy serenade a slumbering Gabby, then sang backup to Roy and Dale in the abbreviated finale, and they performed Tim Spencer's humorous "Jumpin' Bean." Tim again was absent from the film, so the Pioneer lineup included Bob, Lloyd, Pat, Shug, and the Farr brothers. Filmed at Kernville, California, *Roll On Texas Moon* had a cattleman vs. sheepherder theme, with Roy a troubleshooter for a cattle combine and Dale the owner of a sheep ranch. Gabby was at his best as a sheep-hating cattleman adopted by a pet lamb, while the Pioneers helped with chases and a fierce gun battle.

Tim Spencer was back and Shug

"SPORTSMAN" TO THE RESCUE!

Horses eliminate more than twenty pounds of droppings per day. And yet the streets in Western movies are conspicuously clean of horse droppings. "For some strange reason," explained Western director William Witney, "your eye will seek out these distractions on a movie screen. If they are in a pile and the sun is low, they cast a shadow and are even more noticeable."

Therefore, while Westerns were being filmed, a worker was employed to clean up the set between takes. If a horse eliminated right before the cameras were supposed to roll, the cry went up: "Sportsman!" The sportsman would come running with hoe, shovel, and wheelbarrow. The term "sportsman" was a natural for Hollywood, where horse racing was a favorite sport. Anyone who "followed the horses" was called a "sportsman." And the sportsman on a movie set quite literally followed the horses!

William Witney once asked a popular and conscientious sportsman at Republic Studios why he did not find a better job. The reply was emphatic: "And give up Show Biz?"

was out in the next movie, *Home in Oklahoma*. The Pioneer roster was the familiar prewar group: Bob, Tim, Lloyd, Pat, Hugh, and Karl. The movie was filmed on the Flying L Ranch near Dougherty, Oklahoma, so the Pioneers sang Tim's beautiful "Everlasting Hills of Oklahoma." Tim also wrote "Cowboy Ham and Eggs," which Roy and the Pioneers sang with superb harmony at a "Breakfast Club." Roy and Dale sang the other tunes, including the title song. Instead of a production number at the end of the film, Roy and Dale are seen riding down the road singing "Home in Oklahoma." The movie basically is a murder mystery. Again Witney stages a climactic gun battle, while the murderess is shot in the stomach, dying in Roy's arms. Roy Rogers movies definitely were taking a different direction.

Heldorado was filmed at Las Vegas and Hoover Dam. The plot, about black market racketeers working a money scam at the city's gambling clubs, is set against the annual "Helldorado" parade and rodeo in Las Vegas. Roy and Trigger perform at the rodeo, and at the end of the film the Pioneers ride atop a parade float playing and singing the title song. (One of the rewards of watching *Heldorado* today is seeing the Las Vegas of 1946, a far smaller and less glittery town with a decidedly Western flavor.) The Pioneers perform one quick number in a gambling club (Las Vegas still had cozy clubs instead of towering casinos). With few other musical duties, the Pioneers ride in a posse and participate in the plot in other ways. Bob Nolan noticeably enjoys his acting chores, playing scenes with confidence and humor. Cast in a small part was Doye O'Dell, who began to fill in whenever a Pioneer had to be absent.

Heldorado was the last film of 1946, and Roy continued to reign as the Number One Western Star. But late in 1946, Roy suffered a personal tragedy. Arlene, his wife of ten years, died following childbirth. The couple had adopted a daughter, Cheryl, in 1941, and in 1943 Arlene gave birth to another daughter, Linda Lou. On October 27, 1946, a son, Roy Rogers, Jr.—"Dusty"—was born. Six days later, while Arlene was still in a Los Angeles hospital, she was killed by an embolism. Roy's schedule of filming, movie promotions, personal appearances and rodeo shows was busier than ever, and Arlene's parents wanted custody of the children. He bought a home place at Lake Hughes, seventy miles north of Hollywood, installing hired help and his mother with his children.

Just two weeks after Arlene Rogers died, Dale Evans obtained a divorce. Dale's third marriage had deteriorated to the point that she had filed for a divorce late in 1945. During this same period, her son, Tom, graduated from high school and entered military service. Now thirty-four, and with her personal life in flux, Dale became dissatisfied with her predictable role opposite Roy Rogers. "I craved a starring role in a sophisticated picture," she said.

In contrast to Roy and Dale, the Sons of the Pioneers had returned to normal during 1946. The classic lineup of Bob Nolan, Tim Spencer, Lloyd Perryman, Pat Brady, and Hugh and Karl Farr finally came together again for the foreseeable future. The Pioneers had enjoyed their best year of recording, and the demand for personal appearances was greater than ever. During the 1946-47 radio season the Pioneers participated in another "Roy Rogers Show." Sponsored by Miles Laboratories (Alka-Seltzer and One-A-Day Vitamins), the show replaced "The National Barn Dance" on Saturday nights at 9:00 over NBC.

Gabby Hayes and Dale Evans also were part of the cast, prompting *Variety* to comment: "The only thing missing is Trigger."

Although their musical role was being lessened in Roy Rogers movies, the Pioneers were comfortable old pros with whatever acting duties they were assigned. Of course, the Pioneers still had at least one or two numbers per film, which enabled them to demonstrate that they remained in a class of their own. In the first film of 1947, *Apache Rose*, the Pioneers sang the title song around a campfire. "Apache Rose" was written by Glenn Spencer: "Apache Rose/Lovely melody/Of the Golden West/Song of songs to me." The tight harmony of the trio (Bob, Tim and Lloyd) was beautiful and plaintive, while the fiddle and guitar of Hugh and Karl adding striking, inventive instrumentation. This superb performance ranks with any number the Sons of the Pioneers ever put on film.

The title *Apache Rose* came from the name of the tugboat run by Dale. Murders and fistfights and horseback chases filled the film, and the Pioneers stayed busy with the action. There was a strong Mexican presence in *Apache Rose*, and in a gag number the Pioneers donned sombreros, serapes, and fake handlebar mustaches to impersonate a Mexican musical group. Although performed for laughs, "Jose" featured the splendid sounds typical of the Pioneers.

Apache Rose displayed substantial changes in the Roy Rogers format. It was his first film in Trucolor, which showed off Trigger's magnificent coloring to best advantage. Roy's clothing was further toned down, and the tall crown of his white Stetson was flattened and creased to provide a more streamlined look. Bob Nolan also traded in his big black hat for a more subdued tan headwear. Most importantly, Gabby Hayes left the series—this time for good. Now in his sixties, Gabby wanted a less demanding schedule. He refused to renew his contract with Republic, intending to select films on a less regular basis. He made only seven more movies, but in the 1950s he starred in a television series, *The Gabby Hayes Show*.

By now Roy was a Western superstar of immense popularity, but the loss of Gabby Hayes produced an irreplaceable gap in the Roy Rogers movie team. In *Apache Rose*, Republic hired Olin Howlin to play "Alkali," but he was a flop as Roy's sidekick. For the next film, *Bells of San Angelo*, 300-pound Andy Devine was installed as comedic lawman "Cookie Bullfincher." A youthful accident had damaged

ROY ROGERS RIDERS CLUB

During the 1940s, at the height of his popularity, Roy Rogers launched an organization for his young fans. Any child who sent in his or her name and address would receive a "Rogersgram" by "Trigger Express." The membership card to the Roy Rogers Riders Club listed the following goals:

1. Be neat and clean.
2. Be courteous and polite.
3. Always obey your parents.
4. Protect the weak and help them.
5. Be brave but never take chances.
6. Study hard and learn all you can.
7. Be kind to animals and care for them.
8. Eat all your food and never waste any.
9. Love God and go to Sunday school regularly.
10. Always respect our flag and our country.

his vocal cords, and Devine used his high-pitched, broken voice as his principal comedy tool.

He was no Gabby Hayes, but Cookie Bullfincher would be Roy's sidekick for the next couple of years. Pat Brady was given an increasing number of comedy bits in Roy Rogers movies. Pat, of course, had regularly handled comedy in Charles Starrett films, as well as the earlier Roy Rogers oaters, and he was the comedy specialist at live performances of the Sons of the Pioneers. Eventually, Pat would leave the Pioneers to became Roy's full-time sidekick.

William Witney packed *Bells of San Angelo* with murders and shootouts and brutal fistfights. Badly outnumbered in one fight, Roy put up a good battle, but in the end he was badly whipped. Witney often would have Roy beaten up or wounded, but the hero would trounce the bad guys in the end. The Pioneers participated in the action, while providing backup to Roy and Dale, and performing "Lazy Days," "A Cowboy's Dream of Heaven," and a catchy instrumental.

Dale's contract with Republic ran out after *Bells of San Angelo*. Determined to seek stardom in more serious movies, Dale left Republic and the Roy Rogers team. But the roles she hoped for did not materialize, and fans clamored for another pairing of the popular screen couple. Drawn together by their sad pasts and by the personal chemistry that was so obvious onscreen, Roy and Dale began to see each other socially. Their relationship matured rapidly, and the couple married on the last day of 1947. Dale signed another contract with Republic, but the studio thought—incorrectly—that audiences no longer would accept Dale opposite Roy now that they were married. Although Dale eventually would be reunited with Roy onscreen, she would not appear in any more films with the Sons of the Pioneers. Of the classic team of Roy-Dale-Gabby and the Pioneers, suddenly only Roy and the Pioneers remained.

In *Springtime in the Sierras*, Jane Frazee was cast as the leading lady. Dale had played in twenty consecutive Roy Rogers films, and Jane would work in four straight movies. Andy Devine was back as Cookie Bullfincher, while Roy Barcroft was part of a gang that slaughtered and processed out-of-season game. The head of the gang, as in *Home in Oklahoma*, was a murdering villainess. After beating Roy senseless, the gang binds Roy and leaves him in a meat locker to freeze to death. Managing to escape, Roy shoots several gang members with a Winchester, then whips Barcroft following a brutal fight.

The Sons of the Pioneers help with several tunes. With Roy singing lead on Bob Nolan's "A Cowboy Has To Sing," the Pioneers add their trademark harmony yodeling. Tim Spencer was absent from the film, so Shug Fisher—increasingly interested in a movie career—replaced him.

With Roy and Trigger, the Sons of the Pioneers made a cameo appearance in a non-Western Republic film starring Eddie Albert, *Hit Parade of 1947*. Roy and the Pioneers sang "Out California Way."

The Pioneers enjoyed three record hits of their own in 1947. During the first recording session of the year, at RCA's Hollywood studio on January 5, the Pioneers covered three sides, two of which reached the charts. RCA added only one sideman, Neal Boggs, on steel guitar. "Teardrops in My Heart," which was re-recorded on January 27, reached Number Four in July.

A Tim Spencer composition, "Cigareetes, Whusky and Wild (Wild) Women," quickly found an audience. Tim's inspiration for this number was the road life of the Pioneers, specifically a morning after a Chicago performance. Tim awoke to a room full of overflowing ashtrays and half-empty glasses, and to a group of colleagues who showed the effects of a hard night. Like everyone else in the 1940s, the Pioneers smoked "cigareetes," and they were not choirboys. Life on the road was hard—often driving through the night, trying to sleep in a cramped vehicle, snatching a few hours' rest in a hotel, away from home for weeks at a time. Traveling musicians traditionally found a little relaxation with "whusky." And the Sons of the Pioneers, famous not only through their music but through the silver screen, everywhere encountered admiring females, groupies, "Wild (Wild) Women." "Cigareetes, Whusky, and Wild (Wild) Women" was performed with feeling by the Sons of the Pioneers, and it climbed to Number Five on the charts.

One of the songs recorded at the January 27 session was "My Best To You," which eventually reached Number Twelve on the charts. The next session was in New York, with the only sideman steel guitarist, Vaughn Horton, who had written "Teardrops in My Heart." There were three sessions in October at RCA's Chicago studio. Three more sessions followed in November in Hollywood, and the last session of the year was on December 22 in Hollywood.

Altogether 1947 was the busiest recording year the Sons of the Pioneers ever experienced. With the American Federation of Musicians threatening to strike in January 1948, recording companies busily piled up records late in 1947. During the last three months of 1947, the Sons of the Pioneers cut twenty-eight sides. The resulting records, along with re-releases, would be rationed out during the anticipated strike. The strike began as scheduled, in January 1948, and lasted throughout the year, finally ending in December. The Sons of the Pioneers went sixteen months between recording sessions, but a re-release of "Tumbling Tumbleweeds" hit Number Eleven in August 1948, "Cool Water" reached Number Seven the following month, and in February 1949 "My Best To You," recorded two years earlier, made it to Number Twelve.

The last movie of 1947, *On the Old Spanish Trail*, was released on October 15. By this time Gene Autry had filmed his final feature for Republic, *Robin Hood of Texas*. Gene signed a contract with Columbia Pictures and lensed *The Last Roundup*, which was released before the end of the year. With Gene Autry now at a rival studio, Herbert J. Yates was determined that Roy Rogers—and Republic—would remain Number One in the Western genre. Yates decreed that all future Roy Rogers movies would be filmed in color, and feature budgets were increased. Director William Witney was delighted: "More money meant better pictures."

The next picture was *The Gay Ranchero*, released in January 1948. As usual with William Witney, Roy is beaten up and wounded by the bad guys, which looks even more ghastly in color. The villains intend to take over a small airline and airport just across the border in Mexico. There they plan to build a big casino and fly in suckers with a gambling urge. With even greater Mexican emphasis than ever, Sheriff Roy Rogers is helped by bullfighter Tito Guizar and his movie fiancée, fiery Estelita Rodriguez. Jane Frazee runs the airport, aided by

Andy Devine and the Sons of the Pioneers. The Pioneers help Estelita Rodriguez sing a title song, and they ride in a posse. Otherwise, they don't have a whole lot to do.

The Pioneers were busier in *Under California Stars*, with tall Doye O'Dell pinch hitting for Tim Spencer. The film opens at Republic Studios, where Roy completes a movie, then heads for his ranch and a tenth-anniversary broadcast. Roy drives up in a wood-paneled station wagon, and is welcomed to the ranch house by Andy Devine and the Sons of the Pioneers, who sing: "He's rootin' tootin' Rogers/ The King of the Cowboys/ The bravest man upon the silver screen...."

Roy's horse ranch has an army contract (certainly the only army contract for horses in 1948!) that is jeopardized by rustlers, who later kidnap and actually bullwhip Trigger. Jane Frazee is a horse trainer on the ranch working with little Trigger, Jr. The Pioneers sing "Serenade to a Coyote"; they help Roy croon "Little Saddle Pal" to a sleepy boy; they harmonize with Roy on "Dust" during the radio broadcast; and they chime in with Roy and Jane on the title song. Pat Brady's occasional comedy bits are welcome, because Andy Devine's attempts at humor are unusually lame. At the end of the movie, while Roy rescues Trigger, the Pioneers shoot it out with the bad guys.

Bullwhipping Trigger in *Under California Stars* was not enough for "Wild Bill" Witney. In the next film, *Eyes of Texas*, Roy Rogers is bullwhipped, by Roy Barcroft and gang—after the hero is dragged by a runaway horse (this animal was cut off by Trigger, thus saving Roy for the bullwhipping). Roy tries to fight the gang, and is rescued by Andy Devine. Later in the film Barcroft wounds Roy, but his clothes are set on fire by the powder flash. The grisliest touch was murder by a pack of killer dogs, loosed by Barcroft and his boss, an evil villainess who dies by the end of the movie. Western film historians often refer to William Witney as the "Sam Peckinpah of the 1940s." Witney's fights, whippings, and murders hardly compare with Peckinpah's graphic violence of the 1960s and 1970s, but the work of "Wild Bill" was pretty rough for juvenile movies of that day.

In *Eyes of Texas* the Pioneers have a substantial role running a ranch for boys whose fathers were killed in World War II. Pat Brady is the cook. At a ranch party Pat, backed by the Pioneers, performs a comic number written by Tim Spencer about a wild broncho: "He's a Killer! Killer diller! He's the graveyard filler of the West!"

Around a campfire, Pat starts the Pioneers in "Texas Trails," then Roy rides up and sings the verse. The Pioneers also back Roy in "The Padre of Old San Antone," part of which is sung in Spanish. At the climax of the movie, the Pioneers haul out their six-guns and shoot it out with the bad guys.

Eyes of Texas hit the theaters in July 1948, the same month that RKO released *Melody Time*. A Walt Disney production, *Melody Time* featured a twenty-minute segment with Roy Rogers and the Sons of the Pioneers. Aided by clever Disney animation, Roy and the Pioneers tell the story of legendary cowboy Pecos Bill. They sing a beautiful version of "Blue Shadows on the Trail," as well as the ballad of "Pecos Bill." Lensed in splendid Technicolor, with lots of humor and with Roy and the Pioneers in excellent voice, *Melody Time* is one of the most charming and entertaining features the Pioneers ever filmed.

On September 5, 1948, Republic released *Night Time in Nevada*, which would prove to be the final Roy Rogers movie involving the Pioneers. Although there had been substitutions in recent films, usually for Tim Spencer, the classic Pioneer movie roster—Bob, Tim, Lloyd, Pat, Hugh and Karl—appeared in *Night Time in Nevada*. But this movie was a mediocre entry in the Roy Rogers series. Leading lady Adele Mara generated no chemistry with Roy, while Andy Devine again was inadequate as a sidekick. The plot, about rustlers who struck cattle trains, was implausible, and there was not much music. The Pioneers helped with the title song, harmonized on "Sweet Laredo Sue," and with Roy sang a few bars of "Big Rock Candy Mountain."

By 1948 series Westerns were in the midst of a long decline. Production costs were rising rapidly, making it impossible to maintain the once-predictable profit margins. At the same time, public tastes were changing. For decades hundreds of Westerns per year had been filmed, and the old formula was becoming tired. Older, established Western stars were aging visibly, or had died or retired. In 1945, after ten years and sixty movies as a singing cowboy, Tex Ritter no longer could find film work. Even Roy Rogers, firmly established as the King of the Cowboys, would make series Westerns for only three more years.

Republic, always stressing economic efficiency, began looking for ways to cut expenses. Since music was being de-emphasized in Roy Rogers Westerns, it seemed logical to substitute a lesser musical group for the Sons of the Pioneers. When Tim Spencer wrote Herbert J. Yates regarding a contract renewal for his group in 1948, he received the following cold-blooded letter, dated May 7, from the autocratic studio head:

> Because of the foreign market conditions and the shrinkage of domestic boxoffice receipts, the Studio Executive Committee decided to discontinue the services of the Sons of the Pioneers in line with the general economy that we are compelled to pursue in order to stay in business, and which I approved with much regret.
>
> I am grateful of the fact that during the number of years you were part of our studio organization the services rendered were excellent. I think you have a fine group of musicians, and personally I liked each and every one of its members. Let me say in conclusion that it is the Studio's intention to use you from time to time, provided, of course, you will be available.

Republic hired Foy Willing and the Riders of the Purple Sage to replace Bob Nolan and the Sons of the Pioneers in the Roy Rogers series. Willing, a performer from Texas, came to California in 1940 and formed the Riders of the Purple Sage two years later. The group appeared in two Charles Starrett movies and two Monte Hale films, as well as a few other Westerns, before being added to the Roy Rogers cast. Foy Willing usually performed with three other musicians, so the Riders of the Purple Sage presented a smaller group than the Sons of the Pioneers. The Riders also were not as impressive onscreen as the Pioneers, and musically there was no comparison between the two groups.

One way to maintain the quality of Roy Rogers films was to persuade the new Mrs. Rogers to return as leading lady. Dale Evans began playing opposite

ROY ROGERS AND THE BOYS RANCH

Cal Farley's Boys Ranch was begun in 1939 by an Amarillo philanthropist on the site of Tascosa, a Texas ghost town that once was the "Cowboy Capital of the Panhandle." Roy Rogers, who regularly visited orphanages and children's hospitals, inevitably was drawn to this ranch, which offered a wholesome environment for underprivileged boys. Roy and Dale donated their appearance to the fifth annual Boys Ranch Rodeo in 1949, attracting a record crowd.

In 1953 Roy gave 200 pairs of cowboy boots embossed "BR" to the Boys Ranch. Two years later, Roy and Dale hosted the boys at their California ranch. The King of the Cowboys appeared at the twentieth anniversary of Boys Ranch in 1959, and in 1969 he returned for the thirtieth anniversary.

Roy again in 1949. At the same time, Roy began to think that Pat Brady could solve his sidekick problem.

The Sons of the Pioneers had appeared in nearly ninety films. For more than a decade they had been regulars on thousands of movie screens. The resulting recognition led to increased opportunities in radio, recording, and public appearances. But with their movie career virtually at an end, the Pioneers could anticipate that their future would be affected.

Hugh Farr with his "Flyin' Fiddle" and Karl Farr with his "Gallopin' Guitar." The gifted brothers were opposites in temperament: Hugh had a strong ego and temper, while Karl was easy-going and genial. Karl was a bit of a hypochondriac, and a careful dresser.

Top: Song of Arizona *was the first film of 1946. Ken Carson is in front, while Tim Spencer sits in the chair. Rear, L to R: Hugh Farr, Karl Farr, Bob Nolan, Shug Fisher.*

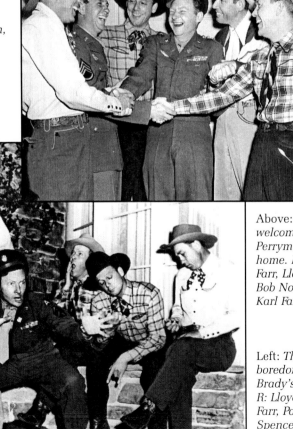

Above: *The Pioneers welcome Sergeants Perryman and Brady home. L to R: Hugh Farr, Lloyd Perryman, Bob Nolan, Pat Brady, Karl Farr, Tim Spencer.*

Left: *The Pioneers feign boredom at Sergeant Brady's war stories. L to R: Lloyd Perryman, Karl Farr, Pat Brady, Tim Spencer, Bob Nolan, Hugh Farr.*

A party at Gabby's ranch for boys in Song of Arizona. *Roy and Dale are at center, while the Pioneers stand onstage.*

Gabby has been temporarily knocked out of action by a bad guy in Song of Arizona. *Behind Roy are Shug Fisher, Ken Carson, and Bob Nolan.*

The boys wore skeleton suits at the party in Song of Arizona. Standing L to R: Hugh Farr, Tim Spencer, Bob Nolan, Roy Rogers, Ken Carson, Karl Farr, Shug Fisher. Bob usually kept an arm up when he sang.

In 1946 Republic placed the Sons of the Pioneers in Monte Hale's first starring film, Home on the Range. *L to R: Adrian Booth, Monte Hale, Shug Fisher, Bob Nolan.*

The Pioneers at a rodeo appearance. Top, L to R: Bob Nolan, Tim Spencer, Ken Carson. Front: Pat Brady, Karl Farr, Hugh Farr.

Roy, Dale, and the Pioneers perform the title song in Rainbow Over Texas. *L to R: Shug Fisher, Hugh Farr, Dale Evans, Roy Rogers, Ken Carson, Karl Farr.*

Roy Rogers faces Jack Holt in My Pal Trigger *as the Pioneers look on. The Pioneers, L to R: Bob Nolan, Karl Farr, Shug Fisher, Hugh Farr, Tim Spencer. Jack Holt was a star of silent Westerns, later a character actor who played Dick Tracy. He was the father of prominent Western players Tim Holt and Jennifer Holt.*

Roy and a chief in Under Nevada Skies. *The Pioneers, L to R: Lloyd Perryman, Bob Nolan, Karl Farr, Shug Fisher (behind Roy's hat), Hugh Farr, Pat Brady.*

The Pioneers welcome Gabby back to his "Golden Horse Ranch" in My Pal Trigger. *Bob Nolan and Lloyd Perryman ride in front, and Hugh Farr can be seen between them in the second pair.*

147

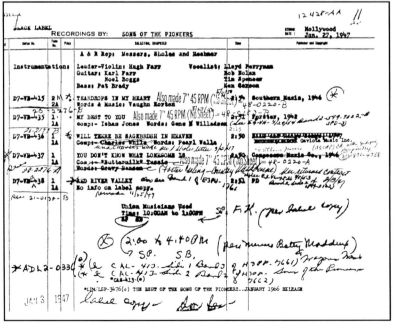

Above: Roll On Texas Moon *was the first Rogers film directed by William Witney, who took Roy's movies in a new direction. L to R: Bob Nolan, Pat Brady, Shug Fisher, Roy Rogers, Hugh Farr, Karl Farr, Lloyd Perryman.*

Right: *Recording sheet for a 1947 session.*

In My Pal Trigger Dale played Gabby's daughter, and the Pioneers were his ranch hands. L to R: Lloyd Perryman, Bob Nolan, Dale Evans, the star of the movie, unidentified actress, Gabby Hayes, Tim Spencer, Hugh Farr, Shug Fisher.

Roy sings to a señorita, backed by four Pioneers: Hugh Farr, Pat Brady, Karl Farr, Lloyd Perryman. Note the new crease in Roy's hat.

Bob Nolan, Gabby Hayes, Dale Evans, and Roy Rogers in a scene from Home in Oklahoma.

Heldorado *was filmed at Las Vegas and Hoover Dam. L to R: Lloyd Perryman, Roy Rogers, Bob Nolan, Shug Fisher, Pat Brady, Hugh Farr.*

Scene from Apache Rose. *L to R: Bob Nolan, bad guy George Meeker, Roy Rogers, Olin Howlin, Dale Evans, Karl Farr. Gabby Hayes had just left the series, and Howlin was a lame sidekick substitute. Dale was skipper of a boat named "Apache Rose."*

Roy Rogers and the Sons of the Pioneers appeared in Hit Parade of 1947, starring Eddie Albert (behind Hugh's fiddle). L to R: Karl Farr, Hugh Farr, Bob Nolan, Tim Spencer, Lloyd Perryman, and Pat Brady (partly obscured by Roy).

Apache Rose was the first film after Gabby Hayes left Republic. Four Pioneers stand beside Roy. L to R: Karl Farr, Tim Spencer, Hugh Farr, Pat Brady.

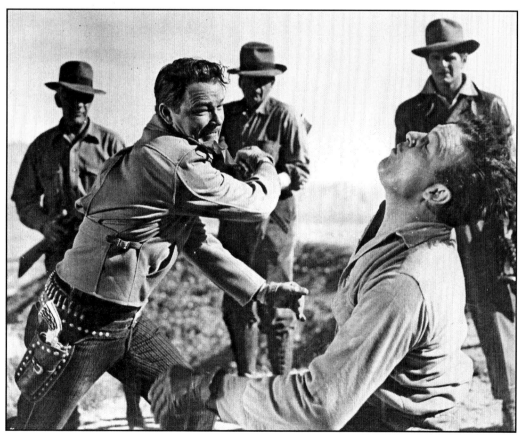

A fight scene in Bells of San Angelo. *"Roy was a great athlete and could ride, fight, dive and jump with the best of the stunt men," testified director William Witney.*

Big Andy Devine (seated at left) was installed as Roy's new sidekick, Cookie Bullfincher, in Bells of San Angelo, *but Pat Brady provided better comedy. L to R: Bob Nolan, Tim Spencer, Lloyd Perryman, Roy Rogers, Hugh Farr, Karl Farr, Pat Brady.*

Scene from Under California Stars. *Pioneers kneeling with Roy, L to R: Karl Farr, Doye O'Dell, Hugh Farr, Pat Brady. (Featured player in front of Pat.)*

Pretty Jane Frazee was Roy's leading lady in five films, including The Gay Ranchero. *The Pioneers seem interested in stealing her away from Roy. L to R: Doye O'Dell (a frequent substitute during this period), Hugh Farr, Karl Farr, Tim Spencer, Bob Nolan, Pat Brady.*

A dressing room scuffle as Bob Nolan struggles for a pocketknife. Spectators, who are offering no help, L to R: Roy Rogers, Karl Farr, Pat Brady, Lloyd Perryman, and a concerned Tim Spencer.

The Pioneers stand behind Roy, Jane Frazee, Andy Devine, and a featured player in Under California Stars. *L to R: Bob Nolan, Doye O'Dell, Hugh Farr, Karl Farr, Lloyd Perryman.*

Poised to make music in Eyes of Texas. *L to R: Pat Brady, Roy Rogers, Bob Nolan, Tim Spencer, Karl Farr, Hugh Farr, and, seated on the bottom stair, Lloyd Perryman.*

Mixing Roy Rogers and the Pioneers with cartoon characters, in 1948 Walt Disney told the story of Pecos Bill—one of the most enjoyable of nearly 100 film appearances by the Sons of the Pioneers.

Sheet music cover for one of Bob Nolan's greatest compositions.

Roy Rogers and daughter Cheryl being filmed at home, while Arlene Rogers looks on.

Roy Rogers with his first child, Cheryl Darlene. Roy frequently entertained at orphanages and children's hospitals. Roy met Cheryl at Hope Cottage in Dallas, and he and his wife adopted her.

OFFICE OF
THE PRESIDENT

May 7, 1948

Mr. Tim Spencer
13049 Oxnard Blvd.
Van Nuys, Calif.

Dear Tim:

I have your letter of May 1st.

Because of the foreign market conditions and the shrinkage
of domestic boxoffice receipts, the Studio Executive Committee decided to discontinue the services of the Sons of
the Pioneers in line with the general economy that we are
compelled to pursue in order to stay in business, and which
I approved with much regret.

I am mindful of the fact that during the number of years you
were part of our studio organization the services rendered
were excellent. I think you have a fine group of musicians,
and personally I liked each and every one of its members.
Let me say in conclusion that it is the Studio's intention to
use you from time to time, provided, of course, you will be
available.

With warmest personal regards to you all, and wishing you
continued success, I beg to remain,

Sincerely yours,

Herbert J. Yates.

HJY:few

*The Pioneers signed a standard seven-year contract with Republic in 1941. But by 1948 B-Westerns
were in decline, and that year Republic finished in the red for the first time in studio history. Among
the many cost-cutting steps was the decision "to discontinue the services of the Sons of the
Pioneers."*

Publicity photo after 1949 retirement of Bob Nolan and Tim Spencer. Clockwise from top: Ken Curtis, Lloyd Perryman, Karl Farr, Shug Fisher, Hugh Farr, Tommy Doss.

8
The Pioneers in Transition

*"We loved our work, and we worked hard to get a distinct sound.
I don't think any group worked as hard."*
—TOMMY DOSS

AT THE SAME TIME that Republic refused to renew the movie contract of the Sons of the Pioneers in 1948, the recording industry still was paralyzed by the strike of the American Federation of Musicians. Therefore it would be necessary for the Pioneers to concentrate more than ever upon personal appearances in order to maintain their career. The Pioneers would have to hit the road and stay on the road.

But Bob Nolan was already forty years old, and so was Tim Spencer. Hugh Farr was forty-five, while Karl was thirty-nine. Although Lloyd Perryman was only thirty-one and Pat Brady thirty-three, not even the younger members of the group looked forward to being on the road constantly.

After a dozen years of steady movie work, the Sons of the Pioneers were at the height of their popularity, and there was no shortage of personal appearance opportunities at rodeos, state fairs, movie theaters, and clubs. The Pioneers often performed four or five times a day, then piled into their stretch DeSoto—with three rows of seats—and drove through the night to their next destination. The relatively modest fees of the day were split evenly, six ways.

Bob Nolan, the best-known member of the group, continued to serve as front man, introducing each number, delivering humorous patter, and telling about his fellow Pioneers. Because Bob's baritone was the strongest voice in the trio, Tim Spencer and Lloyd Perryman usually stood on either side of him, in order to harmonize off his distinctive voice.

The Pioneers opened most shows with "Tumbling Tumbleweeds" and closed with "Cool Water." Each performance featured about ten or twelve interchangeable numbers, including such Bob Nolan compositions as "When Payday Rolls Around," "Home Corral," "Love Song of the Waterfall," "Saddle in the Sun," "Happy Cowboy," "Ridin' Home," and the group's famous opening and closing theme songs. Tim Spencer's regular compositions included the beautiful "Timber Trail," "Cowboy Camp Meeting," and "Graveyard Filler," the comedy number for Pat Brady. The Farr brothers put together popular instrumental tunes—"Farr Away Blues," "Texas Crapshooter," "Improvisations in A"—and the remarkable bass voice of "Foghorn" Farr was exhibited in "Dark Eyes" and briefly in other songs. The recent popularity of Walt Disney's *Melody Time* usually put "Pecos Bill" and "Blue Shadows on the Trail" in the program. Most of each program consisted of original Pioneer compositions, by Bob or Tim or the Farrs. But these tunes had been written largely when the Pioneers had to come up with half a dozen or more Western songs per movie. Now, with no more movie demands to meet, there were fewer new compositions.

By 1947 Tim Spencer had begun to experience vocal difficulties, causing him sometimes to miss a movie, recording session, or personal appearance. By early 1949, after nearly a year of virtually non-stop road appearances, Tim's vocal condition was aggravated. Tim, whose son and daughter now were teenagers, also wanted to spend more time at home. He announced his retirement as a performer early in 1949. Since the 1930s, Tim had taken a lead in handling business affairs of the group, from arranging appearances to collecting fees to dealing with studio heads. The Pioneers wanted him to continue in this capacity, and in 1949 he contracted to serve as business manager. Although Tim Spencer no longer would perform onstage with the Pioneers, for eight more years he would continue a close association with the group he had helped to found.

Bob Nolan was dismayed at the retirement of his longtime associate. "My God, once I lost Tim, for God's sake . . . ," he recalled with emotion to Doug Green and Fred Goodwin. "I mean, he was the brains behind the whole damn thing, so I just lost interest in the whole thing when he left. . . ."

Bob already was disgruntled. He calculated that during the past year he had been at home with his wife, Peanuts, for merely nine days. Bob had a deep need for solitude, but the current nomadic schedule of the Pioneers offered scant prospect of substantial time at home. As the most famous member of the group, Bob long had acted as a front man for each show, "which is one hell of a job," but he received only "my one-sixth" despite these extra efforts. "I was fronting the group and not getting any extra money for it, trying to keep them on their toes, you know, and we were doing an awful lot of traveling. . . ."

In addition, Bob was unhappy with the Farr brothers, who "thought they were too good to attend rehearsals," even though Nolan was still writing and other new material was available. The Farr brothers were brilliant improvisationalists who felt little need of rehearsing; Lynn Farr, Hugh's fifth wife, said that he "never practiced." Years earlier Ken Carson also had complained about the group's lack of rehearsal, although harmonizing often was worked out in the DeSoto during the long hours on the road. But Bob was aware that the endless rehearsals of the early years had helped develop the superior sound of the Pioneers. "They were good musicians, of course," explained Bob. "They were the very best at that time, and people loved them, but they just didn't want to go ahead—they just wanted to sit on their butts and ride along, see."

Bob believed that the problem with the Farr brothers was a principal reason for Tim Spencer's retirement, even though Tim continued to work amicably with the Pioneers for the next several years. Frustrated on many levels, Bob decided to retire only a couple of months after Tim's retirement. Bob informed the other Pioneers that he would leave the group after the current tour played Helena, Montana, in July 1949.

During this period of metamorphosis, Pat Brady also departed the group. Andy Devine had never been a satisfactory sidekick in Roy Rogers movies, and Pat was asked to assume the role. After an absence of several months from movie-making, Pat was delighted to resume his silver screen association with the King of the Cowboys. Pat appeared as the comic character "Sparrow Biffle" in *Down Dakota Way*, the second Roy Rogers film of 1949 (and the fourth without the Sons of the Pioneers). Pat was a natural comedian with great appeal to juvenile audiences, and he also could help Roy and the Riders of the Purple Sage with musical chores. Pat would follow Roy into television in 1951, although years later he would rejoin the Pioneers.

Within a few months during 1949, therefore, the Sons of the Pioneers had to replace half of their roster. For a decade and a half, the group had been remarkably stable. But now their stability and their distinctive sound were drastically threatened. Incredibly, a trio of superb replacements promptly was enlisted.

It proved easy to find a replacement for Pat Brady. As they had done a few years earlier, while Pat was serving in the military during World War II, the Pioneers turned to Shug Fisher. Shug was happy to resume the familiar role of bass fiddle player and comedian for the Sons of the Pioneers.

Shug recently had filmed two Westerns with a talented singer named Ken Curtis. Shug would help recruit the former singing cowboy as a new member of the Pioneer trio. Ken's Western roots were authentic. He was born Curtis Wain Gates on a Colorado homestead on July 2, 1916. When he was six the family moved to Las Animas, Colorado, where his father, Daniel Gates, tried to make a living as a cattleman. During the heart of the depression, Daniel Gates turned to politics, twice winning election as county sheriff. The sheriff's family lived in the county jail, where his wife cooked for the prisoners and his young son worked as a turnkey (years later Ken Curtis would serve as deputy to Matt Dillon of Dodge City, 225 miles east of Las Animas).

Like many other members of the Sons of the Pioneers, his family was musical. Daniel Gates was a fiddler, his wife played a pump organ, one of his sons picked a banjo, and everyone sang. The future Ken Curtis learned to play a saxophone, and he formed a musical trio to help with his father's political campaigns. When he tried college at Colorado Springs, he immersed himself in campus musical activities. In 1938 he ventured to Los Angeles and began working his way into show business. A year or so later, with his banjo-picking brother, Chester Gates, he tried New York.

Returning to Los Angeles, he was hired to replace Frank Sinatra during the crooner's absence from the Tommy Dorsey Band. Dorsey thought the new singer should have a more appealing name, and the twenty-five-year-old Coloradan became "Ken Curtis." Curtis made a few records with Dorsey, and when Sinatra returned to the band, Ken caught on with the Shep Fields Band. But World War II interrupted Ken's career as a band singer. He enlisted in the army in June 1942 and served until 1945.

Soon after his discharge, Ken signed a contract with Columbia Pictures to star in a series of musical Westerns. Beginning with *Rhythm Roundup* in 1945, Ken made eight films during the next couple of years, with Big Boy Williams as his sidekick. But in 1947, when Gene Autry moved from Republic to Columbia, the studio no longer needed Ken as a singing cowboy. A year later Ken starred in two more Westerns for small independent companies. In these two films, released in 1949, Ken's sidekick was his friend and fellow actor-musician, Shug Fisher.

Early in 1949 Ken and Shug were asked to join the Pioneers on a personal appearance tour. Lloyd Perryman faced pressing personal business, while Pat Brady had begun filming at Republic as Roy Rogers' new sidekick. The Pioneers welcomed the popular Shug Fisher back to their ranks on a permanent basis.

By the time Lloyd was able to return to the group, Ken had familiarized himself with Pioneer music. Impressed by Ken's obvious talent as a singer and by his winning personality, the Pioneers invited him to replace Tim Spencer. Ken always was alert to opportunities to advance his career, and he eagerly joined the famous singing group.

Ken was recruited in time to take part in the first Pioneer recording session since December 1947. The musicians' strike finally ended in December 1948, and the Pioneers gathered in RCA's Hollywood studio on April 28, 1949. An accordion and steel guitar were added as backup, while Ken Curtis joined Bob Nolan and Lloyd Perryman in the trio. The group covered the customary four songs: "Riders in the Sky," "No One Here But Me," "Lie Low Little Dogies," and Tim Spencer's "Room Full of Roses." The hit of the session was "Room Full of Roses," which quickly rose to Number Twelve.

With Ken Curtis an immediate success, Bob Nolan hoped that he, too, could be adequately replaced. He well knew, however, that the unusual vibrato of his strong baritone was a major element of the distinctive Pioneer sound. But one night, as Bob and Lloyd Perryman drove over Cahuenga Pass in Los Angeles, the car radio brought the sound of a voice almost identical to Nolan's. "There's my replacement," Bob told Lloyd.

The voice belonged to Lloyd Doss, who was

STARRING KEN CURTIS

Before he joined the Sons of the Pioneers, and before he became known to TV audiences as Festus Haggen of *Gunsmoke*, Ken Curtis was a singing cowboy star. Although Ken was not in the same league with Roy Rogers and Gene Autry, he starred in eleven Westerns:

Rhythm Roundup (Columbia, 1945)
Song of the Prairie (Columbia, 1945)
Throw a Saddle on a Star (Columbia, 1946)
That Texas Jamboree (Columbia, 1946)
Cowboy Blues (Columbia, 1946)
Singing on the Trail (Columbia, 1946)
Lone Star Moonlight (Columbia, 1946)
Over the Santa Fe Trail (Columbia, 1947)
Riders of the Pony Express (Star Craft, 1949)
Stallion Canyon (Astor, 1949)
Don Daredevil Rides Again (Serial, Republic, 1951)

performing with Ole Rasmussen and His Nebraska Cornhuskers at the 97th Street Corral in southeast Los Angeles. Soon Hugh Farr spent an evening at the Corral, afterward talking with Doss. A few days later Tim Spencer called, informing Doss that Bob Nolan intended to retire from the Pioneers and inquiring about his interest in the job. Then Lloyd Perryman phoned with a concrete offer.

"From the first time I heard the group," Doss later related, "I wanted to be one of the Sons of the Pioneers."

Lloyd Thomas Doss first heard the Sons of the Pioneers over the family Victrola at home in La Grande, Oregon. His father was a carpenter, and there were ten children. Lloyd Thomas was born in Weisser, on the western border of Idaho, on September 26, 1920, but two years later the family moved to La Grande, in the mountains of northeastern Oregon. Although raised in a scenic Western region, "I was no cowboy," he later insisted. "I used to ride plow horses bareback, but that was about it."

Lloyd Doss was interested in music from boyhood. His father played accordion while his mother played a pump organ, and his grandfather was a fiddler. Lloyd taught himself to play a harmonica and pick a guitar. "I was all home-learned," he explained. "I never had a lesson."

When he was eleven he won an amateur contest. At dances he pumped musicians for performing tips. On the Victrola he listened avidly to Jimmie Rodgers and Vernon Dalhart, and he was captivated by recordings of the Sons of the Pioneers. When he formed a trio in 1939, he called the group Sons of the Grande Rondo (a regional river). They played Pioneer tunes and performed on the local radio station. Consciously or subconsciously, Doss began singing like Bob Nolan.

When the United States entered World War II, the trio broke up and Doss found work at the Army Ordnance Depot in Hermiston, Oregon. There he met and soon married Naomi Henderson. After the war Lloyd and Naomi moved to La Grande, where he worked as a garbage man and formed a new trio. In 1948 the famous Bob Wills brought his Texas Playboys to play a tour date at Zuber Hall in La Grande. Doss persuaded the Zuber Hall manager to let the Sons of the Grande Rondo to play at intermission. While the trio was rehearsing, Bob Wills arrived and listened to the entire session. Then he astounded Doss with an invitation to join the Texas Playboys as a vocalist.

Although Lloyd and Naomi now had a little boy, they both recognized the enormity of this unexpected opportunity. "We didn't sleep that night," he recalled, since they had to feverishly pack for a sudden move to California. Doss rehearsed with the Playboys in Fresno, then left on a two-month tour. After returning to Fresno, Bob asked Doss to work with his brother's group, Luke Wills and his Rhythm Busters, who were appearing at LA's 97th Street Corral. At an RCA Victor recording session with the Rhythm Busters, a producer complained that Doss sounded just like another RCA artist. Of course, when that other artist, Bob Nolan, heard one of these recordings over a car radio, he recognized the uncanny similarity to his own voice.

Late in 1948 Luke Wills and his Rhythm Busters went on tour, replaced at the 97th Street Corral by Ole Rasmussen and his Nebraska Cornhuskers. Lloyd Doss caught on with Rasmussen and stayed at the Corral, where he was contacted by the Pioneers. Lloyd Perryman asked Doss to join the group in Helena, Montana. And since there already was a Lloyd with the Pioneers, Perryman asked Lloyd Thomas Doss to use his middle name. Tommy Doss traveled to Montana and became a Pioneer on July 15, 1949.

The revamped Pioneer roster was set by the summer of 1949: Lloyd Perryman, Ken Curtis, Tommy Doss, Shug Fisher, and Hugh and Karl Farr. The trio was magnificent: Perryman remained a smooth and gifted harmonizer determined to maintain the traditional Pioneer sound; Curtis had a clear, strikingly beautiful voice; Doss provided the essential, distinctive baritone, so close to Nolan's that it would be difficult to tell them apart on recordings. The Farr brothers still added the brilliant, inventive fiddle and guitar improvisations that provided the wild heartbeat of Pioneer music. Like Pat Brady, Shug Fisher could play the bass fiddle, and his comedy was just as energetic as Pat's.

Despite Bob Nolan's complaints, and perhaps because of the fifty percent roster turnover, Lloyd Perryman insisted upon extensive rehearsals. "We loved our work, and we worked hard to get a distinctive sound," explained Tommy Doss. "I don't think any group worked as hard."

This hard work bred a strong camaraderie between the older members and the new recruits. Lloyd Perryman took the lead in building cohesiveness in the group, and he assumed Bob Nolan's roles as performance frontman or master of ceremonies. Ken Curtis, Tommy Doss, and Shug Fisher all were friendly men with pleasant personalities. Although Karl Farr was nervous and something of a hypochondriac, he too was friendly and likable. Hugh Farr always had displayed the ego and temperament of an artist. But despite his sometimes bumpy personality, he loved to have a good time and was fiercely loyal to the Pioneers.

Part of the group's compatibility was due to harmonious relationships among the wives. "We looked after one another's kids," said Naomi Doss, "just like an extended family." Another son was born to the Doss family after their move to California. Karl Farr had a son, Karl Farr, Jr., and after he divorced and remarried, another son was born. "We had a lot of fun back then," emphasized Naomi. "We had a lot of parties—barbeques and singing."

Naomi learned that her husband "had to have thirty white shirts ready to go at any time" for personal appearance tours that might last two or three months. During the last couple of weeks of a long tour, wives sometimes would join their husbands. If there were kids along, the group might stop for a little fishing. The Pioneers were earning as much as $5,000 per week, which helped smooth over the difficulties of life on the road. "Once, I came back from a road trip and found that Naomi had sold the house and moved," reminisced Tommy Doss. "I didn't know where I lived."

A recording session in Hollywood on December 14, 1949, was the first to feature the new Pioneer group. This session was the first since February and only the second of 1949. But in 1950 RCA Victor produced seven recording sessions, from February through December. The constant touring brought the group into personal contact with their fans, and Sons of the Pioneers fan clubs sprang up across the country. In addition, the Pioneers returned to the movies in 1950.

Ken Curtis was dating Barbara Ford, daughter of acclaimed director John Ford. Ken and Barbara fell in love, and would marry in 1952. Barbara was working as assistant editor on *Wagonmaster*, John Ford's first movie of 1950. The legendary director always used music powerfully in his films. For *Wagonmaster* Ford featured four songs by Stan Jones: "Wagons West," "Rollin' Shadows in the Dust," "Song of the Wagonmaster," and "Chuck-a-Walla-Swing." Ford decided that the Sons of the Pioneers would bring the perfect sound to these songs, and the group was engaged to record the soundtrack. When the Pioneers reported to the soundstage, they were somewhat awed to encounter a full symphony orchestra. At the end of the session the orchestra rose and awarded the Pioneers a standing ovation. In March RCA produced sessions for the Pioneers to record these same songs, but merely arranged for an organ accompaniment. When *Wagonmaster* was released on April 22, 1950, the Pioneers went on a two-week promotional tour for the film.

Like most John Ford Westerns, *Wagonmaster* was filmed in scenic Monument Valley, Utah. Ben Johnson, Harry Carey, Jr., Ward Bond, and Joanne Dru, close friend of Barbara Ford, were the featured players. Although beautifully photographed, *Wagonmaster* was not one of John Ford's major efforts. But already the great director was at work on a more important film, and he intended to use the Sons of the Pioneers onscreen.

Among the most popular of John Ford's cinematic achievements was his "cavalry trilogy." These three movies were romantic, patriotic celebrations of the U.S. Cavalry, based on the character-rich short stories of James Warner Bellah. All three features starred John Wayne and were filmed in Monument Valley. *Fort Apache*, released in 1948, also starred Henry Fonda as a Custer-like commanding officer. Other featured players were Ward Bond, Victor McLaglen, nineteen-year-old Shirley Temple, and her handsome husband, John Agar. *Fort Apache* was a rousing success, and in 1949 Ford released *She Wore a Yellow Ribbon*. Described as "a symphony for the ears and a canvas for the eyes," *She Wore a Yellow Ribbon* featured Victor McLaglen, John Agar, Joanne Dru, Ben Johnson, and Harry Carey, Jr. With John Wayne in superb form, *She Wore a Yellow Ribbon* was an even bigger hit than *Fort Apache*.

John Ford planned a third cavalry film, *Rio Grande*, for 1950. Stirring martial music was a significant element in the captivating atmosphere of the first two cavalry movies, and Ford envisioned the Sons of the Pioneers as an instrument to enrich the musical content of *Rio Grande*. Attired in cavalry uniforms, the Pioneers would play "the regimental singers." (Regiments maintained brass bands for musical occasions, so it was reasonable to devise a group of regimental singers.)

Rio Grande was the most important movie the Sons of the Pioneers had ever helped to film. They spent a month during the summer of 1950 in Monument Valley with Ford, John Wayne, Maureen O'Hara, Victor McLaglen, Ben Johnson, Harry Carey, Jr., and other members of the director's "stock company." In mid-July the cast and crew left Monument Valley to finish the film at Republic Studios, where the Sons of the Pioneers completed their soundtrack work. They were paid $9,000, in four weekly installments of $2,250.

Rio Grande was released in November 1950 to strong reviews. "*Rio Grande* is filmed outdoor action at its best," summed up *Variety*. John Wayne was Hollywood's top money-making star of 1950, and he turned in a virile, heroic performance as Col. Kirby Yorke, struggling to deal with war parties, which crossed the Rio Grande to raid in Texas, then fled back into Mexico. One of many subplots has Yorke trying to win back the love of his wife, Kathleen, played by beautiful Maureen O'Hara.

Early in the film, while Colonel Yorke and Kathleen are dining, the regimental singers gather to serenade the couple with the romantic Irish ballad "I'll Take You Home Again, Kathleen." The Sons of the Pioneers march on-camera looking handsome and dashing in their cavalry uniforms. Off-duty later in the evening, the regimental singers are heard throughout the post singing "Cattle Call" and "Aha, San Antone," a lively tune written by Dale Evans.

Later in the film, with a cavalry column on the march, Colonel Yorke orders, "Singers, give us a tune." With Ken Curtis in the lead, the Pioneers sing "Erie Canal." As the march continues, Yorke again directs, "Singers, sing out!" The Pioneers respond with the cavalry ballad "Yellow Stripes," featuring the rumbling bass of Hugh Farr. Back at the fort, when Colonel and Mrs. Yorke entertain Gen. Phil Sheridan at dinner, the regimental singers are summoned. Ken Curtis again leads another plaintive Irish ballad, "Down By the Glen Side," then the group marches off singing "Footsore Cavalry."

John Wayne, Ben Johnson, and Victor McLaglen were familiar to Western fans of 1950, but so were the Sons of the Pioneers, and like the other veteran actors of *Rio Grande*, the Pioneers brought authority to their roles. Indeed, the Pioneers were given prominent billing in the cast credits. Shug Fisher was awarded extra screen time as a bugler, while Ken Curtis was assigned a couple of lines of dialogue. It was obvious that Ken and Barbara Ford were in love, and John Ford gave the good-looking singer a little extra footage. Scene after scene was enriched by atmospheric music from the Sons of the Pioneers. Of course, *Rio Grande* was a rewarding movie-going experience on many levels. It is an all-time favorite, for example, of Western film expert Brian Garfield: "I can think of very few Westerns that are much better than *Rio Grande*." And the Sons of the Pioneers made a significant contribution to this fine motion picture.

The Pioneers made another film in 1950. Band leader Spade Cooley, self-styled "King of Western Swing on the West Coast," made several films, including *Everybody's Dancin'* in 1950. The Pioneers had backed recordings Cooley made of "Wagon Wheels" and "The Last Round-up," and in *Everybody's Dancin'* the Pioneers sang "Room Full of Roses" and "Cowboy Camp Meetin'."

The Pioneers also had a film appearance in 1951. *Fighting Coast Guard* starred Forrest Tucker, Brian Donlevy, and Ella Raines, and was directed for Republic by Joseph Kane. The Sons of the Pioneers, of course, had been directed by Kane in their first eighteen Roy Rogers movies, from 1941 through 1944. The Pioneers were signed to play a single scene early in *Fighting Coast Guard*, which was a World War II action film. The Pioneers were entertaining at a beachside night spot frequented by trainees from a nearby coast guard base, and they sang "Home on the Range" and "I Love the Prairie Country."

One scene in a minor war movie was not much of a follow-up to *Rio Grande*. Furthermore, in 1951 RCA Victor tried to alter the Pioneer image. Hoping to expand the fan base of the group, RCA publicists announced that the Pioneers had "graduated" to pop music and now performed "Western Pop." But the Pioneers only recorded twelve sides in 1951, a mixture of pop, religious, and Western numbers.

Although these developments were not encouraging, the Sons of the Pioneers scored a major triumph in 1951. They were invited to perform at Carnegie Hall. The Pioneers had worked the Madison Square Garden Rodeo and were no strangers to performing in New York City. But an invitation to Carnegie Hall was special—the ultimate prestige performance.

Thursday, June 7, 1951, was a special evening at Carnegie Hall. Instead of a classical program, there was a Western theme. The master of ceremonies was attired in Western dress, and in the first half of the program, vocal soloists and the Carnegie pop orchestra performed the "Western Suite," selections from *Oklahoma!*, and similar numbers.

Following the intermission, the famous stage was taken over by the Sons of the Pioneers. They sang "Tumbling Tumbleweeds," of course, and other Pioneer classics from "Timber Trail" to "Way Out There," from "Room Full of Roses" to

ROY AND PAT ON TV

In 1951 two former Pioneers launched a successful show on television, the new entertainment medium that was exploding with growth across the nation. When Roy Rogers finished filming *Pals of the Golden West* in 1951, his second seven-year-contract with Republic ended. The star saw the potential of television, but movie studios were battling this new venue, and Herbert J. Yates refused to permit any TV rights in Roy's new contract. Roy would not renew under these conditions, and the King of the Cowboys left the movies for television.

General Foods promptly agreed to sponsor *The Roy Rogers Show*, even though there was not even a pilot episode. A half-hour weekly series was developed. Roy and Trigger—and Roy's German Shepherd, Bullet—lived at the Double R Bar Ranch, while Dale Evans owned the Eureka Cafe in nearby Mineral City. Roy asked Pat Brady to sign on as comic sidekick. Roy then provided a cranky Jeep christened "Nellybelle" which turned out to be *Pat's* sidekick. Curiously, there was no music in the show except over the final credits, when Roy and Dale sang "Happy Trails." Dale composed the number, which became their permanent theme song.

The Roy Rogers Show debuted on December 30, 1951. The program was a huge success among young viewers. Republic continued to re-release Roy's old movies, and he remained the Number One Cowboy Star through 1954, when the list was discontinued. (Roy had been Number One since 1943.) One hundred episodes of *The Roy Rogers Show* were filmed. After the program ended in 1956, Pat Brady would return to the Sons of the Pioneers.

"The Everlasting Hills of Oklahoma." Hugh and Karl were featured on "Farr Way Blues." From *Rio Grande*, the Pioneers performed "I'll Take You Home Again, Kathleen" and "Down By the Glen-Side." From *Wagonmaster* there was "Wagons West," and from *Melody Time*, "Pecos Bill." On the light side they presented "Cigareetes, Whuskey and Wild, Wild Women," and Shug clowned his way through "I Taut I Taw a Puddy Tat." It was a delightful evening at Carnegie Hall, an all-time Pioneer highlight.

In and out of New York during 1951, the Pioneers had the opportunity to make guest appearances on network television, including *The Steve Allen Show* and Perry Como's variety hour. The popular crooner was so impressed during rehearsals that he asked the Pioneers to accompany him on two songs he was about to record, "You Don't Know What Lonesome Is" and "Tumbling Tumbleweeds." Como and the Pioneers both recorded for RCA, so there were no contract difficulties. A short time after appearing on Perry Como's show, Perry and the Pioneers met at RCA's New York studio and completed a busy evening with a recording session.

Through the years the Pioneers provided backup for numerous artists. In 1951 they backed Ezio Pinza, and the previous year they recorded with Spade Cooley. They backed Roy Rogers, of course, along with Gene Autry and Patsy Montana. The Pioneers also recorded with Vaughn Monroe, Johnny Western, Stan Jones, Mason Williams, Rex Allen, Jr., and a group called The Three Suns. In addition to recording more than 470 sides for commercial release under their own name, the Sons of the Pioneers cut another forty-plus sides for a variety of other artists.

A welcome accomplishment of the early 1950s was "The Lucky U Ranch," a network radio show starring the Sons of the Pioneers. In 1950-51 the Pioneers had worked with Rex Allen on a similar show (Allen was the last singing cowboy—introduced by Republic in 1950, he starred in nineteen features before production halted on this type of film in 1954). The Sons of the Pioneers were offered their own show in 1952. "The Lucky U Ranch" originated in the Hollywood studios of KHJ Radio-TV, and was beamed throughout the United States over the 560 stations affiliated with the Mutual Broadcasting System. Armed Forces Radio Service also broadcast the thirty-minute program Monday through Friday to military bases and naval vessels across the world (U.S. forces had been embattled in Korea since 1950). In addition, the program was telecast locally over KHJ.

Sponsored by Planter's Peanut Company, "Lucky U Ranch" was a thirty-minute program which aired Monday through Friday. The Pioneers were aided by accordionist Frankie Messina and Betty Taylor, "the pulchritudinous blonde bombshell of the Lucky U Ranch." Betty played the teacher of "District Number 3" in recurring schoolmarm skits. Ken Curtis developed a hillbilly character, "Dink Swink." (During Pioneer performances, Ken often affected a country hick accent, which he would revive in *The Searchers* and as Festus in *Gunsmoke*.) Bob Nolan and Tim Spencer sometimes appeared on the show to perform with the new Pioneers.

The Sons of the Pioneers had faced major reorganization in 1948, but the revamped group produced an excellent sound, strong in the qualities of traditional Pioneer music. Although the Pioneers no longer were regulars on the silver screen, sporadic film appearances included an important part in a major motion picture. After years of appearing on the radio shows of other stars, the Pioneers had their own network program. And the group achieved the distinction of performing in Carnegie Hall. But only four years into a highly successful transition, the Sons of the Pioneers once again were about to find themselves assailed by the forces of change.

The Pioneers at a standing-room-only performance.

Loading instrument cases aboard their three-seat DeSoto. The Pioneers often practiced their harmonies while driving. When their contract with Republic was not renewed in 1948, the Pioneers had to work the road with almost no breaks.

L to R: Hugh Farr, trio members Tim Spencer, Bob Nolan and Ken Carson, Pat Brady, Karl Farr. The trio liked to sing with Bob in the middle in order to build their tight harmony around his strong baritone.

The Pioneers in a 1948 broadcast over NBC. L to R: Hugh Farr, Pat Brady, Karl Farr, Tim Spencer, Bob Nolan, Lloyd Perryman.

Top, L to R: Shug Fisher, Hugh Farr, Lloyd Perryman. Bottom: Ken Curtis and Tommy Doss.

The Pioneers performing at a rodeo in Mandan, North Dakota. L to R: Hugh Farr, Ken Curtis, Tommy Doss, Lloyd Perryman, Karl Farr, and Shug Fisher.

AGREEMENT

WHEREAS Pioneer Radio Productions (a California corporation) is desirous of appointing Tim Spencer as its General Manager, to handle all of its business affairs, the parties hereto agree as follows:

1. Tim Spencer is appointed General Manager and Secretary of said corporation with the power of handling all of its business affairs, including but not limited to the handling of sales promotion and obtaining distribution and distributorships in connection with the business of the corporation.

2. It is agreed that the incorporators and/or stockholders, when stock has been authorized, and distributed for such corporation, will elect a Treasurer of said corporation, properly bonded, to act in conjunction with Tim Spencer in the collection of all monies due or payable to the corporation, and the payment or distribution of such monies, with the right and power to co-sign all checks in conjunction with Tim Spencer.

3. Tim Spencer agrees to perform all of the duties set forth in paragraphs 1. and 2. in a conscientious and efficient manner.

4. Tim Spencer shall receive no compensation for his services under this contract except as may be specifically authorized at some future times by the corporation.

5. The duration of this contract will be for a period of seven years commencing October 15, 1949. Either Tim Spencer or Pioneer Radio Productions shall have the right to cancel this agreement upon giving ninety days written notice to the other party of the intention so to cancel.

Dated this ____7____ day of _____, 1949.

Tim Spencer

PIONEER RADIO PRODUCTIONS: By
Incorporators of above corporation:

Hugh Farr

Lloyd Perryman

Ken Carson

Ivan Ditmars

Ed Gray

Karl Farr

Pat Brady

Harry Wayne MacMahon

Bob Nolan

Contract officially designating Tim Spencer as the group's "General Manager and Secretary."

During an appearance in Nampa, Idaho, the Pioneers pose aboard the last stage from Murphy, south of Nampa, to Silver City, one of the best ghost towns in the West. L to R: Ken Curtis, Tommy Doss, Lloyd Perryman, Hugh Farr, Karl Farr, Shug Fisher.

Somewhere on the road. By 1949 the Sons of the Pioneers spent most of their time on the road.

In 1949 the Sons of the Pioneers offered a revamped roster that was a blending of the old and new. Standing, L to R: Lloyd Perryman, Ken Curtis, Tommy Doss. Seated, L to R: Hugh Farr, Shug Fisher, Karl Farr.

Playing inside a tent. L to R: Hugh Farr, Ken Curtis, Tommy Doss, Lloyd Perryman, Karl Farr, Shug Fisher.

At the Colorado State Fair. L to R: Hugh Farr, Ken Curtis, Lloyd Perryman, Tommy Doss, Karl Farr. Clowning at right is Shug Fisher.

BOB NOLAN *and the*
SONS OF THE PIONEERS
PROGRAMS

PROGRAM No. ONE

TUMBLING TUMBLEWEEDS
  Theme Song, Composer Bob Nolan
WHEN PAYDAY ROLLS AROUND
  Trio, Composer Bob Nolan
RIDIN' HOME   Sextette, Composer Bob Nolan
TEXAS CRAPSHOOTER
  Farr Brothers—Hugh and Karl, Composers Farr Brothers
LOVE SONG OF THE WATERFALL
  Trio, Composer Bob Nolan
PECOS BILL
  From Walt Disney's "Melody Time", RCA Victor album,
  "Pecos Bill"
MY BEST TO YOU
  Featuring Bob Nolan, RCA Victor recording
TOO HIGH, TOO WIDE, TOO LOW
  Quartet, RCA Victor album "Cowboy Hymns and Spirituals"
IMPROVISIONS IN "A"
  Karl Farr, featuring guitar, Composer Karl Farr
WIND   Trio, Composer Bob Nolan
TEARDROPS IN MY HEART
  Lloyd Perryman, RCA Victor recording
SADDLE THE SUN   Trio, Composer Bob Nolan
MODES OF MADNESS   Pat Brady
COOL WATER
  Sextette, Composer Bob Nolan, RCA Victor album "Cow-
  boy Classics"

PROGRAM No. TWO

HOME CORRAL   Sextette, Composer Bob Nolan
LAST ROUNDUP   Trio, RCA Victor recording
TIMBER TRAIL
  Sextette, Composer Tim Spencer, RCA Victor album "Cow-
  boy Classics"
LONESOME ROAD   Hugh "Foghorn" Farr
BLUE SHADOWS ON THE TRAIL
  Trio, from Walt Disney's "Melody Time", RCA Victor re-
  cording
YOU AIN'T HEARD NOTHIN'
  Pat Brady and sextette, Composer Bob Nolan
CHICO CHICOROTICO   Trio, Composer Bob Nolan
DARK EYES   Karl Farr
COWBOY CAMP MEETIN'
  Sextette, Composer Tim Spencer, RCA Victor album "Cow-
  boy Classics"
WHIFFENPOOF SONG   Quartet, RCA Victor recording
COWBOY'S PRAYER   Ensemble, Arranger Bob Nolan

PROGRAM No. THREE

HAPPY COWBOY   Trio, Composer Bob Nolan
LOVE SONG OF THE WATERFALL
  Trio, Composer Bob Nolan
TEXAS CRAPSHOOTER
  Farr Brothers, Farr Brothers original
BABY DOLL
  Lloyd Perryman and trio, Composer Bob Newman
SOUTH IN MY SOUL   Karl Farr, Composer Karl Farr
GRAVEYARD FILLER   Pat Brady, Composer Tim Spencer

PROGRAM No. FOUR

TUMBLING TUMBLEWEEDS
  Theme Song, Composer Bob Nolan
HOME CORRAL
  Sextette, Composer Bob Nolan
BLUE SHADOWS ON THE TRAIL
  From Walt Disney's "Melody Time"
FARR-AWAY BLUES
  Hugh and Karl Farr, Composers Farr Brothers
MY BEST TO YOU
  Bob Nolan, RCA Victor recording
PECOS BILL
  From Walt Disney's "Melody Time", RCA Victor "Pecos
  Bill" album
TIMBER TRAIL
  Sextette, Composer Tim Spencer
CROWN OF THE CACTUS COUNTRY
  Pat Brady
CHICO CHICOROTICO
  Composer Bob Nolan
COOL WATER
  Sextette, Composer Bob Nolan, RCA Victor album "Cow-
  boy Classics"

PROGRAM No. FIVE

TUMBLING TUMBLEWEEDS
  Theme Song, Composer Bob Nolan, RCA Victor album
  "Cowboy Classics"
HOME CORRAL
  Sextette, Composer Bob Nolan
LAST ROUNDUP
  Featuring Lloyd Perryman, RCA Victor recording
FARR-AWAY BLUES
  Featuring the Farr Brothers, Composers Farr Brothers
MY BEST TO YOU
  Featuring Bob Nolan, RCA Victor recording
PECOS BILL
  Quartet, from Walt Disney's "Melody Time", RCA Victor
  album "Pecos Bill"
BLUE SHADOWS ON THE TRAIL
  Trio, from Walt Disney's "Melody Time", RCA Victor
  album "Pecos Bill"
COWBOY CAMP MEETIN'
  Sextette, Composer Tim Spencer, RCA Victor "Cowboy
  Classics" album
TEARDROPS IN MY HEART
  Featuring Lloyd Perryman, RCA Victor recording
TIMBER TRAIL
  Sextette, Composer Tim Spencer, RCA Victor album "Cow-
  boy Classics"
YOU AIN'T HEARD NOTHIN'
  Pat Brady
COOL WATER
  Sextette, RCA Victor album "Cowboy Classics"

(All programs subject to change)

The five programs performed by the Sons of the Pioneers in 1949 at the Realito Theater in Glen Fall, New York. These various shows were performed everywhere by the Pioneers during this period.

The Sons of the Pioneers were given billing in the ad campaign for John Ford's Rio Grande.

After Pat Brady became part of The Roy Rogers Show on television in 1951, his most famous prop was a Jeep dubbed "Nellybelle."

In 1951 RCA Victor tried to promote the Sons of the Pioneers as a "Western-pop" group, and photographed them as having graduated to pop music. The "graduates" are, L to R: Shug Fisher, Ken Curtis, Hugh Farr, Tommy Doss, Tim Spencer, Lloyd Perryman.

Left: *In 1950 the Pioneers became part of Rex Allen's CBS radio show. Back, L to R: Hugh Farr, Tommy Doss, Lloyd Perryman. Front: Shug Fisher, Ken Curtis, Rex Allen, Karl Farr.*

Below: *In 1950 the Pioneers appeared in the Spade Cooley movie,* Everybody's Dancin'.

The Pioneers in the early 1950s. L to R: Shug Fisher, Tommy Doss, Ken Curtis, Hugh Farr, Karl Farr, Lloyd Perryman. The trio of Doss, Curtis, and Perryman was superb.

Ad for the Pioneers' "Lucky U Ranch" radio program.

The Pioneers in 1953. Clockwise from top: Karl Farr, Deuce Spriggens, Tommy Doss, Lloyd Perryman, Dale Warren, Hugh Farr.

9
Empty Saddles
(1953-63)

"We traveled all over the West together."
—Hugh Farr

EARLY IN 1953 the Sons of the Pioneers became concerned about being tied down by their network radio show. Five days a week the Pioneers had to report to KHJ in Hollywood and perform before a live audience. With only weekends for personal appearance travel, the Pioneers began to realize that they were losing considerable money from extended tour fees. Although it was convenient and pleasant to be able to spend so much time at home, early in 1953 the Pioneers voted to leave "Lucky U Ranch" and go back on the road.

The decision was not unanimous. Ken Curtis and Shug Fisher chose to stay and continue the show. Ken had married Barbara Ford in 1952 and understandably wanted to stay close to home. Furthermore, Ken had journeyed to Ireland to play a small part in John Ford's 1952 classic, *The Quiet Man*, starring John Wayne and Maureen O'Hara. Curtis could expect other movie roles, and Shug Fisher also wanted to be in a position to find film work.

So, Lloyd, Tommy, and the Farr brothers would have to find a trio vocalist and a bass fiddle player. The Pioneers again turned to Deuce Spriggens, who gladly rejoined the group as Shug's replacement. Lloyd received a strong recommendation for twenty-seven-year-old Dale Warren, who had been performing since boyhood. Dale was asked to audition at Lloyd Perryman's house. With Lloyd and Tommy he sang the yodeling song "Way Out There," then he performed "Blue Shadows on the Trail" and "Tumbling Tumbleweeds." Lloyd, Tommy, and the Farr brothers went into the front yard to discuss Dale's performance, then returned to the house and invited him to join the Pioneers.

Nearly half a century later, Dale Warren still leads the Sons of the Pioneers. He has performed with the group longer than any other member, and he has known and worked with every man who has ever been a regular with the Pioneers. Dale Henry Warren was born in Rockford, Illinois, on June 1, 1925. His father and mother, Henry and Wava Warren, were popular professional musicians. "Uncle Henry's Kentucky Mountaineers" featured Henry as comedian, Wava on the piano, and Henry's brother, Grady, on guitar. Although the group had a radio program in Rockford, Uncle Henry's Kentucky Mountaineers appropriately moved its base to Kentucky in the mid-1930s. With a radio show in Louisville, the expanded group became the "Original Kentucky Mountaineers."

In this environment Dale made his musical debut at an early age. Another move took the group to Chicago in 1941. During their six-year stint on the "Summer Time Frolics" over WJJD, Dale served a three-year hitch in the air force. (In 1943 a member of Uncle Henry's group, Ken Carson, left to join the Sons of the Pioneers as a replacement for Lloyd Perryman.) After Henry retired, Dale and Wava led a group on a long tour. In Cincinnati, Dale met fiddler Margie DeVere, who would become his wife. In 1949 Dale and Margie sought opportunity in California. A superb singer, Dale found considerable work, including nearly a year with Foy Willing's Riders of the Purple Sage.

By the time Dale joined the Sons of the Pioneers, the Pioneers and RCA Victor had become dissatisfied with each other. Only eight sides were recorded in 1952, and the Pioneers parted company with RCA. There were no recording sessions in 1953, but the Pioneers finally signed a one-year deal with the Coral label. Coral produced four recording sessions during 1954, in January, April, November, and December. The sessions were held at Coral's studios in Los Angeles. Only two sides were cut at each session, and two of these eight sides were not issued.

When RCA Victor offered a new contract, the Pioneers returned to their old label. The first session was in Hollywood on February 20,

THIS IS YOUR LIFE

In 1953 Ralph Edwards made Roy Rogers the subject of his popular weekly television show, *This Is Your Life*. As customary, Roy was surprised by the host. Edwards began to introduce Roy's family, along with special friends from the past—and, of course, Trigger. There were several touching moments, and at one point Roy shed a few tears. But the highlight of the show was the appearance by the Sons of the Pioneers.

Roy was visibly moved when the group he had helped to form walked onstage. Bob Nolan did not come, but the other old Pioneers took part in the show: Tim Spencer, Pat Brady, Lloyd Perryman, and Hugh and Karl Farr. It was a time for reminiscing.

"We traveled all over the West together," remembered Hugh.

"And it's amazing how far it was between meals," added Karl.

"We were either hungry or we were starving," exclaimed Pat, "so we'd just sing to give our mouths something to do!"

Then the Pioneers began singing "Tumbling Tumbleweeds." Roy joined in, and Hugh inserted brilliant fiddle play. A national television audience was treated to a memorable Pioneer moment.

1955, and included "The Graveyard Filler of the West" and "The Ballad of Davy Crockett," from the popular Disney television series. While the current Pioneers—Lloyd, Tommy, Dale, Hugh, Karl, and Deuce—had recorded for Coral, RCA insisted that the old Pioneers cover the recording sessions. From 1949 through 1952 the trio of Lloyd Perryman, Ken Curtis, and Tommy Doss had made excellent recordings for RCA. But from 1955 through 1957 the RCA recordings would be covered by Bob Nolan, Tim Spencer, Lloyd Perryman, Pat Brady, and Hugh and Karl Farr. This situation somewhat nettled Dale Warren and Tommy Doss, but RCA exerted their contract control, and Dale and Tommy would have to wait another three years to record with the Pioneers.

During this period long-playing albums were introduced, and the Sons of the Pioneers soon plunged into that format. Since the early 1950s nearly four dozen albums have been released featuring the Pioneers. The first Pioneer album, *A Garden of Roses*, was released in 1952. There were three 78 RPM records, encased in the old-fashioned album style, with six tunes related to the theme: "Roses," "Mexicali Rose," "Moonlight and Roses," "Bring Your Roses To Her Now," and Tim Spencer's "Room Full of Roses." Later in the year RCA issued *Cowboy Classics* on a ten-inch 33 RPM LP. The ten-inch records usually carried four tunes on each side, and the eight songs were true Pioneer classics: "Cool Water," "Chant of the Wanderer," "Tumbling Tumbleweeds," "Everlasting Hills of Oklahoma," "Cowboy Camp Meetin'," "Blue Prairie," "Trees," and "Timber Trail." These "classics" had been recorded in 1945 and 1946, and many future albums would be made up of earlier recordings. Also in 1952 another ten-inch LP, *Cowboy Hymns and Spirituals*, featured "The Old Rugged Cross," "Power in the Blood," "The Touch of God's Hand," and five other religious tunes. In 1953 *Western Classics* offered another eight tunes, including "Red River Valley," "Riders in the Sky," and "The Last Roundup." There were no albums in 1954, when the Pioneers recorded for Coral. After the group returned to the RCA label in 1955, the twelve-inch 33 RPM record was in general use. This larger record usually accommodated six songs per side, so that LPs now could offer at least twelve songs.

In 1955 RCA produced seven recording sessions with the Sons of the Pioneers, but nine of the twenty-eight sides went unissued. RCA still hoped to move the Pioneers in the direction of popular music, producing such tunes as "Tennessee Rock and Roll," "Mighty Rock," and "Little Space Man." Rock 'n roll now was America's most popular music, and interest in Western music sagged noticeably. RCA scheduled just one recording session with the Pioneers in 1956. But this was a special session, produced to record theme music from one of the greatest Westerns ever filmed.

The Pioneers had done no film work for five years when John Ford again beckoned, in somewhat backhanded fashion. Ford was developing one of the masterpieces which studded his legendary career. *The Searchers* was based on a gripping novel by Alan LeMay, rich with the grim flavor of the Texas frontier and with powerful characters. Filmed in Ford's beloved Monument Valley, *The Searchers* starred John Wayne and featured actors such as Ward Bond and Ken Curtis, who played a Texas Ranger with the rustic accent he had developed while with the Pioneers. The violent, tragic storyline was relieved by three comic characters, including Ken Curtis' countrified Texas Ranger, Charlie McCorry.

During one scene Charlie courts Laurie Jorgensen, played by Vera Miles. Strumming a guitar, Charlie sings "Gone again, skip to my Lou..." in the beautiful tenor voice that had been enjoyed for years by fans of the Sons of the Pioneers. Group singing included a title ballad and "Shall We Gather at the River," a hymn John Ford liked to use in his Westerns, often at a church service or a funeral. In *The Searchers* the moving hymn is sung both at a funeral and at the wedding of Charlie and Laurie. Upon hearing this hymn, the knowledgeable viewer searches the wedding party expecting to see one or two of the Pioneers in costume.

After location filming ended in August 1955, further work would be completed at Warner Brothers studios in Hollywood. John Ford told Ken Curtis to "get some guys together" to record the soundtrack. Tommy Doss, Lloyd Perryman, and Shug Fisher were summoned. (Shug rejoined the Pioneers at this point, replacing Deuce Spriggens.) With only three members of the group on the job, the Sons of the Pioneers would not be billed on the cast credits. So Ken Curtis, Tommy Doss, Lloyd Perryman, Shug Fisher—and, of course, a full or-

KEN CURTIS

After leaving the Sons of the Pioneers in 1953, Ken Curtis pursued his movie career, aided by the invaluable connection with his father-in-law, John Ford. Following *The Searchers*, Ken landed roles in such major films as *The Horse Soldiers*, *The Wings of Eagles*, *The Alamo*, *Two Rode Together*, and *Cheyenne Autumn*. But Barbara Ford Curtis, like her father, had a serious drinking problem, and her alcoholism eventually led to divorce.

Ken also found work in TV Westerns. In 1962 he played a scruffy, gunfighting hillbilly named Festus Haggen on an episode of *Gunsmoke*. Two years later Dennis Weaver left the show, after nine seasons as Marshal Matt Dillon's sidekick, Chester Goode. Festus Haggen soon was brought back to fill in the void, quickly becoming a regular, alongside Matt, Kitty, and Doc. Ken created a memorable character, staying with *Gunsmoke* until the epic series left the air in 1975.

Ken and character actor Milburn Stone, who played Doc on *Gunsmoke* for twenty years, were a popular duo at rodeos and fairs. Ken also teamed frequently with his old Pioneer pal, Shug Fisher. They were together in several John Ford movies and *Gunsmoke* episodes, as well as in Ken's series, *Ripcord*. When Shug died, at the age of seventy-six in 1984, Ken was at his bedside.

In 1983 Ken starred in another short-lived series, *The Yellow Rose*. He remarried, but never had any children. Following a career that brought him great recognition and popularity—as big band singer, singing cowboy, Pioneer, Festus—Ken Curtis died in Fresno, California, at the age of seventy-four on April 28, 1991.

chestra—recorded the soundtrack. The following March 28, just prior to the film's release in May 1956, the Sons of the Pioneers—Bob Nolan, Lloyd Perryman, Ken Curtis, Pat Brady, and Hugh and Karl Farr—recorded the title ballad for RCA.

The Searchers was a major commercial and critical success. Most film historians rank *The Searchers* among the ten best Westerns of all time, and many rank it as their number-one choice. *New York Times* film critic Roger Greenspan declared *The Searchers* the greatest American film of all time. Brian Garfield stated that "it unquestionably is one of the few Westerns that deserve to be regarded as important works of art." And the Sons of the Pioneers had played their part—albeit unbilled—in creating this epic motion picture.

The next year the Pioneers provided background music for a Disney film, *Andy Burnette*, based on a popular book, *Andy Burnette's Diary*. The Disney Studios were making family movies for their popular television program. The Pioneers, of course, had been prominent in the delightful "Pecos Bill" segment in Disney's 1948 *Melody Time*. In 1959 the Pioneers again collaborated with Disney in the *Saga of Windwagon Smith*. The following year the Pioneers worked on *The Swamp Fox*, starring a youthful Leslie Nielsen as Revolutionary War hero Frances Marion. There were two Disney films in 1961, *Sancho the Homing Steer* and *Legend of Lobo*. After *Johnny Shiloh* in 1962, the Pioneers performed in no further films. But counting early cartoons and shorts, the Sons of the Pioneers had amassed ninety-nine movie credits by the early 1960s.

In addition to *The Searchers*, another highlight of 1956 for the Pioneers was a featured appearance on *The Grand Ole Opry*. For this special show the famous Ryman Auditorium was decorated with a Western set. The show was broadcast over WSM TV and radio. Carl Smith was the host, and such Opry regulars as Jim Reeves, Minnie Pearl, Faron Young, Hank Snow, and Cowboy Copas were present. Tex Ritter was another guest star. The Sons of the Pioneers opened the show with "Happy Rovin' Cowboy" and two other numbers. Opry fans saw Lloyd Perryman, Tommy Doss, Dale Warren, Shug Fisher, and Hugh and Karl Farr. Later in the show the Pioneers brought the house down with their classics, "Tumbling Tumbleweeds" and "Cool Water."

During the late 1950s, weekly Western series became immensely popular on network television. Some series, such as *Gunsmoke*, had originated on radio, while many other shows were generated by the broad interest in the Old West that had been fostered by decades of Western movies. Adult viewers welcomed familiar Western adventures into their living rooms, and for a few years children also enjoyed televised frontier sagas.

A large number of TV theme songs were recorded on RCA Children's Bluebird Records. These were 45 RPM records, and the Sons of the Pioneers were selected to record several of the theme songs. In 1957 the group recorded the ballad from *Cheyenne* (starring big Clint Walker), *The Restless Gun* (John Payne), and *Wagon Train* (Ward Bond). The Pioneers had worked on the 1950 John Ford movie *Wagonmaster*, which starred Ward Bond and was the genesis of the TV series.

In 1958 RCA finally permitted Tommy Doss and Dale Warren to record with the Pioneers. Tommy's voice was almost indistinguishable from Bob Nolan's anyway, and the trio of Perryman, Doss, and Warren produced excellent recordings. This trio recorded the theme music from *Maverick* (starring James Garner) and *Sugarfoot* (starring Will Hutchins) in 1959.

Hugh Farr was not part of these recordings. His last recording session with the Pioneers was on October 7, 1958, in New York. Fittingly, one of the two songs was "My Last Goodbye." An invaluable member of the Sons of the Pioneers, in 1959 Hugh was part of a sad split in the group.

Of course, it was remarkable that the Sons of the Pioneers had not experienced a serious fissure during the group's first quarter of a century. More often than not, musical groups, bristling with artistic temperaments and working in tight proximity, experience disagreements and separations. Even the Beatles, despite their phenomenal success, were able to perform together for less than a decade. Incredibly, the Sons of the Pioneers had suffered no serious internal conflicts during an extremely busy quarter century of successful performance. Pat Brady and Lloyd Perryman temporarily left the group because of military service; Roy Rogers and Pat Brady and Ken Curtis departed to seek success as movie actors; Bob Nolan and Tim Spencer retired. No one left the Pioneers primarily because of hard feelings—until 1959.

Tensions had been building among the Pioneers up to that year. For three years Tommy Doss and Dale Warren had been excluded from recording sessions by RCA. Although they had become part of the recording group in 1958, a certain level of resentment had developed. Most significantly, the group's income had declined steadily during the late 1950s.

The rising popularity of rock 'n roll in general and Elvis Presley in particular cut deeply into the demand for Western music. "When Elvis Presley came in," stated Tommy Doss, "that's when we got hurt. We found ourselves at night clubs singing his songs."

Because of this trend, the Sons of the Pioneers developed a keen appreciation for Marty Robbins, whose enormously successful gunfighter ballad, "El Paso," restored a measure of interest in Western music. Released in the summer of 1959, "El Paso" spent six months on the country charts, including seven weeks at Number One, while also hitting the top of the pop charts. The Sons of the Pioneers recorded their version of "El Paso" for RCA in April 1961.

With the decline in quality bookings, the name "Sons of the Pioneers" seemed to have lost some of its drawing power. Lloyd Perryman joked that "they should go out and work as the 'Six Little Fat Boys.'"

But recent tensions made it harder than in the past for the Pioneers to shrug off the irascible behavior of Hugh Farr. Hugh regarded himself as the last charter member of the Sons of the Pioneers. Hugh contended that the original four members—Roy Rogers, Bob Nolan, Tim Spencer, and himself—had agreed among themselves that the final charter member still working with the group would own the name "Sons of the Pioneers." When it was suggested that Karl Farr also was a charter member, Hugh bluntly insisted that his brother had "simply been an employee of this group since he joined."

According to Lynn Farr, Hugh's wife, Karl was sent to tell his brother that that other Pioneers no longer wanted to work with him. Hugh felt betrayed by Karl, and the brothers became alienated. After appearing on tour in Florida in

February 1959, Hugh left the group. He and his wife then engaged a patent lawyer in Washington, D.C., to copyright the name "Sons of the Pioneers." The copyright application was dated March 2, 1959. Hugh formed five young musicians into a group and, calling themselves the "Sons of the Pioneers," filled an engagement in a Reno hotel. When the older Pioneer group came to the area, Karl appeared at his brother's hotel. "Bud," said Karl, "I'd like to be with you."

Hugh was unyielding. "It's a little late, isn't it, Karl?" The Farr brothers did not shake hands, and never spoke again.

Karl, Lloyd Perryman, Tommy Doss, Dale Warren, and Shug Fisher filed a lawsuit against Hugh over the group's name. The case was heard in the Superior Court of the State of California in Los Angeles on December 15, 1959. On the witness stand, Hugh recounted the origins of the group, and the informal agreement that the last of the charter members would own the name "Sons of the Pioneers." He stated his contention that Karl was not a charter member, and related in detail the grueling rehearsals of the early years. "None of these boys was in on the tough part of it," Hugh said pointedly, "they just come in on the gravy."

Lynn Farr and Lloyd Perryman each testified briefly. Evidence was presented that the Sons of the Pioneers had incorporated in 1957 for business purposes, which created a partnership at that point. Judge Emil Gumpert further reasoned that, through the years, "as the fame or renown of the group increased, the earnings of the group increased, so it would appear that the name gathered value by reason of the efforts of the various partners as they came in and contributed to the success of the group."

Judge Gumpert called a recess and conducted a conference in his chambers, hoping to work out a compromise. He regarded the situation "of a brother pitted against brother" as a "tragedy." Pointing out that "the so-called Ink Spots have four different corporations operating under the name,... it would make the Court personally very happy if some equitable and satisfactory adjustment along those lines could be reached by the parties, but I am not in a position to either urge it or compel it." Proposing that both might each call themselves the Sons of the Pioneers, the judge said, "I was hopeful that that suggestion might be accepted by Mr. Hugh Farr. But the suggestion was rejected by him."

With no other sensible legal recourse, Judge Gumpert ruled that the name would be auctioned to the highest bidder. Because of existing contracts, he decreed that both parties would use the name through April 10, 1960, after which no one could use it until the auction took place. Because there were five Pioneers against one, Hugh was outbid. The overturning of Hugh's federal copyright by a Superior Court was open to legal question, but Hugh chose not to issue a challenge.

Hugh formed a short-lived group, The Country Gentlemen, and later he worked with a few other groups. Then Hugh and Lynn, who played drums and sang, put together an act and worked together for a decade.

The unpleasantness of the trial apparently caused Shug Fisher to leave the group. By the end of 1959 Shug had "retired," even though he soon resumed work as a character actor. Shug was replaced by another popular Pioneer, Pat Brady, free for full-time duty with the group since *The Roy Rogers Show* had stopped airing in 1957. With the departure of Hugh Farr, the other Pioneers elected to work without a fiddle, a decision which markedly altered the group's traditional sound. Accordionist George Bamby began working with the Pioneers in 1959, but he disliked the rigorous travel demands and left the group in May 1960. Soon it was decided to put a fiddle back into the Pioneer sound. A well-known fiddler, forty-seven-year-old Wade Ray, was enlisted as the latest Pioneer. Ray added fiddle backup for a year before departing in 1961.

In 1961 the Sons of the Pioneers suffered a tragic loss. On a personal appearance tour the group played the Eastern States Exposition in West Springfield, Massachusetts. An audience of 4,000 gathered on Wednesday evening, September 20, at the Exposition Coliseum. Karl Farr was soloing on "Up a Lazy River" when a guitar string broke. He seemed unduly upset and left the stage, apparently to repair the broken string. Suddenly, he collapsed and his face turned blue. The show went on while security personnel rushed the stricken musician to the Exposition medical center. The physician on duty injected adrenaline into Karl's heart, but he could not be revived. He had died almost immediately of a massive heart attack. The first member of the Sons of the Pioneers to pass away, Karl Farr was only fifty-two. Amiable and well-liked by other Pioneers, Karl had used his remarkable talents with the group for twenty-six years—half of his lifetime.

Hugh Farr was working in Albuquerque with Jimmy Wakely's band when he was told about his brother's death. He returned to California for the funeral. May Farr, Karl's widow, had him interred at Valhalla in North Hollywood. Hugh Farr encountered the surviving Pioneers at the services, but there was no reconciliation.

Above: *Shug Fisher and Ken Curtis clowning around. Ambitious for careers in film, Ken and Shug declined to go on the road with the Pioneers in 1953.*

Left: *The Pioneers with another American icon, Smokey the Bear. Top, L to R: Deuce Spriggens, Hugh Farr, Dale Warren, Lloyd Perryman. Kneeling: Karl Farr and Tommy Doss.*

The Farr brothers are happy to be surrounded by pretty girls at a Muscular Dystrophy benefit. The book on display is a new volume by Dale Evans Rogers, My Spiritual Diary.

Left: *The Pioneers in the early 1950s. Clockwise from top: Lloyd Perryman, Tommy Doss, Karl Farr, Shug Fisher, Hugh Farr, Dale Warren.*

Below: *Hugh and Lynn Farr in 1966. After leaving the Pioneers, Hugh formed a duo act with his wife. (Courtesy Lynn Farr)*

Above Left: *The Pioneers promoting the Air Force Reserve while performing in Texas in 1956. L to R: Lloyd Perryman, Hugh Farr, Karl Farr, Tommy Doss, Dale Warren, Shug Fisher.*

Middle: *The Pioneers in the late 1950s. Clockwise from top: Pat Brady, Karl Farr, Lloyd Perryman, Tommy Doss, Dale Warren.*

Left: *Ken Curtis earned his greatest fame as Festus Haggen on the long-running television series* Gunsmoke. *Top row, L to R: Milburn Stone (Doc), James Arness (Matt Dillon), Amanda Blake (Miss Kitty), Curtis. Seated: Buck Taylor (Newly) and Glenn Strange (Sam the Bartender).*

The Pioneers of 1974. L to R: Rusty Richards, who had just rejoined the group, Lloyd Perryman, Dale Warren. Front: Roy Lanham.

10
Tumblin' Along the Tumbleweed Trail

*"There never has been, before or since,
a group that could make music
like the Sons of the Pioneers."*
—JOEL MCCREA

FOLLOWING THE DEATH of Karl Farr, Pat Brady and Lloyd Perryman became the only direct links with the early years of the Sons of the Pioneers. Pat had joined the group in 1937, and Lloyd came aboard the next year. Both men had missed a couple of years during World War II, and Pat was absent for several more years while working with Roy Rogers. With over twenty years as a Pioneer, Lloyd led the group in length of service. For more than a decade Lloyd had functioned as leader of the group, and onstage he was the front man. A natural mediator, Lloyd got along well with each of the other members and was a major factor in holding the group together. Lloyd Perryman deserved his unofficial title, "Mr. Pioneer."

It was impossible to replace the uniquely talented Karl Farr in the group he had helped to make famous. But the Pioneers enlisted Karl's friend and admirer, Roy Lanham, a veteran performer with individual gifts of his own. Born in 1923 in Corbin, Kentucky, as a boy he sang enthusiastically in church. When a brother gave him a guitar, Roy learned to play with the ease of a born musician. While he was a high school student in 1939, Roy enlisted with a group of musicians and comedians, Grandpappy and His Gang. Archie Campbell was Grandpappy, and soon Roy was working with Archie on radio station WNDX in Knoxville, Tennessee. In 1940 Roy formed his own group, The Fidgety Four, soon renamed The Whippoorwills. Featuring the jazzy sound of Roy's guitar, The Whippoorwills sang country and pop music with close harmony. The group moved to Los Angeles in 1950 and worked on Smiley Burnette's radio show, then toured with Roy Rogers. The Whippoorwills finally disbanded, but Roy worked steadily as an L.A. studio musician, backing numerous artists on recordings and turning out his own album, *The Most Exciting Guitar*, in 1961. That same year Roy was invited to join the Sons of the Pioneers. Married and the father of a son and two daughters, Roy was a good-humored man who loved his family and his work. He would perform with the Pioneers for more than two decades, until ill health forced his retirement.

For the next couple of years the Pioneers performed with Lloyd Perryman, Tommy Doss, Dale Warren, Pat Brady, and Roy Lanham. But in 1963 Tommy Doss decided to give up touring. "The fast life isn't a life for a family man," he later reflected. "I saw too many entertainers lose their families."

Tommy and his wife, Naomi, began reminiscing about their younger years in rural northeastern Oregon. "We began looking for what had been home for us," he explained. In 1963 the combination store-tavern-post office that was the center of tiny Imnaha was offered for sale. Although Tommy knew nothing about running such a business, he bought it: "I figured I could do anything I set my mind to." Tommy, Naomi, and their younger son moved to Imnaha, Oregon.

Tommy continued to record with the Pioneers through 1967, and occasionally agreed to make a special appearance with the group when a "gravel baritone" was needed. But he settled in happily at Imnaha and declined all over-

WITH ROY AND DALE AGAIN

During the 1950s and 1960s, hour-long musical variety shows were popular on network television. On September 29, 1962, ABC introduced a variety hour with a Western flavor, *The Roy Rogers and Dale Evans Show*, airing on Saturday nights at 7:30. Pat Brady was a regular, and the Sons of the Pioneers were featured in episodes in October and December. The theme of the October hour was "This Is Our Country." The Pioneers sang "Sierra Nevada," which they recently had re-recorded. Later in the show, following an instrumental number, Roy joined the group with his guitar and sang the lead in "Put On Your Old Gray Bonnet." The theme of the later show was "All-Time Western Hit Parade," with movie-TV star Dale Robertson as special guest. The Sons of the Pioneers were part of the opening production number, singing "The Yellow Rose of Texas." The Pioneers performed "Wagon Wheels" with Dale, and later the group offered a fine version of "Cool Water," with Tommy Doss singing lead and Lloyd Perryman plaintively echoing "Water ... water."

But the network pulled the plug on *The Roy Rogers and Dale Evans Show*. At this stage of their careers Roy and Dale were polished, talented entertainers. Dale was especially energetic, attempting to make the show a success through the force of her own gifts and personality. The episodes were wholesome, stressing family, rural, patriotic, and religious values. But by 1962 this mixture of themes proved a bit corny for network prime time, and *The Roy Rogers and Dale Evans Show* left the air on December 29.

tures to rejoin the Pioneers on a regular basis. So in 1963 the Sons of the Pioneers had to replace another key member.

Lloyd Perryman and Dale Warren decided to take the lead and baritone parts, respectively, so that the Pioneers could seek a tenor "who could sing way up in the treetops" like Ken Carson. A great many performers were auditioned before Pat Brady was told about a talented singer-yodeler named Vincent "Rusty" Richards. Born in 1933 in Long Beach, California, Rusty was raised in a musical household. His parents and three siblings sang and played various instruments. Rusty learned to play the guitar, and when he was sixteen he landed his own fifteen-minute show on KLAC-TV, *Song Trail*. Within a year, however, Rusty began a hitch in the Marines. Returning to civilian life, he worked as a stuntman on TV Westerns. Rusty made the acquaintance of Ken Curtis and Burt Reynolds, and he married Amy Fitzpatrick.

After talking by telephone with Pat Brady about a position with the Sons of the Pioneers, Rusty called former Pioneer Ken Curtis to ask his assistance. Curtis contacted Lloyd Perryman, who quickly called Rusty to arrange an audition. After one song, "Tumbling Tumbleweeds," the Pioneers decided to enlist Rusty. In addition to his fine tenor voice, Rusty also provided the Pioneers with their best yodeler since Roy Rogers.

The Pioneers now performed with a trio of Lloyd Perryman, Dale Warren and Rusty Richards, along with guitarist Roy Lanham and bass fiddler-comedian Pat Brady. But RCA still brought in Tommy Doss for recording sessions, so the recording trio during the mid-1960s was Tommy, Lloyd, and Dale. Therefore Rusty Richards did not record with the group, and neither did Pat Brady. RCA provided numerous backup instrumentalists during this period, although Roy Lanham and his guitar always were present in the recording studio.

After three years, in the fall of 1966, Rusty Richards left the Pioneers to tour with Ken Curtis and The Frontiersmen. Rusty began writings songs, but soon decided to settle with his family on a horse ranch near Orange, California. Rusty became a full-time horse trainer, writing articles for *Horse and Horseman* and training the personal mounts for celebrity sweethearts Burt Reynolds and Dinah Shore. In time, however, Rusty Richards would return to the Pioneers for a stint that would last a full decade.

The Pioneers replaced Rusty in October 1966 with a singing fiddler, Billy Armstrong. Born in 1930 in Streator, Illinois, Billy moved with his family in 1935 to Long Beach, California. His mother arranged violin lessons for Billy, who began playing professionally in 1943, with Bob Lively's Dude Ranch Cowboys. Working as a teenager in Country and Western music, Billy adopted the "gouger" style of fiddling. (In C & W terms, a "gouger" would dig in and gouge his fiddle; by contrast, Hugh Farr and Bob Wills were "smooth" fiddlers.) Billy worked with a number of groups, becoming known for his fine tenor voice. The Pioneers invited him to join their group in 1963, but his commitments included a television appearance. In 1965 the Academy of Country Music named Billy the first recipient of their Fiddler of the Year Award, which he was given for thirteen consecutive years. In 1966 the Pioneers repeated their invitation to this superb musician, and Billy Armstrong joined Lloyd Perryman, Dale Warren, Roy Lanham, and Pat Brady in performance at Reno's Holiday Hotel.

Billy tried to adjust his fiddling style toward the Hugh Farr sound. He also found the Pioneer harmony more exacting than anything he had previously experienced. Late in 1966 Billy joined the Pioneers on an extended tour of military bases in the Far East, which lasted until early in 1967. Gen. William Westmoreland authorized presentation of a Meritorious Service Award to the Sons of the Pioneers for "service to their fellow man and allies, above and beyond the call of duty."

Later in 1967 Pat Brady departed the Pioneers. Pat had joined the Pioneers thirty years earlier, leaving for military service and for movie and television work with Roy Rogers. He had once more rejoined the group in 1959. But by the time Pat reached his early fifties, he was suffering from a drinking problem. After separating from the Pioneers in 1967, he divorced his wife, Fayetta, and moved from his Northridge, California, home to Colorado Springs. In Colorado he managed the Pine Cone Ranch, a "fabulous family entertainment center." Pat acquired another Jeep and christened it Nellybelle (the original Nellybelle belonged to Roy Rogers, who eventually displayed it in his museum). Pat performed his old comedy routines for guests at Pine Cone Ranch, and he happily hauled children around in his Jeep.

But his friend John Mette noted that "he was uncomfortable with the lower amp spotlight and wished and wondered why more often the calls did not come that would beckon him to the show stage or the rodeo arena." Pat put together a musical group and played small clubs in and around Colorado Springs. He remarried, taking a young bride named Carol, and they had a son, Pat, Jr. Tragically, the baby was afflicted with Down's syndrome. Personal heartbreak and professional frustrations exacerbated Pat's struggle with alcohol. "The temptation

ALBUMS OF THE 1960s

During the 1960s twenty albums—more than in any other decade—were released featuring the Sons of the Pioneers, including four in 1963 and four more the next year. Seven of the albums were made up of earlier recordings, while RCA produced thirteen LPs by the current Pioneers:

Lure of the West (1961)
Tumbleweed Trail (1962)
Good Old Country Music (1963)
Our Men Out West (1963)
Sons of the Pioneers Sing Hymns of the Cowboys (1963)
Trail Dust (1963)
Country Fare (1964)
Down Memory Trail (1964)
Legends of the West (1965)
The Songs of Bob Nolan (1966)
Campfire Favorites (1967)
South of the Border (1968)
The Sons of the Pioneers Visit the South Seas (1969)

The earliest recordings compiled for a 1960s album were offered in 1964 by Columbia, which re-released ten songs from 1937 for *The Sons of the Pioneers' Best.*

was immense," commented John Mette in his tribute to Pat (... *and i was sensitively touched*), "and he both fought it and gave in to it with great regularity."

Now Lloyd Perryman was the only remaining connection with the movie years that had brought such fame to the Pioneers. Lloyd conscientiously worked to preserve the Pioneer sound, frequently correcting Billy Armstrong on points of harmony. Billy also could not become comfortable with the different style of fiddle play. And soon there were other new members. A bass fiddler-vocalist named Bob Mensor was hired in September 1968, but he departed within six months. Mensor was replaced in the spring of 1969 by thirty-four-year-old Luther Nallie, a fine instrumentalist and tenor from the oil-boom area of Beaumont, Texas. Married and the father of two children, Nallie moved to California to further his career as an entertainer. When he began working with the Pioneers, Nallie was impressed—as other newcomers had been—with the precise phrasing and the breath and volume control demanded of the trio singers. At this point the Sons of the Pioneers were represented by Lloyd Perryman, Dale Warren, Luther Nallie, Billy Armstrong, and Roy Lanham.

But try as he might, Lloyd could not maintain the group's traditional, unique sound with all of the original Pioneers gone. The need had ceased for Bob Nolan and Tim Spencer or one of the other Pioneers to create several new songs for each of six or eight new Western films per year. At this point there was no fresh material unique to the Pioneers, and in 1969 the long Pioneer recording association with RCA was ended. Since 1945 the Pioneers had covered nearly 350 songs and released 27 albums with RCA.

The Pioneers now performed the group's old standards or the hits of other artists. But the newer aggregation sang and played and harmonized well, artfully carrying on the Pioneer tradition in song if not in exact sound. The Sons of the Pioneers were now legends, and "Mr. Pioneer," Lloyd Perryman, was the principal keeper of the flame.

As befitted a legendary musical group, the Sons of the Pioneers began to receive a series of proper honors and awards. In 1967 the Academy of Country Music designated the Sons of the Pioneers as recipients of their first Vocal Group of the Year Award. In 1971 the Academy granted Bob Nolan the Pioneer Award, and in 1977 this same award was given to the entire group. In 1971 both Bob Nolan and Tim Spencer were elected to the Nashville Songwriter Hall of Fame. Also in 1971, on Saturday evening, April 24, the Sons of the Pioneers were feted by the National Cowboy Hall of Fame in Oklahoma City. Western movie stars Joel McCrea and Walter Brennan presented the coveted Wrangler Award for "thirty-eight years as the West's first great singing group." Lloyd Perryman accepted the award, along with Pioneer standouts Ken Curtis, Pat Brady, and Hugh Farr. When the Pioneers started to sing "Tumbling Tumbleweeds," the crowd rose and began to applaud. There were few dry eyes when the Pioneer classic ended.

Joel McCrea spoke for the crowd with his response: "There never has been, before or since, a group that could make music like the Sons of the Pioneers."

This moving occasion proved to be a last hurrah for Pat Brady. Pat returned to Colorado Springs, fighting a losing battle with alcoholism. "Alcohol had been his crutch for a long while," observed John Mette, "both shattering his world and temporarily repairing it." Pat did radio commercials and promotions for a Colorado Springs music store, and he worked at a local Ford dealership. But his health was noticeably affected by his drinking, and on February 26, 1972, Pat checked into The Ark, a rehab center for alcoholics in Green Mountain Falls. Sadly, it was too late—the next day fifty-seven-year-old Pat Brady died of a heart attack.

Hugh Farr came down from Wyoming for the funeral (Pat had not been working with the Pioneers when Hugh had his bitter split with other members of the group). Hugh joined Lloyd Perryman, Dale Warren, and Luther Nallie in performing "Tumbling Tumbleweeds" and "At the Rainbow's End" for their old friend. Roy and Dale could not attend but sent flowers. Pat was buried with full military honors at Evergreen Cemetery.

Pat would have immensely enjoyed the Pioneer reunion that took place less than two months after his death. Friday, April 21, 1972, was declared "Sons of the Pioneers Day" in Los Angeles, and that night, at the Ambassador Hotel, there was a large gathering of past and present Pioneers, relatives, friends, fans, and noted entertainers. At this point the current Pioneers were Lloyd Perryman, Dale Warren, Luther Nallie, Roy Lanham, and Billy Armstrong. Roy Rogers and Dale Evans came and clearly enjoyed socializing with their old comrades. Bob Nolan made a rare public appearance, and a frail Tim Spencer, who had suffered a stroke in 1970, also put forth the effort to come. Hugh Farr, nearing his seventieth year, was present, and Tommy Doss came down from his Oregon village. Ken Carson attended, along with Rusty Richards and Bill Nichols and Shug Fisher. Wesley Tuttle, who had filled in for Tim Spencer in 1937, was warmly welcomed. Following an evening of awards, tributes, speeches and entertainment, all of the Pioneers took the stage and sang "Tumbling Tumbleweeds."

Shortly after this historic Pioneer event, fiddler Billy Armstrong departed the group to pursue other career opportunities. For two years the basic Pioneer lineup was Lloyd Perryman, Dale Warren, Luther Nallie, and Roy Lanham. But in April 1974, lead vocalist Luther Nallie felt compelled to leave the group for family reasons. Although eventually Luther would return, at this point the Pioneers had to regroup. Lloyd Perryman contacted Ken Carson about returning to the group, but Ken had developed a lucrative performing career in Florida and he did not want to resume life on the road. Rusty Richards agreed to return to the Pioneers, bringing back his excellent tenor voice, yodeling talents, and high energy to the group's performances. The Pioneers then enlisted accordionist and musical-arranger-director Billy Liebert.

Liebert had directed numerous recording sessions for Tex Ritter, along with Tennessee Ernie Ford, Kay Starr, Johnny Horton, Ferlin Husky, Merle Travis, and other C&W stars. Liebert was active in radio and television, working as music director for numerous CBS programs originating in Hollywood. A World War II navy veteran, in 1954 he conducted the U. S. Navy Band at the White House and enjoyed the honor of meeting President Eisenhower. Liebert and Dale Warren were married to sisters, Bettie and Margie DeVere, and Billy had worked with his brother-in-law on recordings with Foy Willing and the Riders of the Purple Sage. In 1959 Billy helped the Sons of the Pioneers with arrangements for the album *Cool Water*, then worked with the group on other projects. Lloyd

Perryman asked Billy to perform in 1974 with the Sons of the Pioneers during a two-week engagement at the Nugget Hotel and Casino in Sparks, Nevada. Although there was little time for rehearsal with the Pioneers, Billy provided strong instrumental accompaniment, as well as lively humor. At the end of the Nugget engagement, Billy accepted an invitation to become a member of the Sons of the Pioneers. Dale Warren proudly announced, "Billy's the only one who reads music!"

Now forty years old, the Sons of the Pioneers fielded a trio of Lloyd Perryman, Dale Warren and Rusty Richards, backed by guitarist Roy Lanham and accordionist Billy Liebert. The group which for so long had been a model of stability now dealt with frequent change. With the absence of a fiddle and the addition of an accordion, the Pioneer sound underwent a major alteration.

But the Pioneers' name still was magic, and so were the group's signature songs, "Tumbling Tumbleweeds" and "Cool Water." When the Pioneers performed "Tumbling Tumbleweeds," Billy Liebert observed, "the opening note seemed to charge the air." The Pioneers found themselves performing more than 220 days each year, at clubs and concerts as well as their usual rodeos and fairs.

Pioneer charter member Tim Spencer had been in declining health for several years. After leaving the Pioneers, Tim had focused his efforts on Manna Music, his gospel publishing company. (A major coup was the acquisition of publishing rights to "How Great Thou Art," and in 1955, backed by a large orchestra, the Pioneers recorded a splendid version of the magnificent hymn.) In his early sixties Tim suffered a stroke, and his son Hal took over management of Manna Music. On April 26, 1974, Tim passed away at the age of sixty-five. Along with Len Slye and Bob Nolan, Tim had founded the group that became famous as the Sons of the Pioneers. Under pressure to produce Western music for movies in which the Pioneers appeared, Tim followed the example of Bob Nolan and wrote songs by the score. Sometimes collaborating with his brother Glenn, or with Bob Nolan or Roy Rogers, Tim composed, published, and recorded more than two hundred songs. He wrote "The Everlasting Hills of Oklahoma," "Ride, Ranger, Ride," and "The King of the Cowboys." In 1949 his

ALBUMS OF THE 1970s

Only four albums featuring the Sons of the Pioneers were released during the 1970s. In 1973 RCA produced *Riders in the Sky*, a collection of eighteen recordings from the 1940s, 1950s, and early 1970s.

Fred Goodwin, who was working in radio, was asked by RCA to write the liner notes for *Riders in the Sky*. Fred and Tom Perryman, a future member of the Country Music DJ Hall of Fame, brought the Pioneers to Nashville for a memorable week of performances in February 1973.

In 1976 the current Pioneers recorded eleven songs for *Western Country*, including "Tumbling Tumbleweeds," "Cool Water," "Room Full of Roses," and "When Payday Rolls Around." Also in 1976, Victor Music Industries released *Songs of the Pioneers*, featuring fourteen Victor recordings from 1934, 1935, and 1936. The next year RCA offered *A Country-Western Songbook*, with twelve Pioneer songs recorded from 1960 through 1966.

beautiful "Room Full of Roses" reached the Top Ten, and "Cigareetes, Whuskey & Wild Women" hit the Top Five in 1947 and became a delightful part of the Pioneer stage performance. Pat Brady created a popular comedy routine based upon Tim's "Graveyard Filler of the West." Even after vocal problems forced Tim's retirement as a singer, he continued to help with the group's business affairs for several more years. When the Pioneers staged their memorable reunion in 1972, Tim courageously attended despite his debilitated condition. The event would not have been right without him.

Two years after Tim's death, the Pioneers enjoyed another notable honor. On Friday, September 24, 1976, a star labeled "SONS OF THE PIONEERS" was placed on the world's most famous sidewalk, Hollywood's Walk of Fame at 6841 Hollywood Boulevard. The Hollywood Chamber of Commerce hosted a noontime ceremony before a large crowd. Actress Jane Withers offered a welcome, then television personality Monty Hall took over as master of ceremonies. The reclusive Bob Nolan attended, and so did Roy Rogers, Ken Curtis, and Shug Fisher. Velma Spencer represented her late husband. The 1976 Pioneers included Lloyd Perryman, Dale Warren, Rusty Richards, Billy Liebert, and Roy Lanham. That evening KLAC Radio hosted a "Salute to the Sons of the Pioneers" at the Hollywood Palladium. Rex Allen hosted the show, and Gene Autry paid tribute to the Pioneers. Among the entertainers were Jimmy Wakely, Marty Robbins, Eddie Dean, Johnny Bond, Stuart Hamblen, Ray Whitley, Leon McAuliffe, and Rex Allen, Jr. The sellout crowd was treated by the unexpected appearance of Gen. James Doolittle, the aviation hero who commanded the famous bombing raid over Tokyo in 1942. The Pioneers were recognized for "their pre-eminence in Country-Western music over four decades."

Their pre-eminence was rewarded with a 1977 appearance at the Grand Ole Opry. At the Ryman Auditorium in Nashville, the Pioneers performed a single number, as customary with guests. But the audience response was so electric that host Roy Acuff kept them onstage for two more songs.

That same year the Pioneers experienced another a devastating loss. On April 8, 1977, the group made a stage appearance at Puyallap, Washington, a suburb of Tacoma. The next day Lloyd Perryman was stricken with a heart attack while playing a round of golf. Doctors decided that open-heart surgery was necessary, and Lloyd successfully withstood the difficult operation. He seemed to be recuperating at home, but complications set in and the sixty-year-old entertainer succumbed. "Mr. Pioneer" died on Tuesday, May 31, 1977. He was survived by his wife, Buddy, and his son, Wayne.

KLAC Radio, which had played a principal role in the Hollywood Walk of Fame celebration for the Pioneers the previous September, promptly began to put together a tribute for Lloyd Perryman. The event was scheduled for eight o'clock on Thursday evening at the Shrine Auditorium in Los Angeles. Roy Rogers and Dale Evans agreed to perform, and so did Ken Curtis, Rex Allen, Marty Robbins, Glenn Campbell, Eddie Dean, Jimmy Wakely, Stuart Hamblen, Johnny Bond, and several other artists. The Pioneers, with veteran baritone Rome Johnson taking Lloyd's place in the trio, capped the tribute by singing the group's classic songs.

Lloyd had joined the Pioneers in 1936, at the age of nineteen. Working with the group for more than four decades, he had served as leader of the Pioneers since 1949. Dale Warren now assumed the mantle of leadership. Dale had replaced Ken Curtis in 1952, and through the years he had known and worked with every member of the Pioneers. Dale combined a strong sense of Pioneer heritage with an ambitious vision for the future.

"We've opened up new fields," Dale told an *LA Times* interviewer on August 21, 1977. "When the Pioneers toured before they just did rodeos and fairs, and a few club dates. Now, besides rodeos and fairs, we're doing concerts, TV, colleges, Las Vegas, clubs like the Boarding House in San Francisco." At the Boarding House the Pioneers followed a hard rock band, opening with their old yodeling tune, "When Payday Rolls Around." The youthful San Francisco crowd gave the Pioneers a standing ovation. Other standing ovations followed, and at the end crowd members threw roses at the Western group.

"That kind of opened up as a whole new bag for us," Dale reminisced to Denver's *Rocky Mountain News* reporter Douglas Kreutz on March 26, 1979. "We now play quite a few college concerts in addition to the fairs and clubs and television. The kids like it." Kreutz asked about life on the road. "We've had a lot of fun on the road, all of us together. . . . We're not saints," added Dale.

Kreutz questioned Dale about the technicalities of music. "We read it good enough to know what's going on. It's like the hunt and peck system on a typewriter." Dale also offered a carefully considered musical analysis. "I've always had a saying that Western music is about the outdoors, the mountains and the outdoors in general, and country music is about the indoors, heartbreak songs and things like that. We do some country, but our main bag is Western."

Dale was gratified that "a whole new audience has been created in the last four years." But with each passing year the group increasingly paid homage to the Pioneer traditions during each performance. "We always talk about the past members," said Rusty Richards.

Rusty's comments were made to Eve Zibart, reporter for the *Washington Post*. Zibart interviewed Rusty on March 26, 1979, the day after the Pioneers were honored by the Smithsonian Institution in Washington, D.C. for the group's contribution to Western music. On Sunday evening, March 25, Dale Warren, Rusty Richards, Rome Johnson, Roy Lanham, and Billy Liebert appeared before a sellout crowd at the Smithsonian's Baird Auditorium (in the Museum of Natural History). As part of the Smithsonian's Country Music series, a plaque was presented proclaiming the Sons of the Pioneers to be a "National Treasure." Bob Nolan was acknowledged as the author of the "unofficial anthems of Western song." Following appropriate ceremonies, the Pioneers regaled the audience for an hour and a half. The performance was recorded and placed in the Smithsonian's archives.

"I've never been declared a 'national treasure' before," commented Rusty Richards. "I'm thinking of adding 'N.T.' to my name."

"We're singing a part of the American heritage," Dale Warren explained to Boris Weintraub of the *Washington Post*. "Cowboys have always been romantic for kids. We sing about the West. People come up to us after we sing and they say, 'I had tears in my eyes. You bring back memories.' Nostalgia is what it is. And we do a clean show, for the whole family."

Another Pioneer event of 1979 was the release of Bob Nolan's solo album on the Electra label, *The Sound of a Pioneer*. Bob had not recorded since his last session with the Pioneers in 1957. There were eleven songs on the album, all but two written by Bob. "Tumbling Tumbleweeds" and "Cool Water" were included, of course, along with such compositions as "Wandering," "The Touch of God's Hand," and "Can You Hear Those Pioneers." A perceptive reviewer for the *Milwaukee Sentinel* observed: "It's nice to hear some of the old songs again, delivered with a tenor voice that sounds a little choked up, very lonely and very much in love with his loneliness."

Bob's friend Snuff Garrett produced the album, after finally persuading Nolan to record again. Bob did not want to include "Tumbling Tumbleweeds" and "Cool Water," because these classics had been recorded so many times by the Pioneers. "I didn't want to do them over again, but they convinced me that that's what the people would expect, you know, so I did them," he said. He intended for the album to be his final recording statement, declaring emphatically, "I'm not going to follow up on it at all."

Bob had enjoyed his long retirement. He and his wife, Clara ("Peanuts"), tended the flowers, vegetables, and trees in the garden of their home in the San Fernando Valley. Frequently they retreated to their mountain cabin at Big Bear Lake for fishing and relaxation. Bob's Labrador retriever was named "Sir Tumbleweed." Bob continued to write poetry and songs, but hardly at the frantic pace of his movie years. He sold his library of "well over 2,000" songs to three different music companies. In a 1980 interview with Doug Green and Fred Goodwin, he philosophically considered why some of his best movie songs were never recorded commercially by the Pioneers. Bob explained that "the people who were footing the bill didn't understand—there were certain things that I was writing about that they knew nothing about. They knew nothing about the desert and the plains that were a part of the cowboy's life, and when they don't understand it, they don't like it."

Bob kept in touch with Tim Spencer, and sometimes visited or went fishing with Lloyd Perryman. He attended the Sons of the Pioneers reunion in 1972 and the 1976 ceremony which placed a Pioneer star in the Hollywood Walk of Fame. On April 26, 1980, he attended a testimonial dinner for KLAC Country DJ Dick Haynes at the Hollywood Palladium. The Pioneers and Roy Rogers had agreed to perform, and Bob arrived early to watch the rehearsal. Roy and Bob sat together talking, while Dale Warren, Rusty Richards, Billy Liebert, Luther Nallie and Roy Lanham worked on their numbers. After their performance that night, Roy and the Pioneers were given a standing ovation by the capacity crowd. Dale Warren introduced Bob, stating emphatically, "Whatever success the Sons of the Pioneers have had in these forty-seven years, Bob Nolan made it all possible."

Less than two months later, on June 16, Bob went boating from Newport Harbor with his daughter, Roberta Mileusnich, and his half-brother, Mike. While returning home to the San Fernando Valley, Bob was stricken with a fatal heart attack, dying in Costa Mesa. Roy Rogers was shocked. "He seemed very healthy and happy when I saw him two months ago," said Roy. "He looked the picture of health, like he'd live to be a hundred."

But he was seventy-two, and he may have sensed that the end was near. On

June 8, just eight days before his death, Bob wrote a long personal poem about his favorite subject, "My Mistress, The Desert." In it he referred to specific instructions he had made: "I know I will go back for I've already told the pilot who will take me there/to make the flight in the still of night,/and scatter my ashes in a long, straight line so my mistress can find me there, and she'll smile at me with eyes grown soft through the passing years,/and she'll say, 'Well, what do you know?/My boy is home/to stay.'" Accordingly, Bob Nolan was cremated and his ashes were spread across his beloved desert.

At the end of a long, careful analysis of Nolan and his music ("Western Mystic: Bob Nolan and His Songs," in the October 1986 issue of *The Western Historical Quarterly*), Kenneth Bindas artfully summed up one of the greatest of all Western composers-performers: "In many people's minds he will always be the troubadour of the tumbleweeds, searching for home's cool water." It was fitting that the same year these words were written, Bob's classic "Cool Water" was named to the Grammy Hall of Fame.

Three months before Bob Nolan's death, seventy-six-year-old Hugh Farr succumbed to a lingering illness. Hugh's fifth wife, Lynn, was a Wyoming girl, and they lived in Casper and worked together as a musical act for years. As Hugh aged his temper worsened, and he and Lynn eventually separated. Hugh continued to live in Casper, performing solo despite his health. Lynn pointed out that "he played just as well sick."

A heavy smoker, Hugh suffered from emphysema and heart trouble. He lost weight, had open heart surgery, and moved to a nursing home, but he never stopped smoking. He died on St. Patrick's Day, March 17, 1980, and was buried alongside Lynn's family at Riverton, Wyoming. The Sons of the Pioneers were performing at Reno, and they played a show in his honor.

With the deaths of Hugh Farr and Bob Nolan, Roy Rogers became the only surviving founder of the Sons of the Pioneers. Roy had heart problems of his own, but he remained active and in the public eye. In 1967 the Roy Rogers-Dale Evans Museum opened at their home in Victorville, California. The museum featured a stuffed Trigger, who had died in 1965 at thirty-three (Dale liked to tease that one day she would stuff Roy and mount him on Trigger). In 1967 Roy launched a restaurant chain and within a decade there were 200 Roy Rogers Family Restaurants in the United States and Canada (the chain was sold in 1990 to Hardee's).

Roy and Dale made guest appearances on various television shows, and from 1967 to 1971 they sometimes hosted NBC's *Kraft Music Hall*. In 1974 Roy recorded a nostalgic hit, "Hoppy, Gene and Me." Roy became disgusted with the violent, vulgar Westerns of the 1960s and 1970s: "There's movies today I wouldn't even let Trigger watch." So in 1976 Roy filmed *Mackintosh and TJ*, a wholesome Western in which he played a Bible-reading drifter who helps a troubled teenaged boy.

The Pioneers had made countless appearances with Roy at fairs and rodeos and on radio and television, and in 1978 Roy and the Pioneers came together again on TV's *Hee Haw*. The Pioneers sang "Tumbling Tumbleweeds" to a national audience, announced their hometowns on a regular feature of the show, and backed Roy on "O Carry Me Back on the Lone Prairie."

When Roy and Dale appeared on NBC's popular *Barbara Mandrell Show* in 1981, President Ronald Reagan sent a telegram congratulating them on fifty years of "clean, wholesome entertainment." During the 1980s Roy and Dale co-hosted *Happy Trails Theater*, which showed their old movies over the Nashville Network. The ninety-minute shows featured Roy and Dale and their old co-stars and directors chatting about movie-making at Republic.

While the last charter Pioneer maintained an active profile, the contemporary Sons of the Pioneers continued to appear throughout the country. Both Roy and the Pioneers stressed their rich heritage. And that heritage again was acknowledged in 1980, when the "Original Sons of the Pioneers," along with Johnny Cash and promoter-broadcasting entrepreneur Connie B. Gay, were inducted into the Country Music Hall of Fame. The Hall of Fame plaque featured relief busts of Hugh Farr, Karl Farr, and Bob Nolan, on a top row, and on a lower row, Lloyd Perryman, Roy Rogers, and Tim Spencer. Each bust sported a hat except for Bob's. The busts were labeled with names and birth and death dates, although Roy's had only a birth date. Beneath the busts an inscription read:

ORIGINAL SONS OF THE PIONEERS

The Original Sons of the Pioneers invented Western harmony, one of our most exciting and dignified musical styles, exemplified by their compositions "Cool Water" and "Tumbling Tumbleweeds." Founded in 1933, the group demonstrated their unique vocal stylings in hundreds of films and records. Though the group continues today with new members, the original sextet is remembered and honored for their classic innovations.

Eight years later, Roy Rogers was

COWBOY CHIC

In 1980 the popular John Travolta movie *Urban Cowboy* helped stimulate a growing interest in Western clothing, dancing and music. City dwellers enthusiastically donned cowboy boots, hats and jeans, and drove pickups to Western-style clubs to dance the two-step. Old-time groups such as the Texas Playboys and the Light Crust Doughboys found themselves in demand.

No group benefited more from this surge of interest in Western music than the Sons of the Pioneers. "We're getting ready for one of our busiest summers," observed Dale Warren. "Everywhere we go, there seems to be an increasing interest in the cowboy and the West. City folks are wearing Western clothes, and it was a thrill to see the U. S. Olympic Team in cowboy hats and Western wear at Lake Placid." Dale pointedly added, "We're happy to be part of the new 'Westward Movement,' but we've never been away."

During the summer of 1980 the Sons of the Pioneers would be heard on more than 1,200 radio stations on *Country Crossroads*. Beginning July 17, Roy Rogers would co-host the program for seven weeks, and there would be special tributes to Bob Nolan and Tex Ritter. Personal appearances that summer offer an idea of a typical Pioneer schedule:

July 1-15 .... John Ascuaga's Nugget
(Sparks, Nevada)
July 26 .... Alpine Village Park
(Torrance, California)

elected to the Country Music Hall of Fame, along with Loretta Lynn. Roy thus became the only individual to be inducted twice into the Country Music Hall of Fame.

During the past decade the Sons of the Pioneers had received virtually every significant heritage award that was available to a Western singing group. But the next few years would bring considerable change to the Pioneer roster. In 1980 baritone Rome Johnson left the group, but Luther Nallie, who had left in 1974, was persuaded to return to the Pioneers. The next year accordionist Billy Liebert departed. Since the group now stressed their heritage, Liebert was replaced by a fiddler, Dale Morris. When his tenure proved brief, Tommy Nallie—Luther's younger brother—was enlisted in May 1983. Tommy had a fine tenor voice, and he played drums, guitar, and harmonica.

On Wednesday night, May 25, 1983, a national television audience saw the Pioneers in an episode of *Fall Guy*, a series that starred Lee Majors as a stunt man. Roy Rogers was co-star of the episode, which was entitled "Happy Trails." Opening with black and white scenes from Roy's old movies, the show was "dedicated to a living legend, Roy Rogers, the King of the Cowboys." In addition to the Sons of the Pioneers (none of whom had been with the group during Roy's movies), Jack Kelly of *Maverick* fame also appeared in the episode, and so did James Drury and Doug McClure of *The Virginian*, along with Pat Buttram, Gene Autry's old sidekick. The show began with the filming of a movie scene, as Roy walked onto a porch singing "Cool Water." The Sons of the Pioneers were nearby, just like the old days at Republic, singing backup. In a later scene Roy and the Pioneers combined on "Tumbling Tumbleweeds."

(continued from previous page)

July 31 .... Ramona Bowl (Hemet, California)
August 3 .... Logan County Fair (Lincoln, Illinois)
August 5-9 .... Pike's Peak or Bust Rodeo
            (Colorado Springs)
August 10 .... Taping of Blair Pro Rodeo television
            show (Colorado Springs)
August 15 .... Kutztown Fair (Kutztown,
            Pennsylvania)
August 16 .... Marshall Fair (Marshall, Michigan)
August 17 .... Armada Fair (Armada, Michigan)
August 18-31 .... Sam's Town Hotel and Gambling
            Hall (Las Vegas)
September 3 .... Eastern Idaho State Fair
            (Blackfoot)
September 5-6 .... Bel Isle Club (Bethel Island,
            California)
September 13 .... Republican Committee Conven-
            tion (Bonaventure Hotel,
            Las Vegas)
September 15-19 .... Western Washington Fair and
            Rodeo (Puyallup)
September 26-28 .... With Roy Rogers and Dale
            Evans, Los Angeles County
            Fair (Ponoma, California)
September 29 .... With Roy Rogers and Dale Evans,
            Kern County Fair (Bakersfield,
            California)

There was a strong sense of fun and nostalgia, which was appropriate to the increasingly nostalgic performances of the Pioneers.

In 1984 a veteran harmony singer and versatile instrumentalist, Robert "Sunny" Spencer, became a significant addition to the Sons of the Pioneers. Unrelated to Tim Spencer, Sunny was born in 1929 in Bowen, Kentucky. Grandfather Spencer was a professional fiddler, Sunny's father, a carpenter, played fiddle, guitar and banjo, and his mother played guitar. Sunny sang and played from boyhood, and he began performing with professional groups as a teenager. During a long and varied career, Sunny became noted as a harmony vocalist and for his proficiency on the fiddle, guitar, mandolin, banjo, bass fiddle, clarinet, saxophone, and trumpet. In 1949 he performed with Dale Warren's Jimmy Dale Quartet, beginning a friendship with the future leader of the Sons of the Pioneers. After joining the Pioneers in February 1984, Sunny became the group's lead singer.

A 1984 departure from the group was not amicable. Rusty Richards had enjoyed two stints with the Pioneers, 1963-66 and 1974-84. But there were dis-

THE TUMBLEWEED TRAIL

According to their 1955 publicity release, "the Pioneers are still traveling that Tumbleweed Trail, as strong and alive as ever." They had to be strong to keep up with their nomadic travel schedule. In the fall of 1981, with the Urban Cowboy craze still peaking, the Pioneers had the following quality engagements:

October 1-2 . . . . The Nashville Palace* (airing on NBC-
               TV on Saturday)
November 7 . . . . . . Opryland (Nashville)
October 3 . . . . Nashville Alive, WTBS, Opryland, and
               Grand Ole Opry, WSM, Opryland
               (Nashville)
October 10 . . . . Pioneer Frontier Days, Canyon
               Country (California)
October 27 . . . . Private convention* (Arizona)
November 2-8 . . . . . Cactus Pete's (Jackpot, Nevada)
November 19-21 . . Stetson World's Toughest Rodeo
               (Fort Worth, Texas)
December 2-4 . . . . . Barbara Mandrell and the Mandrell
               Sisters*, NBC Studios (Burbank, California)
*With Roy Rogers and Dale Evans

On Monday, July 16, 1984, Luther Nallie returned to his Beaumont home for a Pioneer engagement in Orlando, Florida. But he would not stay in Beaumont long. "Well," he wrote Fred Goodwin, "I just got home and I will spend one night here and take off for Hememt, Calif—to play at the Ramona Bowl Thursday—Then up to Rio Nido (North of San Francisco about 70 miles) then one day off and open in Lake Tahoe at Harrah's on the 24th of July for one week—"

The Tumbleweed Trail was just as long in the
1980s as it had been in earlier
decades.

agreements in 1984, and late in the year Rusty and the group parted ways. On January 22, 1985, Rusty filed a lawsuit in Ventura County Superior Court. Charging that he had been wrongfully forced out of the group, Rusty sought $1 million in damages and an injunction barring use of the name "Sons of the Pioneers." Also alleging that he had not received his share of the profits from the 1983 fiftieth anniversary album *Celebration*, Rusty asked for an impartial accounting. Dale Warren, Roy Lanham, and Luther Nallie were named in the lawsuit. Like Hugh Farr's 1959 lawsuit, however, this suit ended inconclusively, and the Sons of the Pioneers continued to perform without interruption.

Another Nallie brother, Jack, joined the Pioneers late in 1984, remaining for nearly two years as a bass player. By mid-1986 popular guitarist Roy Lanham was forced to drop out of the group because of health problems. Plagued with cancer and a stroke, he died at the age of sixty-eight on February 14, 1991. (Ken Curtis died two months later.) Roy was replaced in 1986 by another gifted musician, Gary LeMaster.

Gary was born in 1942 in Ashland, Kentucky. His parents sang gospel music, and his father played several instruments. Gary enjoyed harmony singing and began learning a variety of instruments, and while still a boy he started earning money as a performer. Although adept with numerous instruments, Gary became best known as a guitarist. Gary's focus was on rock and pop music, but his career was interrupted by a 1964-66 tour of duty with the army. He married Valerie Spencer, daughter of Sunny Spencer, and Gary and his wife often performed together.

With his Pioneer connection, Gary was asked to fill in for an ailing Roy Lanham at an engagement at Des Moines, Iowa. Soon Gary was asked to fill in again, this time during a three-month engagement at Chuck Camp's Triple C Chuck Wagon in Tucson. In November 1986, after it became obvious that Roy Lanham would be unable to return to the group, Gary agreed to become a permanent member of the Pioneers. He would succeed Roy Lanham and Karl Farr as guitarist, and he also became part of the trio, singing tenor and, when needed, lead and baritone.

The next year another tenor, Daryl Wainscott, was added to the group. For six years Daryl would play the piano and keyboard, vocalize, and arrange numbers for the Pioneers. During this same period, 1988-93, singer-yodeler David Bradley also performed with the Pioneers. David Bradley and Daryl Wainscott both left the group in 1993, replaced by John Nallie, son of Luther, and by fiddler Roy Warhurst. John played keyboard and guitar, and was a talented singer. John, Gary LeMaster, and Dale Warren formed a Pioneer trio that seemed "intensely satisfying" to Dale Warren. Early in 1993 seventy-six-year-old Rome Johnson, who had left the Pioneers in 1980, died of cancer at his home in the Los Angeles area. Rome was survived by his wife, Pat, five sons, and a daughter.

By 1993 the Sons of the Pioneers had become a regular attraction in Branson, Missouri, an enormously popular live entertainment center. The Pioneers began to play Branson in 1983, and as the mountain town became a mecca for heartland Americans, demand increased for the legendary singing group. The Pioneers would open in Branson each May and play through the Christmas season in December, with time out for periodic dates elsewhere.

ALBUMS OF THE 1980s

During the 1980s, thirteen albums were released featuring the Sons of the Pioneers. Seven of these albums were produced by Bear Family Records in 1987; licensed from RCA, they comprised earlier recordings. "Tumbling Tumbleweeds," recorded in 1937, 1946, 1950 (with Perry Como), 1959 and 1963, was on five albums of the 1980s, and there were four versions of "Cool Water."

Let's Go West Again (RCA, 1981). Ten recordings from 1947 through 1957, including "The Searchers" and "This Ain't the Same Old Range."

Sons of the Pioneers (Columbia Historic Edition, 1982). Ten recordings from 1937, including "Song of the Bandit" and "The Devil's Great Grand Son."

Tumbling Tumbleweeds (Reader's Digest, 1982). Twenty recordings from 1959 through 1967. In addition to the title song, classics such as "Cool Water," "Wagon Wheels," and "Riders in the Sky."

The Sons of the Pioneers (Bear Family Records, 1982). Sixteen recordings from 1947 through 1957, including "The Grave Yard Filler of the West."

Empty Saddles (MCA, 1983). Fourteen recordings from 1935, 1936 and 1937, including "Empty Saddles," "I'm an Old Cowhand" and "Blue Prairie."

Celebration (Silver Spur Records, 1983). Twenty-four recordings by the 1983 Pioneers, including "Ghost Riders in the Sky" and "Blue Shadows on the Trail."

Cool Water (Bear Family Records, 1987). Sixteen recordings from 1945 and 1946, including two versions of the title song, along with "Cowboy Camp Meetin'," "No One To Cry To," and "The Everlasting Hills of Oklahoma."

Teardrops in My Heart (Bear Family Records, 1987). Sixteen recordings from 1946 and 1947, including "Blue Prairie" and "My Best To You."

A Hundred and Sixty Acres (Bear Family Records, 1987). Sixteen recordings from 1947, including "The Old Rugged Cross" and "The Last Roundup."

Riders in the Sky (Bear Family Records, 1987). Sixteen recordings from 1947 and 1949, including "Riders in the Sky" and "Room Full of Roses."

Land Beyond the Sun (Bear Family Records, 1987). Sixteen recordings from 1949 and 1950, including "Wagons West" and "Song of the Wagonmaster."

And Friends (Bear Family Records, 1987). Sixteen recordings from 1950 and 1951, featuring songs recorded with Perry Como, Ezio Pinza, the Fontane Sisters, and the Three Suns.

There's a Goldmine in the Sky (Bear Family Records, 1987). Seventeen recordings from 1951 and 1952, including "Ho Le O," "Empty Saddles," and "Home on the Range."

During the winter months they headquartered in Tucson, from 1983 to 1995, playing lengthy engagements at the Triple C Ranch.

The Pioneers of the 1990s added more musical variety than ever before to their act. Of course, the Farr brothers had consistently included jazz elements with their instrumentation, while Pioneer harmony on hymns always had been a popular part of the group's performances and recordings. But now the versatile Pioneers could muster nearly thirty instrument combinations, including Tommie Nallie on drums. "Trail Boss" Dale Warren utilized numerous groupings to provide "an exciting 'lift' to" each performance. A typical performance now included Dixieland, gospel, country, and Western swing, along with traditional Pioneer songs. The group developed "a real crowd-pleaser" entitled "Salute to the Big Bands." In it "the Sons whip through a medley of big band tunes that brings the audience roaring to its feet." At the end of a performance Dale Warren led the group into the crowd for personal greetings, and to autograph Sons of the Pioneers photos, shirts, caps, and their memorabilia—including cassette and CD recordings, of course—that were for sale. The group's publicity stressed that the Sons of the Pioneers were "not getting older—just getting better!"

The Pioneers celebrated their sixtieth anniversary in 1994. In May a Country Music Association representative presented a special achievement award to the Pioneers "before a large cheering audience" onstage at Branson's Braschler Theater. In November, at the annual convention of the Western Music Association in Tucson, the Pioneers were honored before a capacity crowd of more than 2,500 jammed into the University of Tucson's Centennial Hall. In a show that lasted nearly four hours, numerous performers paid "tribute to the Vienna Philharmonic of cowboy crooners—the Sons of the Pioneers." When the Sons of the Pioneers came onstage, they performed in front of a chuckwagon and mini-corral. The group showcased numerous instrument combinations, but made sure to display the tight harmony that had always been the Pioneer hallmark. Roy Rogers and Dale Evans were present, and Roy joined in on "Cool Water" and "Tumbling Tumbleweeds." The big show climaxed with Roy and Dale leading out on "Happy Trails."

Two groups that performed that night included the Sons of the San Joaquin and Riders in the Sky. Only a few years old, the Sons of the San Joaquin are a California group organized to revive the sounds of cowboy music, specifically concentrating on the three-part harmony of the Pioneers. Another trio, Riders in the Sky, was organized in 1977 to capitalize on nostalgia for the beloved B Westerns. Singer-yodeler Ranger Doug (Douglas Green), fiddler Woody Paul (Dr. Paul Chrisman), and sidekick-bass fiddler Too Slim (Fred LaBour) use flamboyant costumes, affectionate humor, original music, and standard tunes (including Pioneer material) to create delightful performances. Both of these popular groups are instrumental in carrying the traditions and sounds of the Sons of the Pioneers into the next century.

In 1995 the Pioneers returned to Oklahoma City to once again receive recognition by the National Cowboy Hall of Fame. Thirty years earlier the Sons of the Pioneers had become the first musical group to receive a Wrangler Award—in special recognition for their contribution to Western music—from the Cowboy Hall of Fame. Now the Pioneers were to be inducted into the Hall.

At a black-tie banquet on Saturday evening, March 18, 1995, the contemporary Pioneers were presented Wrangler Awards by grand old character actors Ernest Borgnine and Jack Elam. Dale Warren accepted Wranglers for Bob Nolan and Roy Rogers, who was unable to attend. Tim Spencer's widow, Velma, and his son, Hal, were present to accept his award. Karl Farr, Jr., collected Wranglers on behalf of his father, his uncle Hugh, and Pat Brady.

A memorable weekend in March 1996 demonstrated the undiminished magic of the Sons of the Pioneers. Fred Goodwin helped arrange a flurry of Nashville bookings for Friday and Saturday, March 22 and 23, including the Pioneers' fifth appearance on *The Grand Ole Opry*. Dale Warren, Gary LeMaster, Luther Nallie, Sunny Spencer, John Nallie, and Roy Warhurst arrived in Nashville on Thursday. On Friday morning they appeared on a radio talk show at WSM's studio off the lobby of the magnificent Opryland Hotel. The lobby quickly filled with fans hoping for photographs and autographs.

Late Friday afternoon the Pioneers taped a guest appearance on *Prime Time Country*, hosted by Tom Wopat and televised over TNN later that evening. The Pioneers sang "Cimarron Roll On," "Along the Navajo Trail," and "Cool Water." While being interviewed by Wopat, Dale introduced Gretchen Carson from the audience. Ken Carson had died in 1994 in Florida, and his widow had come to Nashville to be with the Pioneers during the weekend.

On Saturday morning Sunny Spencer, Gary LeMaster, and Fred Goodwin were guests on another WSM radio talk show. Then the Pioneers visited the Country Music Hall of Fame, attracting a large crowd as they posed for photos in front of their plaque. That evening the Pioneers were televised guests on TNN's *Backstage at the Opry*, hosted by Bill Anderson. The host reminisced about a 1973 Pioneers appearance on the syndicated *Bill Anderson Show*, and "Whispering Bill" joined the 1996 Pioneers in singing "Red River Valley."

The Pioneers were scheduled for both Saturday night *Grand Ole Opry* shows. The first show was televised and hosted by Jimmy C. Newman. The Pioneers sang "Don't Fence Me In" and "Cool Water," which evoked a standing ovation from the big audience. Between shows the

A TRIBUTE TO THE SINGING COWBOY

"Music of the West, A Tribute to the Singing Cowboys" was a 1992 TNN television special that aired live from the Gene Autry Western Heritage Museum in Los Angeles. Starring Clint Black, EmmyLou Harris, and Dwight Yoakum, the show was hosted by Dennis Weaver. On hand to be honored were Gene Autry, Rex Allen, Eddie Dean, Monte Hale, Herb Jeffries, Patsy Montana, Roy Rogers and Dale Evans, and the Sons of the Pioneers.

When the 1992 Pioneers came onstage, a screen behind them featured a black and white film clip of Bob Nolan, Tim Spencer, Ken Carson, Shug Fisher, and Hugh and Karl Farr performing "Tumbling Tumbleweeds." It was announced that "The Sons of the Pioneers have harmonized on over three thousand songs," and Dale Warren, who was in his fortieth year with the group, accepted an award on behalf of the Pioneers.

Pioneers taped a segment for another WSM radio program. The second *Opry* performance was hosted by Little Jimmy Dickens. Using a fiddle, mandolin, electric bass, and two guitars, the Pioneers performed "Ghost Riders in the Sky," "Cool Water," and "Tumbling Tumbleweeds." Afterward the Pioneers signed countless photographs and programs, while the WSM switchboard was flooded with calls from the group's fans.

CONTINUING LEGACY

The Sons of the Pioneers provided music for nearly one hundred movies. And during the 1990s big budget films continued to reprise the most popular of all Pioneer songs. For example, in *The Two Jakes*, filmed in 1990 and starring Jack Nicholson, Nicholson's detective character is driving in the Los Angeles area in 1948. He turns on the car radio, and a Pioneer recording of "Tumbling Tumbleweeds" comes over the airwaves as he motors through the California hills.

In 1991 *City Slickers*, a comedy set in the contemporary West, showcased urban wiseacre Billy Crystal and crusty old cowboy Jack Palance. The leathery Palance, described by Crystal as "a saddlebag with eyes," won an Oscar for Best Supporting Actor. During a scene around a campfire, Palance orders Crystal to accompany him on the harmonica while he recites his favorite song, "Tumbling Tumbleweeds." And in the 1999 comedy, *The Big Liebowski*, another modern cowboy, Sam Elliott, provides a stabilizing influence between the wild antics of Jeff Bridges and John Goodman. Reinforcing Elliott's rugged Western presence is a classic Pioneer recording of "Tumbling Tumbleweeds" on the soundtrack. Nearly half a century after their last appearance on the silver screen, the Sons of the Pioneers still provide an occasional presence in modern movies.

This triumphant weekend in Nashville indicated the legendary status enjoyed by the Sons of the Pioneers in their seventh decade of existence. But on July 6, 1998, the last charter member of the Pioneers died. Roy Rogers was eighty-six, and he had suffered from heart problems for two decades. "Well, Lord," his nurse heard him say, "it's been a long, hard ride." A short time later the King of the Cowboys died in his sleep. He left his wife of fifty years, Dale Evans, along with six children (three others had died from accident or disease), fifteen grandchildren, thirty-three great-grandchildren—and millions of fans and admirers.

Roy Rogers was the founding force behind the Sons of the Pioneers. The group had attained its greatest recognition in the enormously popular Roy Rogers movies, and for decades Roy and the Pioneers had regularly reunited for personal appearances. By the time he died in 1998, the other charter members of the Sons of the Pioneers were already gone: Bob Nolan, Tim Spencer, Hugh and Karl Farr. Other early mainstays of the group who also had died included Lloyd Perryman, Pat Brady, Ken Carson, Shug Fisher, and Ken Curtis. Tommy Doss, who so ably had replaced Bob Nolan's distinctive baritone, was living in quiet retirement and no longer performed.

Only Dale Warren, who had known and worked with every member of the Sons of the Pioneers, remained an active link with the group's first two creative decades. When early performers left the group, every effort was made to replace them with singers of similar vocal qualities. However, eventually the vocal qualities evolved into a noticeably different sound, the instrumental genius of the Farr brothers proved irreplaceable, and the torrent of original tunes from Nolan and Spencer had ceased long ago. Nevertheless, the famed excellence of the Sons of the Pioneers still attracts crowds to road performances and to regular appearances at Branson, Missouri. The group saves two Pioneer classics for last, closing the act with "Cool Water," then singing "Tumbling Tumbleweeds" for an encore. And decades of recordings are readily available for fans of any era of the group, while movies on video offer Bob Nolan, Tim Spencer, Roy Rogers, Lloyd Perryman, Pat Brady, and the Farrs at the prime of their creative and performing powers. The Sons of the Pioneers have established a rich legacy since 1934, and Trail Boss Dale Warren now leads the legendary group along the Tumbleweed Trail into the twenty-first century.

After Karl Farr died and Tommy Doss retired, Roy Lanham (top right) was enlisted as guitarist and Rusty Richards (top left) joined the trio. Bottom, L to R: Dale Warren, Lloyd Perryman, Pat Brady. Lloyd and Pat were the only direct links to the early years of the Pioneers.

The Pioneers were guests on The Bill Anderson Show in 1973, and the finale was a stirring rendition of "Red River Valley" by the entire cast. The Pioneers are seated between Bill, standing at left, and his regulars. L to R: Luther Nallie, Dale Warren, Lloyd Perryman, Billy Armstrong.

Above: *Despite emphysema and other health problems, Hugh Farr continued to fiddle. His wife, Lynn Farr, insisted that "he played just as well sick." Hugh's dog, Rudy, liked to sing along. (Courtesy Lynn Farr)*

Left: *The Pioneer Star at Hollywood's Walk of Fame.*

Above: Grand Ole Opry *appearance in 1973. L to R: Roy Lanham, Billy Armstrong, Lloyd Perryman, Dale Warren, Luther Nallie.*

Left: *The fan club publication* Pioneer News *relates the group's Smithsonian honors. "I've never been declared a 'national treasure' before," remarked Rusty Richards.*

Below: *A* Grand Ole Opry *appearance with Roy Rogers on October 3, 1981. Roy is in the foreground, and Opry legend Roy Acuff stands at far right. The Pioneers, L to R: Doc Denning, Roy Lanham, Luther Nallie, Dale Warren, Dale Morris. (Courtesy Les Leverett)*

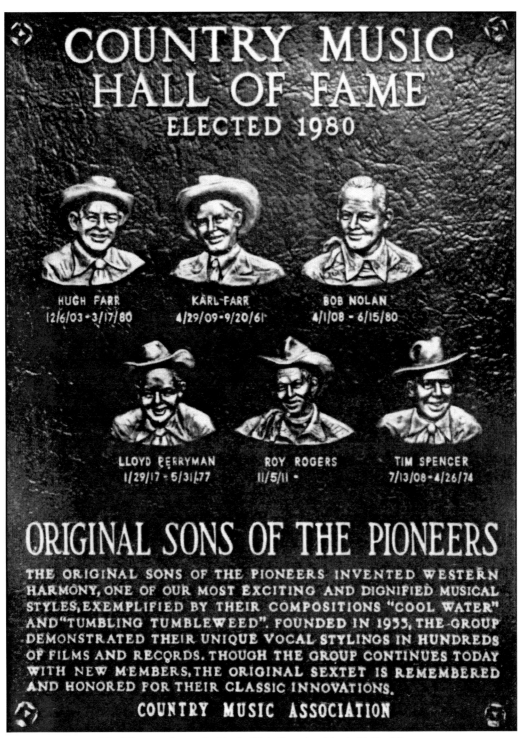

The Pioneer plaque in Nashville's Country Music Hall of Fame.

Above: *The last charter Pioneer remained in the public eye with TV and personal appearances, usually with Dale, and occasional recordings.*

Left: *Roy Rogers with an antelope he bagged. A lifelong hunter, Roy enjoyed chasing rabbits astride a motorcycle.*

Fiftieth anniversary photo of the Pioneers. Top, L to R: Sunny Spencer; Dale Warren, Luther Nallie. Front: Jack Nallie, Roy Lanham, Tommy Nallie. Luther, Jack, and Tommy Nallie provided the first Pioneer brothers since Hugh and Karl Farr.

Atop a stagecoach to Branson, Missouri. L to R: Roy Lanham, Dale Warren, Jack Nallie. Inside the coach: Tommy Nallie, Sunny Spencer, Luther Nallie.

The Pioneers with Hee Haw *star Archie Campbell. L to R: Dale Morris, Dale Warren, Luther Nallie, Archie Campbell, Roy Lanham, Rusty Richards.*

The Pioneers perform with another legendary harmony group, the Oak Ridge Boys.

The Pioneers of 1993. Clockwise from top: Sunny Spencer, David Bradley, Gary LeMaster, Dale Warren, Luther Nallie, Daryl Wainscott.

A sixtieth anniversary tribute was paid to the Pioneers at the 1994 meeting of the Western Music Association in Tucson.

The Tumbleweed Times *is the latest in a long line of Pioneer fan club newsletters.*

The Films of
The Sons of the Pioneers

Each entry includes movie title, star, and studio.

1935   *Radio Scout*, El Brendel (Warner Brothers)
        Bronco Buster (Universal cartoon)
        The Old Homestead, Mary Carlisle (Liberty)
        Slightly Static, Thelma Todd (MGM)
        Romance of the West, Sons of the Pioneers
               (Warner Brothers short)
        Way Up Thar, Joan Davis (Educational)
        Gallant Defender, Charles Starrett (Columbia)

1936   *The Mysterious Defender*, Charles Starrett (Columbia)
        Song of the Saddle, Dick Foran (Warner Brothers)
        Rhythm on the Range, Bing Crosby (Paramount)
        The California Mail, Dick Foran (Warner Brothers)
        The Big Show, Gene Autry (Republic)
        The Old Corral, Gene Autry (Republic)

1937   *The Old Wyoming Trail*, Charles Starrett (Columbia)
        Outlaws of the Prairie, Charles Starrett (Columbia)

1938   *Cattle Raiders*, Charles Starrett (Columbia)
        Call of the Rockies, Charles Starrett (Columbia)
        Law of the Plains, Charles Starrett (Columbia)
        West of Cheyenne, Charles Starrett (Columbia)
        South of Arizona, Charles Starrett (Columbia)
        The Colorado Trail, Charles Starrett (Columbia)
        West of Santa Fe, Charles Starrett (Columbia)
        Rio Grande, Charles Starrett (Columbia)

1939   *The Thundering West*, Charles Starrett (Columbia)
        Texas Stampede, Charles Starrett (Columbia)
        North of the Yukon, Charles Starrett (Columbia)
        Spoilers of the Range, Charles Starrett (Columbia)
        Western Caravans, Charles Starrett (Columbia)
        The Man From Sundown, Charles Starrett (Columbia)
        Riders of Blade River, Charles Starrett (Columbia)
        Outpost of the Mounties, Charles Starrett (Columbia)
        Stranger From Texas, Charles Starrett (Columbia)

1940   *Two-Fisted Ranger*, Charles Starrett (Columbia)
         Bullets for Rustlers, Charles Starrett (Columbia)
         Blazing Six Shooters, Charles Starrett (Columbia)
         Texas Stagecoach, Charles Starrett (Columbia)
         The Durango Kid, Charles Starrett (Columbia)
         West of Abilene, Charles Starrett (Columbia)
         The Thundering West, Charles Starrett (Columbia)

1941   *The Pinto Kid*, Charles Starrett (Columbia)
         Outlaws of the Panhandle, Charles Starrett (Columbia)
         Red River Valley, Roy Rogers (Republic)

1942   *Man From Cheyenne*, Roy Rogers (Republic)
         South of Santa Fe, Roy Rogers (Republic)
         Sunset on the Desert, Roy Rogers (Republic)
         Romance on the Range, Roy Rogers (Republic)
         Sons of the Pioneers, Roy Rogers (Republic)
         Call of the Canyon, Gene Autry (Republic)
         Sunset Serenade, Roy Rogers (Republic)
         Heart of the Golden West, Roy Rogers (Republic)
         Ridin' Down the Canyon, Roy Rogers (Republic)

1943   *Idaho*, Roy Rogers (Republic)
         King of the Cowboys, Roy Rogers (Republic)
         Song of Texas, Roy Rogers (Republic)
         Silver Spurs, Roy Rogers (Republic)
         Man From Music Mountain, Roy Rogers (Republic)

1944   *Hands Across the Border*, Roy Rogers (Republic)
         Cowboy and the Señorita, Roy Rogers (Republic)
         Yellow Rose of Texas, Roy Rogers (Republic)
         Song of Nevada, Roy Rogers (Republic)
         San Fernando Valley, Roy Rogers (Republic)
         Lights of Old Santa Fe, Roy Rogers (Republic)
         Hollywood Canteen, Roy Rogers (Republic)

1945   *Utah*, Roy Rogers
         Bells of Rosarita, Roy Rogers (Republic)
         Man From Oklahoma, Roy Rogers (Republic)
         Sunset in El Dorado, Roy Rogers (Republic)
         Don't Fence Me In, Roy Rogers (Republic)
         Along the Navajo Trail, Roy Rogers (Republic)

1946   *Song of Arizona*, Roy Rogers (Republic)
         Home on the Range, Monte Hale (Republic)
         Ding Dong Williams, Glenn Vernon (RKO)
         Rainbow Over Texas, Roy Rogers (Republic)
         My Pal Trigger, Roy Rogers (Republic)
         Under Nevada Skies, Roy Rogers (Republic)
         Roll On Texas Moon, Roy Rogers (Republic)
         Home in Oklahoma, Roy Rogers (Republic)
         Heldorado, Roy Rogers (Republic)

1947   *Apache Rose*, Roy Rogers (Republic)
Hit Parade of 1947, Eddie Albert (Republic)
Bells of San Angelo, Roy Rogers (Republic)
Springtime in the Sierras, Roy Rogers (Republic)
On the Old Spanish Trail, Roy Rogers (Republic)

1948   *The Gay Ranchero*, Roy Rogers (Republic)
Under California Skies, Roy Rogers (Republic)
Eyes of Texas, Roy Rogers (Republic)
Melody Time, Roy Rogers (RKO)
Night Time in Nevada, Roy Rogers (Republic)

1950   *Wagonmaster*, Ben Johnson (RKO)
Everybody's Dancin', Spade Cooley (Lippert)
Rio Grande, John Wayne (Republic)

1951   *Fighting Coast Guard*, Forrest Tucker (Republic)

1956   *The Searchers*, John Wayne (Warner Brothers)

1957   *The Searchers*, John Wayne (Warner Brothers)

1957   *Andy Burnett* (Disney)

1959   *Saga of Windwagon Smith* (Disney)

1960   *The Swamp Fox* (Disney)

1961   *Sancho, The Homing Steer* (Disney)
Legend of Lobo (Disney)

1962   *Johnny Shiloh* (Disney)

Recordings of
The Sons of the Pioneers

Decca Records

Los Angeles (August 8, 1934)
'Way Out There
Tumbling Tumbleweeds
Moonlight on the Prairie
Ridin' Home

Los Angeles (March 7, 1935)
I Follow the Stream
There's a Round-Up in the Sky
I Still Do
The Roving Cowboy

Los Angeles (March 13, 1935)
When Our Old Age Pension
*   Check Comes To Our Door*
Will You Love Me When My
*   Hair Has Turned to Silver?*
When I Leave This World
*   Behind*
Popeyed (Unissued)

Los Angeles (October 9, 1935)
Over the Santa Fe Trail
Song of the Pioneers
Echoes From the Hills
The New Frontier (Unissued)

Los Angeles (October 16, 1935)
Kilocycle Stomp
Cajun Stomp
Westward Ho
Kelly Waltz (Unissued)

Los Angeles (May 8, 1936)
Hills of Old Wyomin'
A Melody From the Sky
We'll Rest at the End of the Trail

Los Angeles (June 8, 1936)
Texas Star
On a Mountain High (Unissued)

Los Angeles (June 18, 1936)
Blue Bonnet Girl
Ride, Ranger, Ride

Los Angeles (July 3, 1936)
Empty Saddles
Blue Prairie
I'm an Old Cowhand
One More Ride

Los Angeles (February 22, 1937)
'Way Out There
Tumbling Tumbleweeds

Columbia Records

Los Angeles (October 21, 1937)
My Saddle Pals and I
I Love You Nelly
I Wonder If She Waits For Me Tonight
When the Roses Bloom Again
Heavenly Airplane
Billie the Kid
Power in the Blood

Los Angeles (October 26, 1937)
Let's Pretend

Love Song of the Waterfall
Song of the Bandit
Just a Wearying for You
Smilin' Thru
Kelly Waltz
Open Range Ahead
Cajun Stomp
Send Him Home To Me
Blue Juanita (Unissued)

Los Angeles (October 28, 1937)
Cowboy's Night Herd Song
Black Sheep Blues
That Pioneer Mother of Mine
Hadie Brown

Los Angeles (December 14, 1937)
Hear Dem Bells
One More River To Cross
You Must Come in at the Door
Lead Me Gently Home Father
The Devil's Great Grandson

Dwelling in Beulah Land
When the Golden Train Comes Down

Los Angeles (December 16, 1937)
Hold That Critter Down
Leaning on the Everlasting Arms
What You Gonna Say To Peter
At the Rainbow's End
The Touch of God's Hand
The Hangin' Blues (Unissued)
Lord, You Made the Cowboy Happy
   (Unissued)

Decca Records

Chicago (March 27, 1941)
So Long to the Red River Valley
My Love Went Without Water
They Drew My Number
He's Gone Up the Trail
A Love That Ended Too Soon
Cielito Lindo
Cool Water
You Don't Love Me, But I'll Always Care

Chicago (April 1, 1941)
There's A Long, Long Trail
Kelly Waltz
Lonely Rose of Mexico
Wagoner Hoedown
Boggy Road to Texas
Rye Whiskey (Unissued)

Los Angeles (September 3, 1941)
I Knew It All the Time

You Broke My Heart Little Darlin'
How Was I To Know
When the Moon Comes Over Sun Valley

Los Angeles (September 16, 1941)
Pay Me No Mind
Salt River Valley
Tumbleweed Trail
Plain Old Plains

Los Angeles (March 23, 1942)
Private Buckaroo
O-o-oh Wonderful World
I'll Be Around Somewhere
I'm Crying My Heart Out Over You

Los Angeles (December 28, 1943)
I Hang My Head and Cry
Home in San Antone
There's a New Moon Over My Shoulder
Let Me Keep My Memories (Unissued)

RCA Victor

Hollywood (August 8, 1945)
Forgive and Forget
Cool Water
Timber Trail
Stars and Stripes on Iwo Jima

Hollywood (January 7, 1946)
You're Getting Tired of Me
Gold Star Mother With Silvery Hair
You'll Be Sorry When I'm Gone
I Wear Your Memory in My Heart

Hollywood (March 15, 1946)
The Everlasting Hills of Oklahoma
Chant of the Wanderer

Blue Prairie

Hollywood (August 21, 1946)
Trees

Hollywood (September 2, 1946)
The Letter Marked Unclaimed
Baby Doll
A Penny for Your Thoughts
Have I Told You Lately That I Love You

Hollywood (January 5, 1947)
Let's Pretend
Teardrops in My Heart
Cigareetes, Whusky, and Wild (Wild)
   Women

Hollywood (January 27, 1947)
Teardrops in My Heart
Will There Be Sagebrush in Heaven
You Don't Know What Lonesome Is
Red River Valley (Unissued)
New York (June 20, 1947)
You Never Miss the Water Till the Well
Runs Dry
Lead Me Gently Home Father
Too High, Too Wide, Too Low
Out in Pioneertown
Chicago (October 15, 1947)
A Hundred and Sixty Acres
The Sea Walker
Read the Bible Every Day
Chicago (October 16, 1947)
The Last Round-Up
Two Eyes, Two Lips, But No Heart
Cowboy Country
The Bar-None Ranch
Where Are You
Chicago (October 17, 1947)
Calico Apron & A Gingham Gown
Happy Birthday Polka
Let Me Share Your Name
Wind (Unissued)
Hollywood (November 10, 1947)
The Whiffenpoof Song
Hollywood (November 10, 1947)
The Old Rugged Cross
Power in the Blood
The Touch of God's Hand
Rounded Up in Glory
Hollywood (November 24, 1947)
Santa Fe, New Mexico
The Missouri is a Devil of a Woman
Down Where the Rio Flows
My Feet Takes Me Away
Hollywood (November 25, 1947)
Red River Valley
Serenade to a Coyote
Hollywood (December 22, 1947)
No Rodeo Dough
The Missouri is a Devil of a Woman
Sentimental, Worried and Blue
Little Gray Home in the West
I Still Do (Unissued)
Hollywood (April 28, 1949)
Riders in the Sky

Room Full of Roses
No One Here But Me
Lie Low Little Dogies
Hollywood (December 14, 1949)
Let's Go West Again
Love at the County Fair
Wedding Dolls
Wind (Unissued)
Outlaws (Unissued)
Hollywood (February 4, 1950)
Roses
The Eagle's Heart
Land Beyond the Sun
I Told Them All About You
Hollywood (March 10 and 13, 1950)
Wagons West
Rollin' Dust
Song of the Wagonmaster
Chuckawalla Song
Hollywood (July 17, 1950)
Old Man Atom
What This Country Needs
Hollywood (October 16, 1950)
Baby, I Ain't Gonna Cry No More
Little White Cross
America Forever
Daddy's Little Cowboy
New York (December 1, 1950)
Baby, I Ain't Gonna Cry No More
Moonlight and Roses
San Antonio Rose
Bring Your Roses To Her Now
Mexicali Rose
New York (December 14, 1950)
Handsome Stranger
Grasshopper Heart
New York (June 11, 1950)
The Wondrous Word
Lonesome
Resurrectus
The Lord's Prayer (Unissued)
Hollywood (June 20, 1951)
Waltz of the Roses
The Lord's Prayer
Wind
Hollywood (July 26, 1951)
Heartbreak Hill
HoLeO

Hollywood (November 9, 1951)
I Still Do
Waltz of the Roses
Outlaws (Unissued)

Hollywood (February 8, 1952)
Empty Saddles
There's a Gold Mine in the Sky
Old Pioneer
Home on the Range

Coral Records

Los Angeles (January 4, 1954)
If You Would Only Be Mine
Sierra Nevada
Los Angeles (April 19, 1954)
The River of No Return
The Lilies Grow High

Los Angeles (November 22, 1954)
Lovely Little Room
Montana
Los Angeles (December 7, 1954)
Somebody Bigger Than You and I
  (Unissued)
The Mystery of His Way (Unissued)

RCA Victor

Hollywood (February 20, 1955)
The Ballad of Davy Crockett
The Graveyard Filler of the West
I Wonder When We'll Ever Know
Hollywood (February 24, 1955)
The King's Hghway
For the Love of You
Timmy's Tune
Hollywood (March 23, 1955)
The Three of Us
Be What You Want To Be (Unissued)
Epidemic (Unissued)
Tennessee Rock and Roll
Hollywood (March 26, 1955)
Timmy's Tune (Unissued)
Mighty Rock (Unissued)
My Secret Wish (Unissued)
Little Space Man (Unissued)
Hollywood (April 6, 1955)
Tennessee Rock and Roll
Be What You Want To Be
Mighty Rock
Epidemic
Hollywood (April 20, 1955)
A Whale of a Tale
Old Betsy
My Secret Wish
Timmy's Tune
Hollywood (September 9, 1955)
Yaller, Yaller Gold

King of the River
Buffalo
All the Way (Unissued)
Hollywood (December 8, 1955)
The Last Frontier
How Great Thou Art
Hollywood (March 28, 1956)
Song of the Prodigal
The Searchers
Hollywood (March 18, 1957)
Hasta La Vista
Honest True (Unissued)
Hollywood (March 19, 1957)
Roly Poly
Blue Eyes Crying in the Rain
Kaw-Liga
I'll Never Stand in Your Way
The End of the World
Hang Your Head in Shame
It's a Sin
Pins and Needles
No One Will Ever Know
Crazy Heart
Be Honest With Me
Hollywood (March 21, 1957)
Cheyenne
One More Ride
This Ain't the Same Old Range
Hollywood (July 16, 1957)
Wagon Train

The Restless Gun
Battle of the Cowboy-Sailor
The Piney Woods

Hollywood (September 25, 1957)
High Ridin' Woman
God Has His Arms Around Me
Far Enchanted Isle

New York (October 7, 1958)
A Fiddle, a Rifle, an Axe & a Bible
My Last Goodbye

Hollywood (April 9, 1959)
My Calico Girl
Sugarfoot
Maverick
California

Hollywood (June 16, 1959)
Cool Water (Unissued)
Wagon Wheels (Unissued)
Timber Trail (Unissued)
Blue Prairie (Unissued)

Hollywood (June 17, 1959)
Cool Water
Blue Prairie
Empty Saddles
The Last Round-Up

Hollywood (June 18, 1959)
Twilight on the Trail
Wind
Blue Shadows On the Trail
Riders in the Sky
Teardrops in My Heart

Hollywood (June 19, 1959)
Red River Valley
Cowboy's Dream
Ridin' Home
Way Out There

Hollywood (June 23, 1959)
Timber Trail
Way Out There
Whoopie-Ti-Yi-Yo
Ridin' Down the Canyon

Hollywood (June 24, 1959)
Tumbling Tumbleweeds (Unissued)
Wagon Wheels
Way Out There
Tumbling Tumbleweeds

Hollywood (November 11, 1960)
Cimarron (Roll On)
Saddle Up

Pecos Bill
Take Me Back to My Boots and Saddle
   (Unissued)

Hollywood (November 17, 23, 25, 1960,
and December 2, 7, 30, 1960)
Take Me Back to My Boots and Saddle
Carry Me Back to the Lone Prairie
Along the Navajo Trail
A Cowboy Has to Sing
Wanderers
Silver on the Sage
Ragtime Cowboy Joe
Chant of the Plains
The Cowboy's Lament
Yippi-Yi, Yippi-Yo
There's a Gold Mine in the Sky
When the Bloom is on the Sage
My Adobe Hacienda
Cimarron (Roll On)
The Cattle Call
Hills of Old Wyoming
There's a Gold Mine in the Sky
Saddle Up

Hollywood (April 19, 1961)
El Paso
There's a Home in Wyomin'
Tumbleweed Trail

Hollywood (April 20, 1961)
The Lilies Grow High
Song of the Pioneers
Song of the Trail

Hollywood (August 28, 29, 31, 1962)
The Singing Hills
Dusty Skies
Along the Santa Fe Trail
Ole Faithful
Chant of the Wanderer
Sierra Nevada
San Antonio Rose
South of the Border
*When My Blue Moon Turns Over to
   Gold Again*
High Noon
Columbus Stockade Blues
When It's Night Time in Nevada

Hollywood (November 23, 1962)
How Will I Know Him
The Place Where I Worship
The Woodman's Prayer

All Wild Things
Suddenly There's a Valley
He Walks with the Wild and the Lonely
Star of Hope
The Mystery of His Way
Hollywood (December 14, 1962)
I Believe
Wonders of God's Green Earth
Lord, You Made the Cowboy Happy
God Speaks
Hollywood (March 27, 1963)
The Utah Trail
By a Campfire on the Trail
Trail to San Antone
Trail Herdin' Cowboy
Hollywood (March 28, 1963)
Trail Dust
There's a Long, Long Trail
Over the Santa Fe Trail
The Oregon Trail
Hollywood (April 1, 1963)
We'll Rest at the End of the Trail
Trail Dreamin'
Autumn on the Trail
Silent Trails
Hollywood (November 18, 1963)
I'll Hold You in My Heart
Crazy Arms
Greenfields
Have I Told You Lately That I Love You
Hollywood (November 19, 1963)
I Still Do
My Heart Cries Out for You
Cold, Cold Heart
Ramona
Hollywood (November 21, 1963)
Song of the Bandit
Almost
Catttle Call Rondolet
Listen to the Mockingbird
Hollywood (June 18, 1964)
Gone
Among My Souvenirs
Memories
Four Walls
Mockin' Bird Hill
Hollywood (June 19, 1964)
Memories Are Made of This
Sleepy Rio Grande

By the River of the Roses
Vaya Con Dios
Hollywood (June 20, 1964)
Bonaparte's Retreat
Born To Lose
Left My Gal in the Mountain
Supersonic Suzy
Hollywood (December 9, 1964)
The Strawberry Roan
Billy the Kid
Little Joe, the Wrangler
Jesse James
Hollywood (December 10, 1964)
Destiny
Ringo
Me and My Burro
Green Ice and Mountain Men
Hollywood (December 11, 1965)
O Bury Me Not, On the Lone Prairie
Buffalo
Outlaws
The Shifting, Whispering Sands
Hollywood (January 18, 1966)
I Follow the Stream
A Sandman's Lullaby
The Boss is Hangin' Out a Rainbow
One More Ride
Hollywood (January 19, 1966)
A Summer Night's Rain
Cottage in the Clouds
You Are My Eyes
Half Way Round the World
Hollywood (January 21, 1966)
Song of the Prairie
Night Falls on the Prairie
At the Rainbow's End
Following the Sun All Day
Hollywood (September 8, 9, 12, 1966)
Roll Along Prairie Moon
Moonlight on the Colorado
Carolina in the Morning
I Love You Truly
That Lucky Old Sun
Somewhere in Wyoming
Don't Fence Me in
It Happened in Monterey
When It's Springtime in the Rockies
Leanin' on the Ole Top Rail
Be Honest with Me

I Can't Help It
Hollywood (December 14, 15, 1967)
  South of the Border
  You Belong to My Heart
  Spanish Eyes
  Love Me With All Your Heart
  Rosa
  A Gay Ranchero
  Margretta
  Mexicali Rose
Hollywood (December 16, 1967)
  Gringo's Guitar
  Maria Elena
  Yours
Hollywood (November 12, 1968)
  King of the Fools

Song of the Land I Love
Tumbling Tumbleweeds
Hollywood (May 12, 13, 14, 1969)
  Blue Hawaii
  Far Enchanted Isle
  Tiny Bubbles
  Stars Above Hawaii
  Pali Wind
  Harbor Lights
  Hawaiian Lullaby
  Walkin' in the Sand
  Beyond the Reef
  I'll Remember You
  Isle of Golden Dreams

Albums of
The Sons of the Pioneers

A Garden of Roses (RCA, 1952)

Cowboy Classics (RCA, 1952)

Cowboy Hymns and Spirituals (RCA, 1952)

Western Classics (RCA, 1953)

25 Favorite Cowboy Songs (RCA, 1955)

How Great Thou Art (RCA, 1957)

One Man's Songs (RCA, 1957)

Wagons West (RCA, 1958)

Cool Water (RCA, 1959)

Room Full of Roses (RCA, 1960)

Westward Ho! (RCA, 1961)

Lure of the West (RCA, 1961)

Tumbleweed Trail (RCA, 1962)

Good Old Country Music (RCA, 1963)

Our Men Out West (RCA, 1963)

Sons of the Pioneers Sing Hymns of the Cowboys (RCA, 1963)

Trail Dust (RCA, 1963)

Tumbleweed Trails (RCA, 1964)

Country Fare (RCA, 1964)

The Sons of the Pioneers' Best (RCA, 1964)

Down Memory Trail (RCA, 1964)

Legends of the West (RCA, 1965)

The Best of the Sons of the Pioneers (RCA, 1966)

The Songs of Bob Nolan (RCA, 1966)

Campfire Favorites (RCA, 1967)

San Antonio Rose (RCA, 1968)

South of the Border (RCA, 1968)

Tumbling Tumbleweeds (RCA, 1969)

The Sons of the Pioneers Visit the South Seas (RCA, 1969)

Riders in the Sky (RCA, 1973)

Western Country (Granite-ATV Music, 1976)

Sons of the Pioneers (Victor Music Industries, 1976)

A Country-Western Songbook (RCA, 1977)

Let's Go West Again (RCA, 1981)

Sons of the Pioneers (Columbia, 1982)

Tumbling Tumbleweeds (Reader's Digest, 1982)

The Sons of the Pioneers (Bear Family Records, 1982)

Empty Saddles (MCA, 1983)

Celebration (Silver Spur Records, 1983)

Cool Water (Bear Family Records, 1987)

Teardrops in My Heart (Bear Family Records, 1987)

A Hundred and Sixty Acres (Bear Family Records, 1987)

Riders in the Sky (Bear Family Records, 1987)

Land Beyond the Sun (Bear Family Records, 1987)

And Friends (Bear Family Records, 1987)

There's a Goldmine in the Sky (Bear Family Records, 1987)

Bibliography

Books

Adams, Les, and Buck Rainey. *Shoot-Em-Ups*. New Rochelle, NY: Arlington House, Publishers, 1978.

Barabas, SuzAnne and Gabor. *Gunsmoke, A Complete History and Analysis of the Legendary Broadcast Series*. Jefferson, NC: McFarland & Company, Inc., Publishers, 1990.

Davis, Elise Miller. *The Answer is God, The Inspiring Personal Story of Dale Evans and Roy Rogers*. New York: McGraw-Hill Book Company, Inc., 1955.

Davis, Ronald L. *John Ford, Hollywood's Old Master*. Norman: University of Oklahoma Press, 1995.

Dick, Bernard F., ed. *Columbia Pictures, Portrait of a Studio*. Lexington: The University Press of Kentucky, 1992.

Dixon, Wheeler W. *The "B" Directors, A Biographical Directory*. Metuchen, NJ, and London: The Scarecrow Press, Inc., 1985.

Everson, William K. *A Pictorial History of the Western Film*. New York: The Citadel Press, 1969.

Finler, Joel W. *The Hollywood Story*. New York: Crown Publishers, Inc., 1988.

Garfield, Brian. *Western Films, A Complete Guide*. New York: Rawson Associates, 1982.

Gentry, Linnell. *A History and Encyclopedia of Country, Western, and Gospel Music*. St. Clair Shores, MI: Scholarly Press, Inc., 1972.

Griffis, Ken. *Hear My Song, The Story of the Celebrated Sons of the Pioneers*. Northglenn, CO: Norken, 1974.

Hardy, Phil. *The Western*. New York: William Morrow and Company, Inc., 1983.

Hirschhorn, Clive. *The Universal Story*. New York: Crown Publishers, Inc., 1983.

Holland, Ted. *B Western Actors Encyclopedia*. Jefferson, NC: McFarland & Company, Inc., 1989.

Hurst, Richard Maurice. *Republic Studios: Between Poverty Row and the Majors*. Metuchen, NJ: The Scarecrow Press, Inc., 1979.

Kennett, Lee. *G. I., The American Soldier in World War II*. Norman: University of Oklahoma Press, 1987.

Kingsbury, Paul, Alan Axelrod, and Susan Costello, eds. The Country Music Foundation. *Country, The Music and the Musicians, From the Beginnings to the '90s*. New York: Abbeville Press, 1988.

Larkin, Rochelle. *Hail, Columbia*. New Rochelle, NY: Arlington House, Publishers, 1975.

Lyles, Allen. *The Western*. New York: A. S. Barnes and Company, Inc., 1975.

Magers, Boyd, and Michael G. Fitzgerald. *Westerns Women*. Jefferson, NC: McFarland & Company, Inc., Publishers, 1999.

Malone, Bill C. *Country Music, U. S. A*. Austin: University of Texas Press, 1985.

Martin, Len D. *The Columbia Checklist*. Jefferson, NC: McFarland & Company, Inc., Publishers, 1991.

McCloud, Barry, and contributing writers. *Definitive Country, The Ultimate Encyclopedia of Country Music and Its Performers.* New York: The Berkley Publishing Group, 1995.

McClure, Arthur F., and Ken D. Jones. *Western Films, Heroes, Heavies and Sagebrush of the "B" Genre.* New York: A. S. Barnes and Company, 1972.

McDonald, Archie P., ed. *Shooting Stars, Heroes and Heroines of Western Film.* Bloomington: Indiana University Press, 1987.

Moore, Thurston, ed. *Pictorial History of Country Music, Vol. 3.* Denver, CO: Heather Enterprises, Inc., 1970.

Phillips, Robert W. *Roy Rogers.* Jefferson, NC: McFarland & Company, Inc., Publishers, 1995.

Pitts, Michael R. *Western Movies.* Jefferson, NC: McFarland & Company, Inc., Publishers, 1986.

Place, J. A. *The Western Films of John Ford.* Secaucus, NJ: The Citadel Press, 1973.

Rainey, Buck. *Sweethearts of the Sage.* Jefferson, NC: McFarland & Company, Inc., Publishers, 1992.

Rogers, Dale Evans. *Dale, My Personal Picture Album.* Old Tappan, NJ: Fleming H. Revell Company, 1971.

Rogers, Roy, and Dale Evans, with Jane and Michael Stern. *Happy Trails, Our Life Story.* New York: Simon & Schuster, 1994.

Rogers, Roy, Jr., with Karen Ann Wojahn. *Growing Up with Roy & Dale.* Ventura, CA: Regal Books, 1986.

Rothel, David. *The Gene Autry Book.* Madison, NC: Empire Publishing Company, Inc., 1988.

———. *The Singing Cowboys.* New York: A. S. Barnes & Company, Inc., 1978.

———. *Those Great Cowboy Sidekicks.* Waynesville, NC: WOY Publications, 1984.

Storm, Gale. *I Ain't Down Yet.* Indianapolis: The Bobbs-Merrill Company, Inc., 1981.

Terrace, Vincent. *Television Specials, 3,201 Entertainment Spectaculars, 1939-1993.* Jefferson, NC: McFarland & Company, Inc., 1995.

Torrence, Bruce T. *Hollywood: The First Hundred Years.* New York: Zoetrope, 1982.

Tuska, Jon. *The Filming of the West.* Garden City, NY: Doubleday & Company, Inc., 1976.

West, Richard. *Television Westerns.* Jefferson, NC: McFarland & Company, Inc., 1987.

Whitburn, Joel. *Top Country Singles 1944-1993.* Menomonee Falls, WI: Record Research, Inc., 1994.

Witney, William. *Trigger Remembered.* Huntsville, AL: Golden Rule Printing, 1989.

Articles

Atkinson, Terry. "Western Rock: Son of the Sons of the Pioneers." *Los Angeles Times* (August 21, 1977).

"Autry, Gene." *Current Biography* (December 1947): 24-26.

Barter, Frieda. "Sons of the Pioneers, Together Again." *Country and Western Jamboree* (March 1956): 12.

Bindas, Kenneth J. "Western Mystic." *The Western Historical Quarterly* (October 1986): 439-456.

Buckley, Daniel. "Sons, 'Tumblin' Tumbleweeds' gather no moss at festival here." *Tucson Citizen* (November 15, 1994).

Campbell, Jackie. "'Sons of Pioneers' strive to preserve mystique." *Rocky Mountain News*, Denver, CO (January 20, 1978).

Crowther, Bosley. "Fighting Coast Guard." *The New York Times Film Reviews* (May 12, 1951).

Davenport, Gene. "The Sons of the Pioneers, Half a Century of the Tumbleweed Trail." *Country Sounds* (November 1986): 14-17.

Edwards, John. Spotlight Feature Story No. 13, *Country and Western Spotlight*, No. B (November 1956): 8-9.

Elwood, Philip. "Classic Western Swing." *San Francisco Examiner* (March 2, 1977).

Fairchuck, Joan. "Tribute to the Sons of the Pioneers." *Rex Allen Fan Club Journal* (1973).

"For Songs of the West, You'll Enjoy the Lucky U Ranch Hour." *The Sea Hawk* (December 1952): 13,16.

Gilliam, Stanley. "Country-Western History Comes Alive." *Sacramento Bee* (July 25, 1975).

Green, Douglas B. "Sons of the Pioneers." *Country Music Magazine* (October 1998): 34-36.

Hardesty, Will. "Sons of the Pioneers still drifting along with the tumbleweeds." *Rocky Mountain News*, Denver, CO (January 16, 1976).

Hieronymus, Clara. "Sons of the Pioneers Perform at Cheekwood." *Nashville Tennessean* (June 26, 1983).

Highberger, Mark. "Singing Cowboys: Hanging a Tune on the Velvet Moon." *Signal Mountain, Northeast Oregon's Own Historical Magazine* (Summer 1998): 11-14.

Klinka, Karen. "Museum Black-Tie Gala Pays Tribute to American West." *The Daily Oklahoman*, Oklahoma City (March 20, 1995).

Kreutz, Douglas. "Sons of the Pioneers: Cowboy Crooners still know how to please after 45 years." *Rocky Mountain News*, Denver, CO (March 26, 1979).

Lancaster, Jimmy. "Sons of the Pioneers receive Wrangler Award." *Branson Tri-Lakes Daily* (April 26, 1995).

Robinson, Tom. "Carrying on a Cowboy Tradition." *Music City News* (August 1983): 10.

Roden, Jim. "Roy and the Heroes." *Dallas Times Herald* (December 20, 1974).

"Rogers, Dale Evans." *Current Biography* (September 1956): 56-57.

"Rogers, Roy." *Current Biography* (March 1948): 531-533.

"Rogers, Roy." *Current Biography* (October 1983): 29-33.

Shewchuk, Cyd. "'Sons of the Pioneers' keep making old-fashioned country music." *Colorado Springs Sun* (September 16, 1974).

"Sons of the Pioneers." *The Chronicle of Country Music* (September 1976), 1.

"Sons of the Pioneers Double On Networks and Screens." *The Rhythm Round-Up* (February 1940): 4.

"Sons of the Pioneers Rewarded—Finally." *The Oklahoma Journal*, Oklahoma City (October 2, 1972).

"Sons of the Pioneers' Lloyd Perryman dies." *Pasadena Star News*, California (June 1, 1977).

"There's Nothing Plastic About Bob Nolan's Music." *Milwaukee Sentinel* (August 31, 1979).

Weintraub, Boris. "The Enduring Myth: Sons of the Pioneers." *Washington Star* (March 25, 1979).

"Western singer succumbs." *The Tacoma News Tribune* (June 1, 1977).

Zibart, Eve. "Sons of the Pioneers: Memories of a Waning Way of Life." *Washington Post* (March 26, 1979).

Zwisohn, Laurence. "Roy Rogers." *The Sons of the Pioneers Historical Journal* (December 1992): 9-11.

Interviews

Rex Allen	Tennessee Ernie Ford	Wade Ray
Eddie Arnold	Olive Jones	Roy Rogers
Chet Atkins	Debbie Lanham	Hal Spencer
Opal Berry	Roy Lanham	Tim Spencer
Ken Carson	Bobbie Mileusnich	Velma Spencer
Eddie Dean	Smokey Montgomery	Cliffe Stone
Tommy Doss	Luther Nallie	Wesley Tuttle
Dale Evans	Bob Nolan	Bob Wagoner
Hugh Farr	Doye O'Dell	Jimmy Wakely
Karl Farr, Jr.	Lloyd Perryman	Dale Warren
Lynn Farr		

Recordings and Movies

Of primary importance in researching the Sons of the Pioneers was the study of their performances on recordings and films. The authors have listened to most of their recordings and viewed almost all of their movies, which have been collected by Fred Goodwin. The Pioneer recordings and movies are listed in the appendices, and many are available for purchase. In addition, Fred Goodwin has collected several videotapes of Pioneer appearances on various television shows.

Pioneer TV Performance Videos

Purina Grand Ole Opry (1956).
Bill Anderson Show (1973).
Hee Haw (May 1978).
Fall Guy (May 25, 1983).
Music of the West, A TNN Tribute to the Singing Cowboys (1992).
Prime Time Country (March 22, 1996).
Opry Backstage (March 23, 1996).

Miscellaneous

Adams, Thomas J. *The Sons of the Pioneers (a tribute)*. 1996.
"Bob Nolan, Bio." Press Relations Dept. Elektra/Asylum Records, Los Angeles, n.d.
Great Western Heroes Reunion & Hall of Fame Induction, Orlando, FL. Program, July 12-15, 1984.
Karl Farr, Lloyd Perryman, George Fisher, Lloyd T. Doss, Dale Warren vs. Hugh Farr. Superior Court of the State of California for the County of Los Angeles, Case No. 721111. Testimony Transcript, December 15, 1959.
KLAC Radio, Los Angeles, to tribute Lloyd Perryman. Press Release, June 9, 1977.
Pepper Rangers Gazette. Published at 10-2-4 Ranch, Hollywood, California, 195.
Pine Cone Ranch, Colorado Springs. Brochure.
Pioneer News. 1978-1979. Fred Goodwin Collection, Murfreesboro, TN.
Roy Rogers Homecoming Day, Portsmouth and Cincinnati. Program. September 6, 1982.
Roy Rogers, King of the Cowboys. American Movie Classic Original Production. Galean Films, Len Morris, director.
"Roy Rogers: King of the Cowboys." Press Conference Transcript. Century Plaza Hotel, Los Angeles, July 7, 1992.
The Sons of the Pioneers Historical Journal. 1988-1992. Fred Goodwin Collection, Murfreesboro, TN.
"Sons of the Pioneers, Living Legends for 60 years." Press Release (July 30, 1996), 5 pp.
Sons of the Pioneers Press Release. Fred Goodwin Collection, Murfreesboro, TN.
Sons of the Pioneers, Programs, Realito Theater, Glen Falls, NY, 1949.
Sons of the Pioneers Reunion-Tribute. Video. Embassy Room of the Ambassador Hotel, Los Angeles, April 21, 1972.
Tumbleweed Times. Official Newsletter for the Sons of the Pioneers. 1989-1996. Fred Goodwin Collection, Murfreesboro, TN.
The Western Heritage Awards, National Cowboy Hall of Fame, Oklahoma City. Program, March 18, 1995.
Zwisohn, Laurence. *Sons of the Pioneers, Wagons West*. Album Essay.
———. *Sons of the Pioneers & Roy Rogers, Songs of the Prairie*. Album Essay.

Index